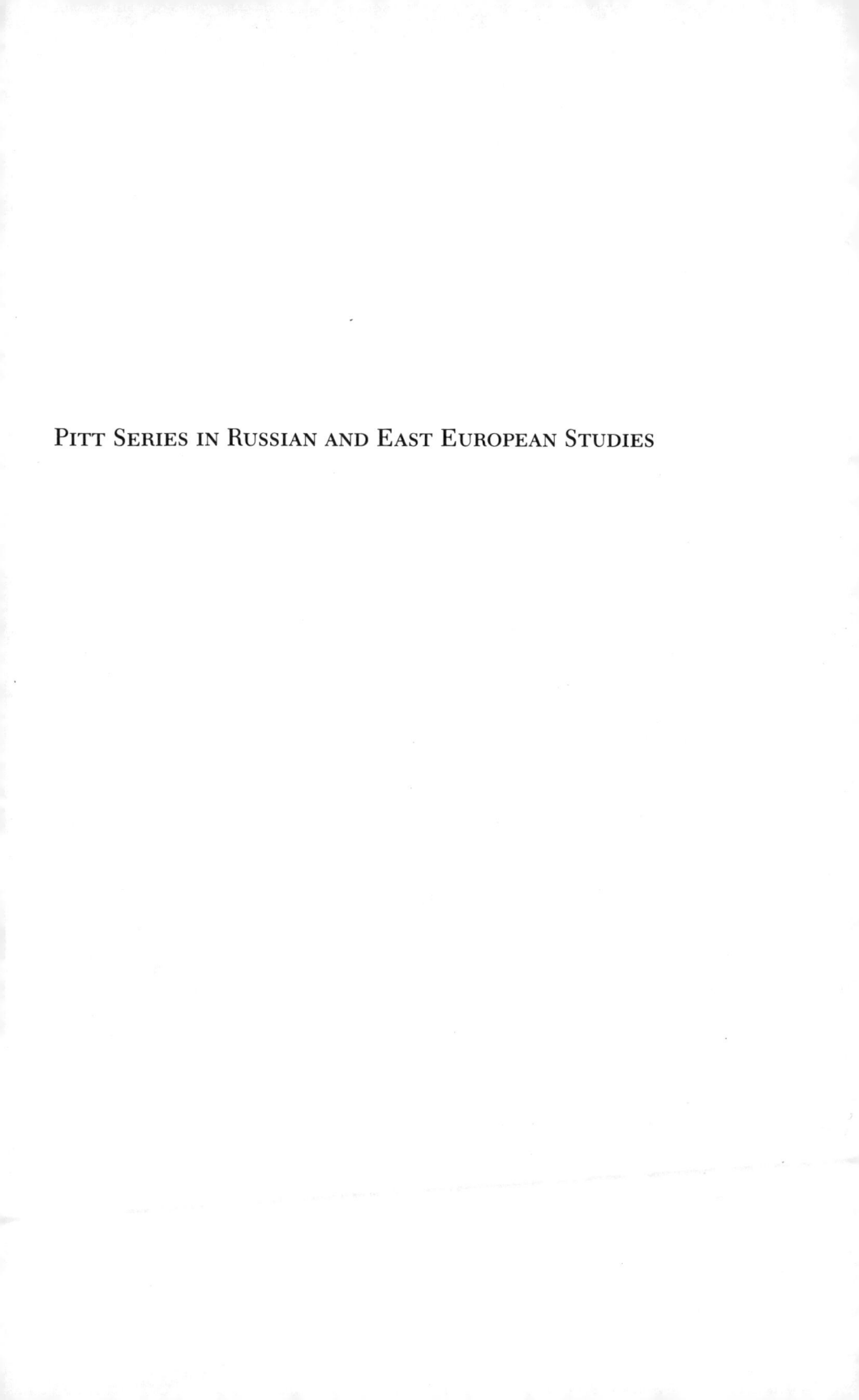

Pitt Series in Russian and East European Studies

A Russian primary school classroom at the turn of the century (*Zhiponucnoe obozrenie*, 1904).

Gender, Class, and the Professionalization of Russian City Teachers, 1860–1914

Christine Ruane

University of Pittsburgh Press
Pittsburgh and London

Pitt Series in Russian and East European Studies no. 24.

Published by the University of Pittsburgh Press, Pittsburgh, Pa., 15260
Copyright © 1994, University of Pittsburgh Press
All rights reserved
Manufactured in the United States of America
Printed on acid-free paper

Library of Congress Cataloging-in-Publication Data

Ruane, Christine.
   Gender, class, and the professionalization of Russian city teachers, 1860–1914 / Christine Ruane.
      p.   cm.—(Pitt series in Russian and East European studies : no. 24)
   Includes bibliographical references (p.   ) and index.
   ISBN 0-8229-3864-2 (acid-free paper)
   1. Teachers—Russian—History—19th century. 2. Urban schools—Russian—History—19th century. 3. Education and state—Russia—History—19th century. 4. Women teachers—Russia—History—19th century. 5. Russia—Social conditions—1801–1917. I. Title.
II. Series: Series in Russian and East European studies : no. 24.
L82832.4.R8R8   1994
371.1′00947—dc20   94-30861
                                                                                        CIP

A CIP catalogue record for this book is available from the British Library.
Eurospan, London

Portions of this work are based on research first published in *The Russian Review* 50, no. 2 (April 1991). Copyright 1991 Ohio State University Press. All rights reserved. Other material was previously published in "Divergent Discourses: The Image of the Russian Woman Schoolteacher in Post-Reform Russia," *Russian History* 20 (1993). Permission to reprint from these sources is gratefully acknowledged.

Contents

Acknowledgments ix

Introduction: The Rise of a
Professional Consciousness 3

1 Pedagogy and Professionalization 21

2 City Teachers' Daily Lives: The Development of a
Professional Ethos 42

3 Women Teachers and Professionalization 62

4 Politics and Professionalization, 1860–1905 87

5 The Revolution of 1905 128

6 City Teachers After the 1905 Revolution 164

Conclusion: Pedagogy, Professionalization,
and Politics 185

Appendix 199

Notes 209

Bibliography 235

Index 249

For Jimmy, with love

Acknowledgments

A CENTRAL THEME OF THIS BOOK IS THE SEARCH FOR EXCELLENCE IN teaching, and particularly those qualities which superlative teachers possess. During my days as a graduate student, when my interest in Russian schoolteachers first began, I benefited from three such excellent teachers. Nicholas V. Riasanovsky shared with me his vast knowledge and unbounded love for Russian history. In seminars and over many cups of coffee, he taught me the rigors and rewards of studying a country and culture that were not my own. Reginald E. Zelnik imparted to me the skills necessary to become a social historian. Through his insightful criticism and his own scholarship, Reggie showed me that historical meaning is substantially enhanced by the study of the daily lives of ordinary people. Both men directed this manuscript through its various stages and through their wisdom and counsel made it a better book. Finally, I would like to thank Lynn Hunt for the example she set for me, a young woman graduate student searching for a role model. Even though I was not officially her student, she encouraged me to push myself intellectually and not to be satisfied with historical certainties. If this book successfully challenges some long held ideas about Russian history, it is due in no small part to her example and advice.

I have also benefited from the support of family, friends, and colleagues. My parents encouraged my intellectual curiosity and integrity at an early age and constantly supported my efforts to pursue an academic life throughout a long apprenticeship. A number of friends—Lynn Mally, Suzanne Desan, Elisabeth Domansky, Jerry Hinshaw, and Jean Fletcher—supported me at various points during the writing of this book. Their interest and support made my endeavors seem less solitary. I also want to give special thanks to a wonderful colleague and friend, Mike McTighe, who helped me to clarify the central themes of this book. It saddens me that he did not live to see the book to its completion. I am grateful to colleagues at Washington University—Nancy Berg, Milica Banjanin, Nancy Grant, Iver Bernstein, David Konig, Max Okenfuss, and Richard Walter—who helped me to mature both as a scholar and as a teacher.

ACKNOWLEDGMENTS

Generous funding from a variety of sources helped to bring this book to completion. This research was assisted by a grant from the Joint Committee on Soviet Studies of the Social Science Research Council and the American Council of Learned Societies, with funds provided by the National Endowment for the Humanities and the Ford Foundation. The International Research and Exchanges Board funded a research trip to the Soviet Union in 1982–1983. I received additional funding from the National Endowment for the Humanities and Washington Unversity.

I had the good fortune to work in a number of libraries and archives on this project. The libraries at the University of California at Berkeley, the University of Illinois, Stanford University, Helsinki University, the Hoover Institution, and the Library of Congress provided excellent working conditions. Special thanks to Helen Sullivan at the University of Illinois library for tracking down some hard-to-locate materials. In the former Soviet Union, I spent many productive hours in the Library of the Academy of Sciences and the Saltykov-Shchedrin library in Leningrad and the Lenin Library in Moscow. I thank the staffs at the Central Historical Archive, the Leningrad City Archive, and the Central State Archive for the October Revolution for helping to locate essential materials. In particular, I wish to thank Svetlana Gimien, my *sotrudnitsa*, and Grigorii A. Tishkin, my advisor, for making my stay in Leningrad so productive. These individuals and their institutions opened their doors so that I could learn the art of archival research.

I am grateful to Catherine Marshall, Jane Flanders, Jonathan Harris, and others at the University of Pittsburgh Press for their help. The suggestions of the two anonymous readers allowed me to clarify some important points in my argument.

Finally, I am greatly indebted to my husband, Brad, who entered my life at a very difficult time and whose love, support, and encouragement have sustained me through difficulties. His skills as a historian have made this work a better book. My son, Jimmy, has taken as great an interest in my work as I have in his growth and maturity. He has helped me to understand that teaching, at its best, is a two-way street.

Gender, Class, and the Professionalization of Russian City Teachers, 1860–1914

Introduction: The Rise of a Professional Consciousness

IN 1861 TSAR ALEXANDER II USHERED IN A NEW ERA IN RUSSIAN history, the Era of the Great Reforms. Beginning with the emancipation of the serfs, the tsar and his ministers created a new set of institutions—a Western-style judiciary, new organs of local self-government, universal military service—through which Russia would be administered. In freeing the serfs from their bondage to the nobility, the government wished not only to remove a sore on the body politic but also to provide sufficient manpower so that Russia could become a modern military force supported by a strong industrial and agricultural base. In order to facilitate these economic changes, Alexander hoped to create a civil society of juridically free subjects based on the rule of law and civic responsibility. He wanted ordinary Russians, after years of blindly following the autocrat's decisions, to act on their own behalf and share the responsibility for government policies and actions. Thus, the purpose of the Great Reforms was nothing less than the total transformation of Russia.[1]

Despite the far-reaching intent of the reforms, problems remained. Many of the reforms were half-measures. The emancipation freed the serfs from the juridical authority of the landlord only to bind the peasants to the land and the commune. Other reforms, such as the university statute, the censorship laws, and city government regulations were modified or abolished when they appeared to create serious social tensions. Although these changes were not a full retreat from the reforms, they marked a reluctance on the part of the Russian government to pursue the reforms to the fullest extent. In the end, the government wanted to pursue the reforms without making any major social or political changes and without permitting the growth of an autonomous civil society. This was an impossible goal, given the nature of the reforms themselves.

One key element that was missing from the reform legislation was any change in the social structure. According to Russian law, all men and women were born into a particular *soslovie* (estate), and their social ranking determined their position and function within society. These social categories—nobility, clergy, townspeople, and peasants—reflected an older way of life, which the Russian government was attempting to preserve de jure if not de facto. For example, peasants, now free to seek employment in the newly created factories without the permission of their landlord, remained peasants under the law. The government's refusal to abolish the estate system meant that many Russians had divided social identities in the late nineteenth century. Newer identities based upon work coexisted with older identities determined by birth. In the case of workers, this situation proved explosive. The Russian working class became revolutionary because it carried with it the grievances of both workers and peasants.[2] But workers were not the only social group with divided identities. As we shall see, professionals too were pulled in different directions by their conflicting social identities.

For the Great Reforms to have been truly transformative, Russia needed a new social system. Individual Russians who performed new kinds of work wanted to be rewarded for their labors. While the government agreed to devolve responsibility for the nation's administration, it continued to reward success by the old standards—making promotions in the government and military ranks, awarding medals for service, and granting personal nobility. This is one of the many paradoxes of late nineteenth-century Russian history: the government's reforms undermined the very social system they were intended to perpetuate. What could have been a sustained cooperative effort between state and society to create a modern industrialized nation became a continual struggle of the government and old privileged elite against the newer elites.

Against this background, Russian civil society emerged. If they were going to carry more obligations as citizens, members of the new civil society wanted civil rights and freedoms as well. Once again government policy was inconsistent, however. Although the thrust of the reforms was to create a land of citizens from a land of subjects, the government remained for the most part reluctant to share its power and authority with civil society. It continued to circumscribe citizenship throughout the last years of imperial rule, and looked upon any attempt to change the status quo with suspicion and mistrust.

Despite government inconsistency, increasing numbers of Russians began to participate in the economic, social, and political life of their country as never before. Men and women, educated in the newly reformed schools, sought employment in the expanding sectors of the Russian economy—in industry, commerce, and public service. They were part of a new, modern Russia, and they wanted to create a new arena where rights could be asserted and defended and where new voices could have legitimacy in shaping "public opinion."

One set of important actors in this process of social transformation were the professions.[3] When the government decided to reform, it needed large numbers of employees to staff the new institutions—the courts, the zemstvos, and the schools. To satisfy this need, the state created new educational institutions to train competent experts for these positions. Most of these experts were not part of the government bureaucracy, but became part of what was known as the "free" professions, although the professions in Russia were never as "free" as their West European counterparts. Not fitting into any of the existing social categories, these professional men and women formed a new group with their own interests, concerns, and aspirations. As such, they became a critical part of the new civil society.

The rise of the professions was one of the most important events in postreform Russia.[4] Despite some superficial similarities, Russian professionals were fundamentally different from their Western counterparts. In order to understand the complex nature of the Russian professions, it is necessary, first, to review traditional models of professionalization in Western Europe and the United States and, second, to demonstrate why it is difficult to apply these models to the Russian case. Finally, by understanding how the Russian case is different, we can propose a new model to explain Russian professional development. Russian professionals did not become part of a burgeoning middle class as they did in the West; rather, they constituted a new social group, the professional intelligentsia.

The sociologist Talcott Parsons has asserted that "the emergence of the professional complex . . . [was] the crucial structural development in twentieth century society."[5] This was particularly true in Western societies, where professional development was preceded by the growth of democratic political institutions and a middle class. Nowhere was this crucial connection more apparent than in the United States. In the democratic United States the professions became a powerful source of the political, social, and economic power of the middle class. If business was the quintessential career choice for

Americans of humble origins seeking to enter the middle class, the professions became increasingly the preferred choice of educated Americans who wished to remain middle class.

By the twentieth century American professional and middle-class values had become so intertwined that they appeared inseparable. Because the majority of professionals came from the middle class, those values that helped them achieve middle-class status were the standards that also shaped professional development. Just as the proponents of the middle class supported notions of self-reliance, individualism, and autonomy, the new American professions incorporated these same qualities. American professionalization can be seen as part of a national development—professional attitudes and values sprang from the middle-class values of the vast majority of members of a profession.

The American experience of professional development has influenced scholars studying the rise of the professions. According to Parsons, the essential characteristics defining a profession were formal technical training, the development of demonstrable skills in the application of that training, and the creation of specific institutions designed to ensure that these skills would be used in a socially responsible way. Parsons particularly emphasized the autonomy of the professions: completely independent of government control, these "communities of the competent" were the opposite of bureaucracy and bureaucratic modes of organization.[6] At the same time, Parsons incorporated into his model of professional development those American middle-class values that proved so definitive; in so doing, he universalized those values as essential to all professional development.

Recently, the Parsonian model has come under attack from a number of scholars of differing viewpoints. Some sociologists have criticized Parsons's view of the professions as a benign social force. According to a model developed by Magali Sarfatti Larson, the organizational task of a profession has been to create a distinctive commodity to be produced, find a market for such a commodity, and convince the new recruits to the profession to accept economic and social sacrifices of training, which will be rewarded later with greater social and economic status.[7] This model emphasized the role of professions in extending capitalist mechanisms into new areas. Despite the importance of this critique, the fundamental characteristics defining professions—technical expertise and autonomy—have remained the same.

INTRODUCTION

Historians have criticized both the Parsons and Larson models for their dependence on evidence from the United States and Great Britain. After analyzing professionalization in continental European countries, several scholars have concluded that neither model adequately explains professional development. Scholars of the French professions have pointed out that, far from being the "antithesis of bureaucracy and the bureaucratic mode of work organization,"[8] professions have flourished as a direct result of their dependence on the French government: "In France, professional groups in search of fiscal support, social legitimacy, and some measure of intellectual independence usually discovered that the most effective way to attain their goals was through cooperation or even 'collaboration' with the central state and its bureaucracy."[9]

In a major new work, Harold Perkin has further criticized the traditional Anglo-American model by analyzing in a new way the development of professions in England since 1880. According to him, "professional society is based on human capital created by education and enhanced by strategies of closure, that is, the exclusion of the unqualified."[10] Perkin sees a conflict that emerged in Great Britain between the entrepreneurial ideal based on competition in the open market and on the self-made man, and the professional ideal that emphasized expertise and merit, awarded by other experts. Unlike Parsons, he argues that the role of the state is crucial in promoting the professional ideal, for in almost all cases, the state creates the need for the professional's services. Moreover, Perkin divides professionals into public sector professions, which benefit directly or indirectly from state aid, and private sector professions, which do not. These two groups compete for the society's resources and this competition has become "the master conflict of professional society."[11]

Women's historians have also come to criticize all existing models for ignoring the role of women in professional development. The authors of a recent article on women in the professions conclude:

> The primary actors in the standard works are inevitably male. The working definition of "profession," in sociology and history, excludes fields dominated by women because they seem to lack qualities of autonomy and expertise central to professional power. Even in those historical works that have examined a predominately female profession, such as social work or education, the issue of gender is overlooked.[12]

Thus, women are excluded from the history of the professions both as individuals and as members of distinct professions. Indeed, those professions where women have dominated are not even considered "real" professions.[13]

All these critiques are still based on an Anglo-American model of professionalization. Scholars still emphasize technical expertise, autonomy, and the formation of professional institutions as a way of assessing the degree to which a profession has coalesced. Moreover, underlying these criteria for professionalization is the assumption that the membership of any profession will be from the middle class. Even the feminist critique of existing professional models makes this assumption.[14] Accordingly, any group that does not attain full autonomy, clear control over educational requirements and ethical standards, and a predominately middle-class membership cannot be classified as a "true" profession.

The Anglo-American model has had an enormous impact on the Western scholarship concerning the Russian professions. In the first place, Western historians seek autonomy in their subjects. Under an autocratic political system, however, Russian professionals never had the same control over their professional lives as did their colleagues in the West. The government had no intention of surrendering its authority, nor did it intend to give any group within society any kind of autonomous standing. It looked upon any attempts to establish autonomy as a threat to its security and disciplined those audacious enough to make such demands with exile and other forms of punishment. This placed Russian professionals in a difficult position: how could they establish their professional autonomy without jeopardizing their livelihood?

Applying the Anglo-American model to Russia presents a second difficulty: Russia had no well-developed middle class from which the professions could draw their members.[15] The "middle," according to nineteenth-century Russian social categories, consisted of townspeople who were occupied in trade and commerce. This group was one of the sources for members of the new professions in Europe and the United States, but not in Russia. Russian merchants were particularly bound by traditional attitudes toward their place in society and were not interested in becoming members of the new professions. If they wanted to "move" socially, they tried to move into the nobility.[16]

Finally, the professions and other middling groups failed to develop self-interested politics during the last years of tsarist rule. To claim to represent all social groups (*vsesoslovnyi*) in politics or to speak on behalf of the lower classes was easier than to articulate a clear agenda for enhancing their political power within Russia. As one historian has observed, "If the criterion of middle-class identity is the attainment of common political action, then Russia failed to develop a middle class. . . . Merchants split along regional and ethnic lines, professionals argued over authority and status, writers and intellectuals agonized over where they belonged. Would-be leaders of a new middle class found the right words but emerged with relatively few followers."[17] In Russia professionalization was not coterminous with middle-class development.

Because Russian professionals do not appear to conform to the criteria of the Anglo-American model, most Western scholars have seen Russian professionalization as a failure.[18] Virtually every work on the Russian professions emphasizes their inability to control educational requirements and ethics. Particularly serious in the view of most scholars was the inability of Russians to establish autonomous professional societies that could have helped the professions achieve some of these goals. Because they did not fit the Anglo-American model, Russian professions allegedly never became "true" professions. The "failure" of Russians to create Western-style professions then becomes part of the explanation as to why the Russian bourgeoisie failed to defend its class interests in the Revolution of 1917.[19]

In my view, to describe professionalization as a failure is to miss the real story of Russian professional development.[20] Russian professionals were involved in an exciting and important process of social transformation in late imperial Russia. While it is true that Russians did not create Western-style professions, they transformed state service by dedicating themselves to the new ideal of public service, and in doing so, created a new work ethic for those occupations. Although they were never able to transform their professional organizations into fully autonomous institutions, these same organizations helped to foster a professional consciousness among the members. This sense of themselves as professionals was in the end the most important criterion for Russians—they believed that they were professionals and acted accordingly, even when it brought them into conflict with the tsarist government, their chief employer. The end result of this exciting and painful transformation was the creation of a new social group, the professional intelligentsia, who became major players in twentieth-century Russian history.

The professional intelligentsia and the radical intelligentsia had a common origin, namely, the traditional service elite composed of the nobility, the bureaucracy, and the clergy. In the autocratic system the social contract between tsar and people was based on service. All Russians, regardless of rank, were to serve the tsar; in return, he agreed to provide them security and domestic tranquility. For the nobility, service to the tsar meant participating in the military or the government bureaucracy. In exchange for loyal service, the gentry received land and serfs. As the inequities of this system became more apparent, an intelligentsia developed in Russia.[21] It criticized the old service ethic and offered a new one in its place. Service, according to the intelligentsia, meant service to all Russians and not just the tsar. The intelligentsia particularly emphasized the need to eschew any political or economic self-interested activity in order to serve the lower classes, whose labor had provided the elites with their privileged position in society. These two service ideals—one to the state and the other to the people—differed in many ways, but they had one thing in common. In return for selfless devotion, the service providers would receive benefits. In the case of the nobility and the bureaucrats, the government would give them titles, medals, and privileges. The intelligentsia received more intangible items—recognition from "the people" and the knowledge that they were helping to destroy the autocratic system, either by acts of violence or by their refusal to participate in it.

After the reforms were implemented, a new service ethic flowered among the professionals. Working in the new government-sponsored institutions, many professionals were dependent upon the government for their livelihood. But, given the divided identities of the period, these professionals combined the noble and intelligentsia ideals and dedicated themselves to serving both government and people. In doing so, they created a third service alternative, public service. No longer willing to be the abject servant of either the state or the people, professionals believed that their specialized education and practical experiences made them "experts" and, as experts, they should be awarded certain status and privileges in Russian society. In contrast to the revolutionary intelligentsia, they wanted to live in relative comfort and enjoy the pleasures of family life. To achieve this, they needed higher salaries and freedom from police surveillance. Just as important, they wanted freedom in their work to act according to their professional principles and training. The professionals tried to create a public sphere where they could discuss their common concerns in order to then bring about changes in domestic policy. These changes suggest that professionals were developing new values in postreform Russia. Public service, autonomy, self-reliance, and individualism were the values that shaped this new professional ideal, but professionals also remained embedded in the older tradition of service. This development of a professional public service ethic that combined older ideals with new values meant that Russian professionals developed a unique professional consciousness that distinguished them from Western professionals and profoundly affected their professional behavior in the public sphere they were helping to create.

This mix of old and new ideals and attitudes had far-reaching consequences on Russian professional development. In the realm of work, professionals were redefining service in ways that clearly threatened the status quo. However, their political behavior was still influenced by older traditions that put professionals in a difficult position. Arguments favoring self-interested politics had already been discredited by the radical intelligentsia's rhetoric. Moreover, professionals' sense of a shared identity was still coalescing in 1905 and had not overcome serious class and gender differences. As a result, professionals did not act politically as a unified force, but were divided between those who proposed to speak for the common interests of the professions and those who claimed to speak for the classes that they served. Thus, as professional political behavior in 1905 demonstrated, there was no self-conscious professional middle class in Russia, but rather a professional intelligentsia that fell back on older notions of political behavior. It is these divided identities, a combination of new professional values and older political attitudes among the intelligentsia, which make the Russian professionals a distinct historical phenomenon.

In order to understand the rise of a Russian professional intelligentsia, this study examines professionalization among city teachers. Teachers offer a unique perspective from which to study professionalization for a number of reasons. In the West, teachers are not ordinarily considered part of the "true" professions because of their status as public employees. However, in Russia virtually all professionals worked for government-sponsored institutions. Since there was no significant dichotomy between public and private employees, Russian teachers were not seen as second-class professionals or semi-professionals, as often happened in the West. As Nancy Mandelker Frieden has observed in her study of Russian doctors: "Professionalization in Russia was Janus-faced: a bid for control over training and careers combined with dependence on the state."[22]

Teachers were key players in the attempts to reform Russian society. The expansion of educational opportunity was central to the government plan for a modern Russia. In a country where few people had any sort of formal schooling, both government and society placed great importance upon literacy. Nineteenth-century Russians possessed a remarkable faith in the power of enlightenment to overcome the poverty, ignorance, and backwardness that were keeping Russia from claiming her rightful place among the great world powers. Even peasants understood the importance of literacy for their economic survival.[23] The real debate in Russia was not over the need for literacy, but over access to education and the kind of education available. On this question there was no unanimity of opinion, and teachers attempted to play a prominent part in the debate over education and educational opportunity that continued throughout the nineteenth and early twentieth centuries.

A full discussion of these educational debates is beyond the scope of this book. However, it is important to understand the general outlines of the issues that provide a backdrop for the professionalization of city teachers. The general government policy throughout the period under study was to educate Russian children for their station in life. The children of the elite had access to the best schools at all levels of the school system. Children of the lower classes received only a few years of primary education, just enough to make them better workers, but not enough to give them ideas about improving their lives or the political system. Or so the government thought. As a result of this philosophy, graduation from the lower schools did not automatically entitle one to entrance to secondary or higher schools. Difficult entrance examinations and high tuition fees kept the lower classes out of these schools, reserving them for the children of the elite. In addition, a multiplicity of schools, each with a different curriculum, served the "needs" of a particular part of the population. Schools designated for the nobility and the bureaucracy offered a liberal arts curriculum, while children of merchants and artisans were expected to attend vocational schools.[24] This system of limiting access to certain kinds of education based on social station was called the Tolstoi system, named after Count Dmitrii Tolstoi, the minister of education who devised it.

At its very inception, this caste system of education came under attack. For pedagogical and political reasons, educators within and without the Ministry of Education argued against the injustice of such a system. According to one historian, three main groups participated in the education debates. The first group, centered around the Ministry of Education, supported the Tolstoi system. The second group argued for a democratic school system, one in which any child could receive a university diploma. This group wanted to introduce a ladder system of education with a curriculum based on the liberal arts or general education. The third group was also interested in expanding educational opportunity, but believed that Russian schools should emphasize vocational education rather than liberal arts. As a result of these debates, other government ministries, most notably the Ministry of Finance, stepped into the realm of educational policy and introduced new kinds of vocational schools. The Ministry of Education had high-level discussions about reforming the Tolstoi system, but in the end these debates brought no meaningful changes.[25]

Even though this public debate about education did not bring about any significant reforms, it did bring teachers into the public eye. The government saw teachers as key participants in the success of the tsarist educational program. The intelligentsia acknowledged the importance of enlisting teachers' support in changing the educational system. And everyone recognized the teachers' role in combatting illiteracy. In the countryside, rural teachers were weapons in the fight against peasant backwardness. In the cities, teachers were necessary to help transform the illiterate urban classes into a modern industrial work force. It was essential that factory workers, for example, obtain the skills necessary for their work and for their survival in the cities; and the teacher was the expert who could provide these skills. If Russia was to compete with the rest of the world, the success of the city teacher's role as cultural agent was critical.

Who were these city teachers? One is immediately struck by their social profile. Unlike their counterparts in Western Europe and America, who had middle-class origins, in Russia city teachers came from the traditional service groups—the nobility, the civil and military bureaucracy, and the clergy.[26] This difference in origins suggests the important changes in social status that were occurring in postreform Russia. It was no longer enough to be born into the elite; it was now necessary to work in one of the new professions to keep one's status. Although teaching was not held in the same high regard as other professions in Russia, it was still a way to guarantee social success. City teachers' social origins were also quite different from those of rural teachers. In the 1870s the Ministry of Education inaugurated a policy of hiring peasant men to serve as teachers in the village schools. The ministry believed that these men would be less susceptible to revolutionary propaganda and make better teachers of peasant children than men from urban Russia.[27] Thus, from its very beginning, the teaching profession was sharply divided into two distinct groups, city and rural teachers. These divisions were not based solely on where the teachers worked, but also on their social origins. This meant that as teachers tried to create a new social identity based on common interests, they had to overcome the inequities of the older social system that divided them, as well as their own individual identities, which were also divided. Given the complexity of Russian social relations, this task proved extremely difficult.

Unlike rural primary schoolteachers, who were scattered all over the countryside and had few opportunities to discuss their problems, city primary and secondary teachers were able to meet often and discuss their concerns. This ability to meet repeatedly, both formally and informally, without unduly arousing the suspicions of the police gave them an advantage in developing a sense of professional identity. Moreover, city teachers also met with members of other professional groups. Because membership in the various professional societies was not limited solely to one occupational group, teachers could join or participate in other professional societies, thereby gaining practical expertise in running such organizations. In addition, by joining other voluntary associations that promoted Russian intellectual and cultural life, teachers furthered their understanding of Russia's serious social and political problems and became an integral part of the newly emerging public sphere.

The most important group of city teachers were those who worked in St. Petersburg and Moscow, and it is they who are the focus of this study. Teachers were the largest professional group in the two capitals. According to the 1897 census, there were almost twelve thousand teachers who worked in Petersburg and Moscow; by 1912 Moscow alone had more than sixteen thousand. More important for the teachers' professional movement, over half of all city teachers worked in the two capitals.[28] Teachers in Moscow and Petersburg shared similar problems with other city teachers. All suffered from low pay, poor working conditions, overcrowding in the classroom, an increasingly demanding curriculum, and a majority of pupils suffering from the ill effects of poverty, malnutrition, and abuse. These problems typified life in city schools for all teachers who worked in them.[29] What made teachers in Petersburg and Moscow different from their colleagues was that they were the best educated, the most articulate and the most active of all city teachers. Living in the two capital cities allowed these teachers to witness and sometimes participate in the important changes that were occurring in Russian social, political, and intellectual life. These advantages meant that Moscow and Petersburg teachers were the first of all city teachers to articulate a professional ethos. Because they were the leaders and much of the membership of the city teachers' professional movement, their experiences had a profound influence on the entire professional movement.[30]

Despite the advantages of working in the capital cities, teachers had difficult lives. In teachers' accounts and government reports, a number of common themes emerge. The secondary schools were tightly controlled by the various government agencies that administered them. The rigid curriculum and teaching methods made for a rather dry and formal approach to learning. Relations between pupils and teachers were further strained because teachers were expected to supervise their pupils' activities both in and outside the classroom. Many secondary schools did not have the necessary facilities or equipment to teach some of the required subjects, and there was frequent overcrowding, particularly in the lower grades. The primary schools were encumbered by a difficult administrative structure: the Ministry of Education and the cities attempted to share responsibility for the schools but their areas of competency were poorly defined. Battles over jurisdiction were frequent, with teachers often caught in the middle. The city governments added more schools as quickly as they could, but they could never keep up with the demand for primary education. Limited by insufficient tax revenues, the cities were faced with too many children to educate with the available monies.[31]

Particularly in the area of primary education, Moscow and Petersburg teachers worked in very different school systems. Moscow began its municipal primary schools in 1867 when the city set up five schools to provide a basic education for girls, who were barred from enrolling in the government primary schools. When the Ministry of Education essentially turned over responsibility for urban primary education to the cities in 1870, Moscow quickly set about the task of providing an elementary education for both boys and girls, during the last quarter of the nineteenth century. Each school consisted of three grades, usually with one teacher per grade. Teaching and administration within the school was coordinated by a head teacher. By contrast, Petersburg school officials started their municipal school system later than Moscow (1877) and established one-room schoolhouses throughout the city. In the Petersburg schools, there was one teacher who instructed all three grades. The end result was that there were more schools in Petersburg than in Moscow, but each city educated the same percentage of the school-age population. For example, in 1898, Petersburg had 341 schools with 19,985 pupils, while Moscow had only 136 schools but 18,045 pupils.[32] These structural differences were important to the teachers. Although Moscow's city government is often regarded as more democratic than that of Petersburg, its schools were more bureaucratic than the Petersburg one-room schoolhouses. Moscow teachers had to follow the instructions of the head teachers, who received their instructions from a variety of city and government officials. Petersburg teachers had greater freedom to instruct their pupils as they saw fit, with only occasional interference from outside officials.[33] When Petersburg city officials abandoned the one-room schoolhouse in favor of the more centralized and bureaucratic schools used in Moscow, the teachers perceived this as a challenge to their status as professionals.

Despite the centrality of Moscow and Petersburg teachers to prerevolutionary Russian social history, no history of these teachers exists. There are several reasons for this lacuna. Working in the best schools and under the best conditions, teachers in Moscow and Petersburg were the elite of the profession. In a country where so many were less fortunate, city teachers were reluctant to complain too loudly about their plight. Instead, they devoted their energies to trying to improve working conditions for all teachers. City teachers focused much of their public speaking and writing on the plight of rural teachers; they spoke less frequently about their own problems and concerns.

With the 1917 Russian Revolution and the advent of a Soviet school of historiography, city teachers virtually disappear from the public record. Soviet historians have centered on rural teachers as a kind of proletariat of the profession. Yet the reasons for this glorification of the plight of rural teachers have gone beyond a simple empathy for the disadvantaged. By arguing for local control of the schools and teacher control over the classroom, ideas antithetical to the Bolshevik ruling elite, city teachers participated in a serious struggle with the Bolshevik Party for control of the profession after 1917. Once the supporters of a central bureaucratized school system gained control of the profession, city teachers and their views were rarely, if ever, mentioned in historical studies.[34]

The other reason for their studied silence on city teachers in Soviet historiography is that much of that history concerns the history of women in Russia. Soviet historians, in general, were not interested in the condition of women. The historians who have studied women have written almost exclusively about those socialists working for women's issues, and have ignored the "bourgeois" feminist movement that developed in Russia at the turn of the century. The underlying assumption of much of this historiography is that women's problems are not different from men's and do not need separate treatment. Thus, with the exception of one article published in 1941, the problems of women teachers in prerevolutionary Russia have not concerned Soviet historians.[35]

Unfortunately, recent Western historiography has repeated these errors of omission. For example, two recent books do briefly discuss women teachers, but primarily in a negative way: women allegedly could not be effective teachers in rural schools because they were "outsiders" in the villages. More important, it was claimed that women teachers did not play a significant role within the profession, even though their numbers increased dramatically in postreform Russia.[36] Instead, I will argue that women teachers were quite explicitly discriminated against in tsarist Russia. Men administrators and teachers alike belittled women's role in the classroom and in the profession. By defining women as outsiders, men teachers were attempting to exclude women as unqualified, thereby raising their own status. Perkin terms this the "strategy of closure." Women developed their own unique identity as teachers, based on traditional models of female behavior, and they continued to struggle to gain a rightful place in the teachers' professional organization throughout the period under study. In Russia as elsewhere, gender played an essential role in teachers' professional development in Russia.[37]

Until now, historians have written primarily about the role of women in the Russian revolutionary movement, women's struggle for education and the women's liberation movement.[38] The role of women professionals has not been analyzed, even though their acceptance into occupations that had been traditionally within the male sphere marked an important step toward women's equality. In Russia, as in other Western countries, women labored mightily to achieve positions within the professions. Through hard work and determination, women gained admission. In the case of teaching, acceptance was easier because teaching was seen as part of women's "natural" work. And by 1914, more women were employed in teaching than in any other profession. By examining the role of women teachers, we will understand better the challenges all women faced in becoming full-fledged members of a profession.

In order to fill this serious gap in our historical knowledge, this study seeks to understand the role teachers in St. Petersburg and Moscow played in their profession and in their society. Who were these teachers who worked in Moscow and Petersburg? What were their hopes and aspirations for themselves and their country? What kind of a profession did they envision? Frustrated by their inability to act as independent, competent experts in the face of government opposition, city teachers began to demand greater control over their occupation and its members. These demands were, in turn, informed by the values, attitudes, and self-definition taking shape as part of Russian teachers' professional ethos.

As part of their attempts to create a profession, city teachers tried to establish a new self-definition. Nineteenth-century literature and society contained three competing images of teachers. In one image, a dedicated and passionate revolutionary lived in desperate poverty while trying to teach reading and revolutionary zeal to his pupils. In another image, "the man in the footlocker" portrayed by Chekhov in a short story of the same name, the schoolteacher was a cog in a machine, a person who did his job each day and returned to his hovel unaware of the life around him. In the final image, the teacher-bureaucrat taught children, not because he loved learning or his pupils, but only because he wanted to advance himself in the government hierarchy and receive monetary rewards and greater social status. City teachers wanted to replace these images with one of their own creation: "the soul of the school." This phrase symbolized for them the changes they wished to make in their own consciousness and that of their fellow Russians. Instead of being considered dull and boring pedants, bureaucrats seeking self-aggrandizement, or wild-eyed revolutionaries, Russian teachers wanted to be viewed as well-trained specialists who cared about their students and their country.

By using such a powerful image as "the soul of the school," city teachers were insisting that without their support and skills, the schools would surely die and the hopes for a better future for all Russians would be imperiled. When the government did not respond to their calls for reform and tried to inhibit their professional development, city teachers began to call for the creation of a new school in Russia. According to their vision, this new school would be governed by local officials, parents, and teachers equally, with little interference from outside authorities. In the classroom, teachers would teach as they saw fit, guided by their pedagogical training and practical experience. The entire school system would be dedicated to providing education to any child, regardless of social origin.

City teachers soon realized that this new school required a new Russia in which to prosper. In postreform Russia the autocracy followed a contradictory course that appeared to encourage reforms but was never completely willing to implement them. City teachers grew frustrated with a government policy that simultaneously encouraged and discouraged professionalization. Finally, teachers' frustration drew them into the nascent political liberation movement. Thwarted in their desire for educational reform, city teachers saw political reform as the essential prerequisite. Linking professionalization and politics in their professional movement, city teachers were drawn inexorably into the revolutionary crisis that enveloped Russia in 1905.

The first three chapters of this book examine the construction of city teachers' professional identity. Pedagogical training and shared experiences both in and outside the classroom helped to make city teachers aware of their common interests and concerns. Chapter 1 discusses city teachers' pedagogical training. Despite different types of teacher training available, their education instilled in them a sense of professional purpose. Chapter 2 delineates the common problems teachers faced in the school system, problems that encouraged teachers to talk of a shared identity. If pedagogical training and classroom experiences caused teachers to speak of a common identity, gender emphasized the serious differences that divided the profession. As chapter 3 shows, men teachers and administrators developed discursive methods for trying to keep women at the periphery of the profession. By defining women as outsiders to the profession, they did not have to take seriously the challenge that women teachers presented to male authority within the profession. This tendency to ignore serious divisions along not only gender but also class lines would prove problematic in city teachers' quest for a unified profession. For their part, women teachers refused to accept their status as outsiders and continued to work to find a meaningful place for themselves in the profession.

The three remaining chapters deal with city teachers' attempts to institutionalize and publicize their professional consciousness among all the teachers. Chapter 4 examines the chief devices—mass organizations and national meetings—that city teachers used to articulate their professional goals. At the same time, the city teachers' professional movement became closely linked to the Liberation movement. This political and professional discontent exploded into revolutionary fervor during the Revolution of 1905, the subject of chapter 5. It was at this time that the diverse professional and political interests that had been submerged in the common fight for professional status now splintered the teachers' professional movement. In understanding their participation in the breakup of the national teachers' professional movement, we will see the extent to which city teachers' attitudes and values were shaped by their professionalization. Chapter 6 shows the continued efforts of city teachers to achieve many of the institutional and political demands they had unsuccessfully put forward during the 1905 Revolution. City teachers' actions between 1907 and 1914 demonstrate the ways in which their professional consciousness promoted the new values of autonomy, self-reliance, and individualism within the context of a public service ethic.

It is important to stress that this study remains a collective biography. It is difficult in any society to reconstruct the lives of individual teachers, but particularly so in Russian history. School records are scattered and incomplete. Few city teachers wrote about their lives or concerns and those who did frequently wrote anonymously. In fact, teachers could and did lose their jobs for writing unflattering portraits of the schools and their officials. The voices and deeds of individual men and women teachers remain muffled in this study. Yet, as a group, city teachers' collective stories and actions provide an essential case study of the emergence of the teaching profession and of their role in Russian civil society.

1 Pedagogy and Professionalization

TEACHING HAD NEVER BEEN AN EXALTED OCCUPATION IN RUSSIA. Before the 1860s, most primary schoolteachers had been priests or seminarians who accepted teaching positions either to supplement their income or to provide employment until they received a parish assignment. There were frequent reports that some rural teachers were barely literate. Nevertheless, they managed to secure a teaching job during the winter months, when there was no field work to perform.[1] In the cities tutors and governesses, many of them foreigners with a poor command of Russian, taught the children of the upper classes. Although secondary schoolteachers were university graduates, they were not held in high regard by Russian society; most were considered dry, boring pedants. Moreover, many secondary schoolteachers looked upon their work as a career advancement in the government bureaucracy, rather than as meaningful, productive work. Teaching was not an end in itself, but the means to obtain a more lucrative career in the bureaucracy.[2]

With the inauguration of the Great Reforms, the Ministry of Education began an empire-wide effort to improve the quality of education that all Russians received. If Russia was to compete as a modern industrialized nation, it needed a well-trained, literate corps of workers, technicians, and managers. In order to achieve this goal, the Ministry of Education reformed all existing educational institutions, including the universities and secondary schools. The ministry also gave local governments the initiative to establish new primary schools throughout Russia. But it was not enough to provide more schools; the quality of teaching needed improvement as well.

Given the low opinion most Russians had of teachers, the Ministry of Education had set itself a difficult task. In order to achieve improved classroom instruction, education officials embarked upon a government-sponsored professionalization program. To raise the status of teaching, the ministry began to emphasize the important work teachers performed for their society. The ministry raised educational qualifications, hired full-time teachers, and raised their pay as part of this effort. The task of training Russia's future subjects was too vital to be entrusted to barely literate peasants and priests. Instead, ministry officials wanted a dedicated corps of teachers to bring science, progress, and civilization to the people. In order to serve as cultural missionaries, Russian teachers, like other professionals, needed to become "experts" in their chosen field and to make a life-long commitment to their profession. Once they had mastered their field of expertise, they could be entrusted with their noble mission.

A central component of government-sponsored professionalization was the creation and implementation of better teacher training programs.[3] In 1872 teachers' institutes were established to train advanced primary schoolteachers; teachers' seminaries for men primary schoolteachers were introduced in 1875; and the first pedagogical courses for women were opened in 1859. By 1880 a new system of teacher training programs was in place. The desired end of government-sponsored professionalization was improved teacher cadres. In Russia, better teacher training included academic specialization for advanced teaching, child-centered pedagogy at the primary level, and the inculcation of political loyalty to the regime. As these principles suggest, the government program tried to implement new approaches to teacher training while remaining firmly rooted in the autocratic tradition. For teachers intending to teach at the secondary levels, professionalization meant academic specialization and mastery of a discrete body of knowledge. For primary schoolteachers, professionalization meant an emphasis on pedagogy, particularly on child-centered pedagogy. Child-centered pedagogy, a new philosophy of education developed by the Swiss educator Johann Pestalozzi, encouraged more pupil-teacher interaction based on the child's interests, and an approach to learning that was more democratic than the traditional rote memorization. The goal of this pedagogy was to foster a child's self-esteem and autonomy through learning. Nineteenth-century Europeans thought of it as a "scientific" theory because it was based upon insights from the new science of child psychology. After their training in this new "scientific" pedagogy, primary schoolteachers would become "experts" in child development.

The final principle guiding the ministry's teacher training programs was the political reliability of all teachers. The ministry permitted only those students with spotless political records to enter teacher training programs. In addition, officials proceeded to construct a curriculum for these programs so that future teachers received what the government believed to be just enough knowledge to teach effectively, but no extraneous information that might cause political discontent. Through this type of teacher preparation, the ministry hoped to create a corps of professional public servants who were loyal to the regime.

These three principles guiding the ministry's policies—specialized training, child-centered pedagogy, and political reliability—provided a strong basis for the professionalization of teachers. Teachers began to see themselves as important contributors to Russian society. Many accepted wholeheartedly their mission to bring enlightenment to Russia's future subjects, and they saw this work as a career that conferred meaningful social status. But, at the same time, their adoption of a professional self-identity brought them into conflict with the same Ministry of Education that had sponsored their professional development. The ministry was interested in creating a professional elite only so long as it did not challenge the ministry's leading role in the educational policy. And yet, the very pedagogy that teachers were encouraged to use in the classroom emphasized the development of an individual's self-esteem and autonomy. Thus, the ministry's teacher training program contained contradictory elements. Self-esteem and autonomy were good for children, but not for their adult teachers. As teachers grew more conscious of themselves as professionals, they began to resent the government's concern for political reliability, which thwarted their quest for autonomy. Teachers complained bitterly of the strict and arbitrary regime at teacher training programs and rightly argued that it ran counter to their professional training.

Teacher training programs, like so many other schools in Russia, helped to create a sense of corporate solidarity among the students. But this solidarity was frequently created in opposition to the government and its officials, who were, after all, the future employers of many of these teachers. This oppositional attitude became an integral part of teacher training so that even before they joined the profession many teachers came to view the ministry as hostile to their work as dedicated professionals. The tension between the ministry as the initiator of professionalization and the newly professionalized teachers permeated all their joint activities.

To understand how teacher training shaped the professional identity of city teachers, we will look at the efforts of the Ministry of Education to improve their education. The majority of teachers in Petersburg and Moscow graduated from three kinds of institutions—

the universities, the women's pedagogical courses, and the teachers' institutes. Each of these institutions helped future teachers to feel themselves part of a new and important profession.

The Universities

In order to teach in any secondary school, it was essential to have a university diploma.[4] The first Russian university had been founded in 1755 in Moscow, but it was not until 1802 that Alexander I created six more universities. By 1905 Russia had ten universities located in the major cities. Russian universities had a long and difficult history. The Ministry of Education attempted to reform the universities in 1864 by granting them an unprecedented degree of autonomy. In 1881, following the assassination of Alexander II and two decades of student demonstrations, the ministry rescinded some of this autonomy, an action that only served to antagonize faculty and students. According to one recent study, Russian universities were caught between those who wished Russia to remain an autocracy and those who wanted a democratic Russia. The ministry's ambivalent policy created serious tensions within the universities that were never resolved.[5]

The purpose of the Russian universities was to train scholars and civil servants for all the government ministries, not to serve as teacher training programs. Nevertheless, when the Ministry of Education decided to make a university degree the requirement for secondary schoolteachers, it had to determine how to provide the necessary training for those who wished to teach.

There were two teaching methodologies in Russia by mid-century. The first was the traditional rote and memorization method. Following this pedagogy, teachers conducted classes by giving their pupils assignments to memorize. The students came to class the next day prepared to recite what they had learned; there was no class discussion and very little explanation by the teacher. This was the teaching methodology that prevailed in Russian primary and secondary schools until the Great Reforms.

In the early nineteenth century Russian educators learned of a new pedagogy that was particularly influential in German-speaking countries. First articulated by Johann Pestalozzi, a Swiss educator, and later expanded upon by Friedrich Froebel and Johann Herbart, this method was based on new theories of child development and psychology, and was called child-centered pedagogy. Child-centered pedagogy tried to foster the development of the whole child—intellectual, moral, and physical—and thereby encourage a child's self-esteem, individuality, and independence.[6] Pestalozzi met Alexander I during the Napoleonic Wars and impressed him with his new approach to learning. Upon returning to Russia, Alexander asked Count Sergei Uvarov to study his ideas further, but Uvarov expressed serious doubt about their applicability to Russia. Despite this lack of official sanction, Russian educators continued to discuss child-centered pedagogy. Finally, Konstantin Ushinskii, Russia's most famous educator, popularized many of the concepts of child-centered pedagogy in Russia and created a Russian national pedagogy that emphasized an interactive pedagogy between teacher and pupil. Although Ushinskii was persecuted by the government, his ideas became influential and provided a real alternative to the traditional rote method.[7]

In its plans to prepare secondary schoolteachers at the universities, the Ministry of Education had to choose between two pedagogical methods: the traditional rote method or the newer child-centered pedagogy. After much vacillation, in 1867 the Ministry of Education adopted the philosophy that "pedagogy is only a skill, which comes in the process of work."[8] This meant that university students received no specialized pedagogical training at all, only the specific knowledge of their academic discipline.

This lack of methodological preparation gets to the heart of the Ministry of Education's reluctance to insist on pedagogical training for men secondary schoolteachers. Child-centered pedagogy emphasized the development of a child's self-esteem and self-motivation. These qualities were antithetical to the teaching and entire philosophy of education that the minister of education, Count Dmitrii Tolstoi, had introduced into Russian secondary schools. Tolstoi saw these schools as training grounds requiring more discipline, not greater freedom. While Tolstoi saw real advantages in using child-centered pedagogy to teach primary schoolchildren, he disapproved of it for young adults.[9]

As a result, university students who chose teaching as their career were not required to take any courses in pedagogy. Rather than creating a separate department as some had wanted, the Ministry placed pedagogy within the philosophy department at Russian universities. The students took classes in their areas of specialization, but the professors did not take time to discuss the topics that might concern a future teacher, such as what textbooks to use or how to present new material. As one critic put it, "Professors saw in their students not future secondary schoolteachers, but future researchers, recruiting from these students candidates for professorships." Upon graduation, these young men went into the classroom without any prior experience and faced their new job without any supervision. Because of their lack of preparation, many men quickly became disenchanted and left the profession.[10]

Because acquisition of knowledge was and is such a central part of professionalization, secondary schoolteachers came to identify themselves as specialists in their chosen field as well as teachers. Those teachers who did not give up after the first exhausting years of teaching did as much as they could to participate in their academic disciplines. Many wrote articles, monographs, and textbooks. When such meetings were permitted, secondary schoolteachers attended scholarly conferences in their area of specialization. Thus, in some ways, they resembled university professors, who also shared a double identity in their disciplines and in their profession.[11]

Problems persisted because of the decision not to provide pedagogical training for university students. A high turnover rate among secondary schoolteachers created a chronic shortage of qualified teachers. The complaints about the quality of teaching in the secondary schools persisted. In 1898 the Ministry of Education called upon the curators of the educational districts to discuss these problems and recommend some changes. The curators set up a commission to study the problem, but they immediately divided among themselves as to the remedy. Supporters of the existing system of teacher training believed that the university provided excellent training, not only in a student's area of specialization, but also in the other required subjects. University graduates could and did teach their students without any need for special courses in pedagogy or methodology.[12]

Other educators did not concur and felt that some reform was essential. Most critics agreed on the need for additional pedagogical courses, but disagreed over the length of study—one summer or an additional two years of study. A more significant point of disagreement was whether pedagogical training courses should be offered through the university. P. Ivanovskii suggested that, instead of creating a new department of pedagogy, the university should have a staff of specialists with different areas of expertise, who could be called upon to provide information in the different departments as needed.[13] Despite these disagreements over implementation of the reforms, all agreed that university students needed a background in child psychology, hygiene, the history of pedagogy, and teaching methodology if they were to become better teachers.[14]

In addition to pleading for better academic training for future students, some critics of the existing system argued that other measures were necessary. One proposal suggested that new secondary schoolteachers should be under the direct supervision of the director of the school for three years to get practical guidance on how to improve their teaching.[15] Another supporter of reform, S. Zenchenko, proposed the establishment of teachers' clubs to provide a forum to discuss problems. This last suggestion led to complaints that, in order to have better teachers, the system needed to provide better salaries and incentives to keep qualified people in the teaching profession.[16]

In its published report, the government commission recommended that the universities create special pedagogical courses emphasizing both theoretical and practical teacher training.[17] The Ministry of Education, however, always in need of more teachers, refused to jeopardize the meager supply by making the educational requirements more demanding. Moreover, the ministry remained committed to using traditional rote and memorization method in the secondary schools, making any change a moot point. Accordingly, these measures were never adopted and teacher training for men secondary schoolteachers remained unchanged until after the Revolution of 1917.

What government policy toward teacher training in the universities did achieve was to encourage a sense of corporate solidarity among the students. There is a growing literature in Russian history on the importance of schools in forming lifelong support networks and common bonds among graduates. Richard Wortman has written eloquently on the importance of the School of Jurisprudence in the creation of a newly conscious corps of lawyers in the 1860s. Daniel Brower has described the development of a nihilist counterculture at the Russian universities, and Barbara Alpern Engel has discussed the formation of women's networks among the intelligentsia.[18] University students, easily identifiable in their uniforms and caps, developed a consciousness of themselves as a distinct group within Russian society, the *studenchestvo*. The shared experiences of Russian undergraduates helped to unite them in their differences with the faculty, the administration, and the government. Even though there was disagreement about the meaning of student identity, no one seriously doubted its existence.[19] Equally important, the curriculum at the universities introduced students to the literature and terminology of their new field, and thereby helped to create a professional consciousness and identity. At the same time, these men formed common bonds that could be renewed through correspondence or by becoming colleagues at the same school. Especially for teachers lucky enough to find jobs in the cities, there were ample opportunities to continue and strengthen these school friendships in the workplace. As the professional movement began to grow, these teachers constantly referred to their shared identity and fate. A professional ethos among secondary schoolteachers emerged first in Russia's universities.

Women's Pedagogical Courses

Pedagogical training for women was somewhat different. As will be discussed at greater length in chapter 3, women occupied an ambiguous position within the teaching profession. They usually taught only for a few years before they married and pursued their "natural" role—the care of their children. Because of their short stay in the profession, women were seen as less "professional" than their male colleagues, who devoted their whole working lives to public education. Despite this perception of women teachers, the Ministry of Education remained committed to professionalizing all teacher training programs. However, attempts to provide better teacher training for women created a constant tension between those who saw women as temporary educators and wanted women's pedagogical training to make them better mothers, and those who saw women as professional educators and wanted to create a more "scientific" and therefore more "professional" training for them.

The decision to hire women teachers was the result of the introduction of child-centered pedagogy in Russia and a vigorous debate on "the woman question." Because child-centered pedagogy was seen as a successful way to teach young children, it brought about important changes for women. Many educators insisted that the best teachers of young children were those who understood the moral and physical development of children. Because this had been traditionally the woman's role within the family, women came to be seen as the best teachers for the primary schools. Yet most educators felt that it was necessary to educate women for their "natural" role. Nature, after all, was capricious and unpredictable. Since there were many examples in nineteenth-century Russia of poor mothers, women's "natural" abilities were not foolproof. Moreover, reliance upon natural abilities ran counter to the growing professional movement. Professionalization stressed acquired skills, expertise, and science—positive knowledge that could be regulated and verified. According to this perspective, women could not be allowed to follow their own instincts, but instead had to be trained according to the latest pedagogical theories in order to be both better mothers and teachers. In short, women had to be trained to become women.[20]

These changes in pedagogical theories and women's education coincided with a debate over "the woman question" in Russia during the 1850s and 1860s. This debate emerged, as did so many other "burning questions" in nineteenth-century Russia, following the Crimean War debacle. The decision to emancipate the serfs and reform Russian society caused the educated elite to rethink social relations among all members of society, even between men and women. The debate on the woman question began as a narrow concern for women's education, but quickly developed into a full discussion of women's place in society, including women's right to seek meaningful employment outside the home.

Before 1850 most Russians did not believe that women should prepare themselves for an independent and autonomous life. Like other Europeans, they subordinated education to women's position in the family: women's education was to prepare them to be excellent wives and mothers. This attitude was accepted by educated Russians without question until mid-century.[21]

In 1856 the publication of "Questions of Life," an article by the noted physician and educator, N. I. Pirogov, challenged this view. In that article, Pirogov roundly criticized the current state of women's education, which emphasized the arts and foreign languages. He argued that women were educated to become like dolls, purely decorative. Instead, Pirogov challenged Russian society to educate women for the betterment of society. As future mothers and teachers, women directly influenced their children's development and thereby the development of Russia.[22]

Pirogov's indictment of education had an enormous effect on the educated public. According to D. D. Semenov, one of the new breed of professional educators and a future official for the Petersburg city schools, Pirogov's article caused everyone to rethink the purpose of education.[23] The proponents of women's emancipation argued that women should acquire a good liberal arts education, which would allow them to gain economic independence through work. Through work, women could develop meaningful lives separate from those of their families and husbands. This view was publicized by Chernyshevskii in his widely read novel, *What is to Be Done?* Such prominent educators as K. D. Ushinskii advocated complete equality in the education of both sexes.[24] For women, this meant less emphasis on the decorative arts and more time devoted to math, science, and history. Opponents of women's emancipation continued to insist that women should adhere to their traditional roles as wives and mothers. Nevertheless, even conservatives agreed that women's education, as it existed in the 1850s, was woefully inadequate—it created mindless creatures who could neither manage a household nor converse intelligently with their husbands. The conservatives, too, wanted educational reform, but only to prepare women in a very practical way to be better wives and mothers.

Despite the disagreement about the goal of women's education, both sides concluded that major reform was needed in women's education. In 1858 the Ministry of Education and the Department of the Institutions of the Empress Maria opened women's gymnasiums and pro-gymnasiums. After a protracted debate, Alexander II authorized the opening of women's higher courses in 1872.[25] The young woman was to be educated in order to be "the teacher of mankind, above all a citizen-mother, and not a fashionable doll."[26]

As the mixing of the terms "teacher" and "citizen-mother" suggests, the idea that women's education served as a preparation for marriage and motherhood, women's role according to the older service ethic, was never completely rejected, and the reforms were a compromise with the conservatives. Russian society still saw teaching in the public schools as preparation for women's traditional role—women teachers became substitute mothers for their pupils until they had their own children. Because of the link established between teaching and gender, the values associated with good teaching and, especially, with the care of young schoolchildren were seen as "feminine" values. As one Russian educator wrote as late as 1905, "the education of children is a woman's specialty."[27] And while this meant that women could be accepted as teachers, it also meant that teaching began to be marked as women's work, thereby lessening its appeal as a career choice for men, as the rapid feminization of the teaching profession after 1900 demonstrates.[28]

In order to prepare women for their work as schoolteachers, the Ministry of Education and the Department of the Institutions of the Empress Maria introduced pedagogical training courses for women in the gymnasiums in 1859. At first the courses consisted of a year of study in addition to the regular curriculum; after a while young women took courses in their seventh and eighth years at school. Completion of these pedagogical courses allowed a young woman to teach in the primary schools.

The purpose of the gymnasium course was to "acquaint the students with the science of pedagogy: to prepare them to read pedagogical articles independently, to interest them in pedagogical questions, to broaden their intellectual outlook, and to ensure their continuing participation in the field of pedagogy."[29] Young women studied general pedagogy, didactics, teaching methodology, and the history of pedagogy. They also studied the physical and moral development of the child, including methods of encouraging a child's curiosity and mastery of the environment.[30] Thus, the purpose of the courses was to make pedagogical training scientific and progressive in the hope that women would take their education into the classroom and into their homes.

To supplement this theoretical instruction, women students served as assistants in the lower classes of a gymnasium and selected a particular special subject. This demonstrates that growing specialization was becoming a part of women's pedagogical preparation, even though there were few primary schools that required such specialization.[31] The pedagogical courses appealed to the Ministry of Education because they were a fairly quick and inexpensive way to supply teachers for the growing number of new primary schools.

However, Russian educators and parents were not entirely satisfied with this type of pedagogical training. Russian parents complained that their daughters, all of whom were intended to be wives and mothers, knew nothing about the care and upbringing of children, despite their education. As one critic stated the problem, "The pedagogical program gives too much attention to pedagogical technicalities, studying moral and intellectual development and too little time to the physical upbringing [of children]; it [the program] exclusively views the future schoolteacher as a *sexless professional* and completely ignores these future wives and mothers as educators in the family circle" (emphasis added).[32] This view clearly shows the attitude of many Russians toward women teachers—pedagogical training and teaching were intended to enhance women's "natural" abilities as wives and mothers, not to make them into "sexless professionals."

Those educators who viewed women's role in education more seriously criticized the teaching methodology used in the courses. They felt that the courses offered a superficial review of many subjects without dealing in much substance. Brakengeim pointed out that while young women read selections from Locke, Rousseau, Ushinskii, and Pirogov, they read without any historical understanding of the authors.[33] In addition, the subject matter in the courses was often presented in a dry and boring fashion. This criticism was applied to much of the teaching at the secondary level in Russia. E. D'iakonova argued that if young women were taught in such a dull manner, they would also teach their pupils and their own children in such a fashion.[34] These criticisms of the pedagogical courses reflected the conflicting attitudes toward women's education. Some parents and educators still emphasized the primacy of family for their daughters; they wanted more time devoted to pedagogical training so that their daughters might become better wives and mothers. At the same time, many educators wanted more pedagogical training for women because women had proved themselves to be good teachers. Although these educators still acknolwedged women's "natural" role in the home, teaching was rapidly becoming women's "natural" profession. In order for women to succeed in this profession, educators argued, more extensive training and job supervision by men were needed. The result was the periodic lengthening of women's pedagogical courses in late imperial Russia to allow for more subjects and greater specialization.[35] Nevertheless, the dual nature of women's pedagogical education remained.

Women could also obtain permission to teach in the women's gymnasiums, the lower classes of the male gymnasiums (after 1906), and primary schools by graduating from one of the higher women's courses. The higher women's courses had been established in 1872 with the opening of the Moscow Higher Women's (Guerrier) Courses, followed by the St. Petersburg Higher Women's (Bestuzhev) Courses in 1878. The history of these courses was long and stormy. Their main purpose was to provide young women with a university-type degree without allowing them into the already-established universities, then exclusively for men. Since a university degree was necessary for men who were to teach at the secondary level, it was only logical that women secondary schoolteachers be required to have an equivalent educational background. Thus, the Bestuzhev and Guerrier courses provided training for teachers at both the secondary and primary levels.[36]

Even at the women's higher courses, however, the same conflict over the purpose of women's general education and pedagogical preparation remained. According to one recent history of the Bestuzhev courses, the director of the courses told the auditors to work hard "but not with the aim of preparing yourself for any kind of professional activity, no—you are preparing for life, mainly family life."[37] As a result, there was no specialized pedagogical training required for women interested in becoming teachers. Like men secondary schoolteachers, women graduates had advanced academic knowledge, but virtually no practical teaching experience.

Despite this lack of pedagogical training, most of the graduates of the women's higher courses became teachers either at the secondary or primary level. The figures for the Bestuzhev graduates illustrate this very well. Between 1882 and 1896, 1,346 women completed the higher courses in St. Petersburg. Of this number, 514 women or 71.1 percent went on to become teachers, of which 200 were teaching in city primary schools. The next largest group consisted of graduates working as headmistresses and teachers in secondary schools. The third largest group were women engaged as tutors giving private lessons. The others were either teaching in rural schools, serving as assistants in institutions of higher learning, or working as music teachers. In a similar survey of Bestuzhev graduates conducted in 1909, the proportion of women involved in teaching was 67 percent.[38]

It is difficult to assess the effect of pedagogical training on Russian women teachers: they spoke little of their experiences. According to a recent study of rural education, most zemstvo schoolteachers believed their general knowledge was adequate but felt themselves deficient in their understanding of pedagogy. This was particularly true for women gymnasium graduates. Others felt they lacked sufficient classroom experience rather than pedagogical knowledge.[39]

One exception to the teachers' silence on the impact of pedagogical training on their performance in the classroom was an anonymous article by a Petersburg teacher in 1893 in *Russkaia shkola*. Writing about her first year as a teacher in the Petersburg schools, she recalled that her chief difficulty was her inexperience with children from the lower classes. The gulf between her own upbringing and the home life of her new pupils was wide. Much of the article detailed her attempts to understand and deal with her pupils and their parents. When she found a subject that interested the children, she acknowledged that she did not stick to rigid lessons plans but allowed them to ask questions for as long as they wanted. In permitting her pupils' interests to govern the lessons, this teacher was clearly following the precepts of the child-centered pedagogy she learned during her training. However, this meant her pupils spent less time learning to write and count: one child could not learn to count beyond the number three after three years of schooling. Discipline posed a particular problem—her expectations for order and silence in the classroom were higher than her pupils could maintain. She attributed her problems to her failure to account for the individual personalities of her pupils, and when she lowered her expectations, she and the children got along much better. The tone of the article suggested that despite her education and even a year's previous teaching experience, this teacher felt quite unprepared for the challenges of her position.[40]

As this young women's experience illustrates, the problems for most new teachers were not in devising the correct lesson plans, but rather in relating to their pupils. The heavily supervised student teaching that most young women experienced during their coursework was inadequate preparation for the classroom. It took two or three years of daily struggle for most teachers to gain confidence in their teaching ability. Moreover, these problems were not unique to Russian women teachers; they reflect a problem with pedagogical training in general. How can educators instruct teachers to provide structure and flexibility within the classroom, to teach large groups of children and still account for individual differences in ability and interests? How can teachers instruct children who are malnourished or abused? Teachers face these problems even in our own time.

One of the stated purposes of the pedagogical courses was to interest teachers in pedagogical questions so that they would continue to sharpen their teaching skills. In that area, women teachers who found jobs in the cities were better able than many rural teachers to keep abreast of the pedagogical literature. Both Moscow and Petersburg had libraries for teachers that subscribed to all the leading educational journals. In Petersburg, teachers were periodically permitted to hold meetings where pedagogical issues were discussed; during the 1870s they also met weekly with school officials to discuss problems.[41] Some school administrators actually encouraged teachers to write articles for the educational journals. In 1892 fifteen Petersburg teachers had written articles and, just two years later, thirty teachers had published.[42] Despite continuing difficulties for many women, all of these activities show a high level of pedagogical commitment on the part of teachers and suggest that at least some city teachers took their pedagogical training seriously and felt themselves to be a part of a newly emerging profession.

Like the universities, women's teacher training programs created a sense of community among their graduates that persisted well after graduation. Many of these schools had active alumni organizations that tried to keep track of graduates and occasionally provide material assistance to those who needed help. The Bestuzhev courses had just such an organization, and alumnae continued to meet well into the Soviet period.[43]

Finally, the emphasis on pedagogy as a scientific endeavor gave women teachers the chance to think of themselves as professionals and as equals to their male colleagues. Although they attended separate institutions, women were acquiring expertise in a discrete area of scientific inquiry. Thus, like the secondary schoolteachers, women's introduction to their professional identity and community came through their pedagogical training.

Teachers' Institutes

If the universities provide an example of specialized academic training and the women's pedagogical courses show the influence of child-centered pedagogy on Russian primary schoolteachers, the teachers' institutes are the best example of the third component of the Ministry of Education's teacher training program: the importance the government placed on Russian teachers' political reliability. It was not enough that the Ministry permitted only those with unblemished records into the programs; it also wanted to ensure that the teachers stayed loyal to the regime after graduation. The institutes present the most egregious example of how this preoccupation permeated the institutions and helped to create among teachers an increasingly antigovernment professional ethos.

Most men who taught in city primary schools were employed in advanced primary schools. The purpose of these schools was to provide a more extensive education than could be provided in the three-year primary schools. In order to train teachers for these new schools, the Ministry of Education created the teachers' institute (*uchitel'skii institut*). Ministry officials hoped the teachers' institute would educate graduates better than either the teachers' or the clerical seminaries, both of which had terrible reputations as teacher training programs. Because the advanced primary schools were initially just for boys, the ministry employed only men teachers, who were considered better suited to teaching young boys than were women. This meant that the institutes were also open to men only.

Despite the government's attempt to create a unique teacher training program for men primary schoolteachers, the teachers' institutes resembled the rural teachers' seminaries. Both institutions had the dual purpose of providing teachers with a more advanced educational training and ensuring the political reliability of the individuals involved. However, because the institutes were located in the cities, the Ministry of Education worried that the students would be exposed to those pernicious urban elements—gambling, prostitution, and more important, radical politics—that could make them unreliable teachers. Through strict regulation of what went on both inside and outside the classroom, the ministry hoped to insulate students from urban vices. As a result, the teachers' institutes became the most oppressive of all the pedagogical institutions.[44]

The student profile at the teachers' institutes was a bit different from that of other teacher training programs. In order to attract students to the new institutes, the Ministry of Education established a scholarship program that granted full scholarships to most entering students in return for six years of service after graduation. The ministry hoped to attract graduates of the advanced primary schools to the institutes and thereby maintain a continuous supply of teachers for these schools. This policy did not succeed, however. Although most students who attended the institutes received scholarships, the majority were former teachers from the rural primary schools, many of whom were graduates of the teachers' seminaries. In 1902 forty-two students at the Petersburg Teachers' Institute were graduates of teachers' seminaries, while only eighteen had graduated from the advanced primary schools.[45] Most of the students came from the lower classes, with peasants representing the largest social group. In social composition, the institutes were similar to the teachers' seminaries intended primarily for rural teachers (see Appendix, table 7).[46]

Another feature of the student profile was the students' age: the institute students tended to be older than most students at other teacher training programs. Among the seventy-one students attending the St. Petersburg Teachers' Institute in 1902, eighteen were between the ages of fifteen and nineteen, while thirty-seven were between the ages of twenty and twenty-four, and seventeen were between the ages of twenty-five and thirty. Students at the teachers' institutes were not for the most part adolescents, but rather adults, many of whom had worked for some years before returning to school. With a diploma from the teachers' institute, rural teachers could escape the isolation of teaching in the countryside and obtain work in the cities without having to leave their chosen profession.[47]

The Ministry of Education devised a curriculum to provide future teachers with only that knowledge necessary to teach in the advanced primary schools. The course of study at an institute was three years in duration, with much time spent in the classroom (see Appendix, table 8). Since teachers at the advanced primary level taught all subjects for each class, each student needed to do well in all subjects. Classes were conducted using the recitational approach with no class discussion allowed. Only in Moscow and Petersburg did the faculty lecture to the students with periodic drill sessions.[48]

Since one of the Ministry of Education's aims in creating the teachers' institutes was to keep the students out of trouble, the teachers' institutes established a rigid structure within which the students were given very little free time (see Appendix, table 9). Because almost all of the students boarded at the institutes, this type of control was fairly easy to implement. Each hour of the day was accounted for, and the students had few opportunities to go to the theater or other public places. They even complained that it was difficult for them to return home for the school holidays during their three-year stay at the institutes. In addition to the constant surveillance by the faculty, an elaborate system of student monitors reported unauthorized activities of other students.[49]

In this tightly supervised atmosphere, future teachers were expected to concern themselves only with educational matters. During their first two years at the institute, they studied the subjects they were expected to teach. The third year was devoted to acquiring practical teaching skills. Initially, students planned practice lessons; faculty then critiqued them and suggested improvements. During the second semester, students taught lessons in the advanced primary school affiliated with the teachers' institute. Each student spent two weeks teaching Russian, mathematics, history, geography, and science, thereby covering the entire curriculum. By graduation the students had spent eight weeks in the classroom.[50]

What did all this close supervision and rigorous educational program mean for the graduates of the institutes? Were they more effective as teachers as a result of this training? According to M. Demkov, a director of the Moscow Teachers' Institute and a leading educator, the answer to these questions was a resounding yes. Writing many years after the demise of the teachers' institutes, he commented:

Thanks to the work and efforts [of the directors, teachers, and students at the institutes], toward the end of the nineteenth century it was possible to say that the teachers' institutes had significantly improved the quality of the pedagogical education and methodological training of elementary teachers. [The institutes] prepared many conscientious and knowledgeable city teachers who worked with honor in the pedagogical field and developed a love for the city schools among the population.[51]

Not everyone agreed with Demkov's assessment, however. In an article published in 1904 in the influential journal, *Vestnik vospitaniia*, the anonymous author criticized the notion that the teachers' institutes provided a solid educational program. The curriculum had not been reviewed since it was established in 1872 and was greatly in need of reform. According to this critic, there were too many subjects to cover in too little time. As a result, coverage was shallow, and often the same textbooks were used to instruct the future teachers as were used by the pupils. There was no attempt to expand the knowledge of the students at the institutes. The author also calculated that students spent only one twenty-third of their time studying pedagogy; this put it in last place on their schedule.[52]

Criticism can also be found in the memoirs of the institutes' alumni. One relevant example is that of Aleksandr Nasimovich, who went to work for a merchant in Kostroma at the age of fourteen and decided six years later that he wanted to become a teacher. In the fall of 1900, he went to study at the "temple of knowledge," the Moscow Teachers' Institute, and spent his first few days there reading in the institute's excellent library. He quickly became disenchanted, however. He found the lessons boring and concerned with petty details that did not interest him. Worst of all, according to Nasimovich, the faculty at the school treated the students as if they were gymnasium students rather than adults.[53] The real problem at the institutes was that former teachers were taking classes side by side with recent graduates of the advanced primary schools. Like Nasimovich, the other adult men found the institutes geared toward the abilities of the adolescents. These men complained that the institute curriculum was not all that different from the curriculum of the teachers' seminaries, which many of them had already attended. As one graduate of the institutes put it, there could never be a sense of shared identity among the students at the institutes because of the hostility between the adults and the adolescents. This hostility was more than just a generation gap. He argued that Russian school life so polarized teachers and students that the former teachers and students could not get along with one another even though they were now all students. He told the story of one former teacher, now a student at a teachers' institute, who wanted his younger colleagues to give up part of their main meal to help feed the hungry during the famine of 1891–92. The young students refused, saying they did not want to mutiny (*buntovat'*).[54] This antagonism between students certainly made their three-year stay difficult.

In 1909 graduates of the teacher's institutes were asked to rate the education they had received. Of the 548 respondents, only 33 thought their education adequate. According to them, the chief problem with the institutes was the narrow curriculum. These teachers wanted a more advanced education in all subjects, but especially in modern Russian and European literature. One-third of the survey respondents also wanted an expanded course in psychology, pedagogy, and methodology. These were not immature adolescents, but responsible professionals who wanted to know about Russia's place in the modern world. They felt unprepared by the brief introduction they received in the institutes.[55]

After this rather gloomy report enumerating the flaws of an institute education, the compiler of the survey still concluded that the institutes were not a total failure. Despite the many flaws in the curriculum and administration of the institutes, the graduates acquired a basic understanding of pedagogical theory and a sense of themselves as belonging to the community of teachers.[56] Thus, even the teachers' institutes, the worst pedagogical training programs in Russia, managed to convey to their students a sense of professional identity.

Pedagogy and teacher training programs are not held in high regard in most modern societies. Everywhere problems in the schools are blamed on the teachers and their inability to instruct their pupils effectively. The qualities of good teaching are just as elusive now as they were to nineteenth-century Russian educators. This rather negative view of teacher training has influenced much writing on teachers and their attempts to professionalize. As one scholar has argued, teaching is a "semi-profession," in large part because there is no perceived canon of specialized knowledge that belongs exclusively to the teaching profession and that teacher training programs can convey to their students.[57]

While there is some truth to this critique of teacher training, the experience of Russian schoolteachers suggests another interpretation. To judge from the evidence presented here, Russian teachers felt that their training did impart a distinct attitude toward their work and their view of themselves as teachers. Pedagogical training in postreform Russia became more extensive and included more time studying theory and practice. Child-centered pedagogy, adopted from Western Europe, developed in primary schoolteachers a distinct way of teaching that differed from earlier methods. Even though secondary schoolteachers did not receive specialized pedagogical training, they considered themselves specialists in a particular field, and many felt committed to introducing pupils to their own specialized knowledge. Although their area of expertise differed, what is important is that both groups felt themselves to be technical specialists.

The adoption of child-centered pedagogy also meant that women could be hired as teachers for the first time. Because women were educators in the home, many believed that with proper training women could now be educators in the school. The difficulty was that women were educated to be both teachers and mothers. It was a woman's gender plus her pedagogical training that qualified her for her job. This argument was never made for men teachers and their training. Because women's pedagogical training always had a dual purpose, it created problems for women teachers, as we will see in chapter 3.

In addition to specialized training, a sense of community developed among graduates of these various programs. The students felt they were a part of something larger than themselves, a nascent teaching profession. This sense of corporate solidarity began with their shared experiences in the classroom as students and grew as they shared experiences as teachers. Without this sense of community, it would have been more difficult for teachers scattered all across the vast Russian empire to professionalize. It was, of course, easier for teachers who were located in one city to establish these contacts with former classmates, and the alumni organizations of teacher training programs were an important source for the creation of just such a teachers' network.

At the same time, this sense of community had an antigovernment tinge to it. Strict discipline and constant surveillance of students by their teachers in the training programs created ill will among many, if not all, teacher candidates. The contradictions in government policy toward teacher preparation were immediately apparent—the Ministry of Education was attempting to train a professional corps of civil servants, not professional educators. From the very beginning, this government-sponsored professionalization sowed the seeds of discontent and frustration that would lead to a direct confrontation between teachers and their employers in 1905.

Despite the lack of uniformity of teacher training programs in postreform Russia, these programs formed an important part in the professionalization of Russian teachers and the creation of their professional ethos. Graduates of these various programs thought of themselves as competent individuals who had important expertise to utilize in the battle against illiteracy and ignorance in imperial Russia. Russian pedagogical training gave teachers a common vocabulary, common values, and work habits with which they could articulate their professional concerns. This corporate solidarity, in turn, laid the groundwork for the development of a teachers' professional consciousness in imperial Russia.

2 City Teachers' Daily Lives: The Development of a Professional Ethos

LIFE IN THE CITY CLASSROOM WAS NOT EASY FOR MOST TEACHERS. Primary schoolteachers worked in overcrowded classrooms with children who were frequently malnourished, sick, or abused. Secondary schoolteachers were more fortunate—their pupils suffered less from the effects of an impoverished background. But teaching in Russian secondary schools presented its own set of problems. The strict discipline, rigid curriculum, and pedantic nature of much of the teaching engendered a rebellious attitude in the pupils, who often saw their teachers as enemies. While this rebelliousness is characteristic of adolescents, many parents and teachers believed that Russian schools exacerbated the problem. Regardless of their position in the educational system, city teachers shared similar problems. They instructed too many pupils with not enough textbooks or school supplies. Moreover, the division of authority between central and local school officials was ambiguous, and teachers were frequently caught in the middle of conflicts among school authorities. Teachers themselves often differed with school officials concerning how to conduct their work. Yet teachers had very little power to implement change. They often spoke of feeling forgotten and alone in their efforts to provide instruction.

What is of interest to historians about this rather dreary picture of city teachers' workaday lives is the teachers' reaction. Having graduated from government-sponsored professional programs, many teachers believed they should be granted greater authority in the classroom. Instead, teachers found a school system where, in their view, arbitrariness, police authority, and traditional religious and political values held sway. Teachers faced a myriad of state and local officials who tried to tell them how and what to teach. Many teachers were also offended by the rules and regulations governing their public and private lives, rules that violated their new identity as professionals.

The response of city teachers to this situation varied. Some, like Chekhov's "man in a footlocker," withdrew completely from the difficult situation in which they found themselves. Others tried to advance within the educational system by becoming part of the administrative elite. But more and more teachers found it difficult to remain aloof from the problems they faced in the schools. Taking the precepts of their professional training seriously, they found that their attitudes toward their work conflicted with those of school officials. These conflicts between officialdom and city teachers forced them to articulate their own approach to education and their place as teachers within Russian society. The values that emerged from their daily lives and experiences as teachers in turn helped to solidify their professional consciousness, which had been fostered in the teacher training programs.

What were these values? City teachers, like all professionals, believed that Russian society should award status and power to those who valued and possessed education and specialized knowledge. Underlying this faith in education, expertise, and reason was teachers' emphasis on the importance of the individual. Rather than work in a rigidly bureaucratic system, they wanted to instruct their pupils in a more flexible environment that took individual needs and abilities into account. Teachers also wanted to be free of petty government interference in their professional lives and to be rewarded for the valuable service they performed for the good of society. Individualism, self-worth, autonomy, and technical expertise were the values shaping teachers' professional identity.

This new professional consciousness ran counter to both the prevailing autocratic tradition and the ethic of the radical intelligentsia that had evolved during the nineteenth century. City teachers wanted to replace the traditional official political culture, which emphasized loyalty and service to the tsar, with a system that valued individual initiative and expertise. At the same time, teachers rejected the traditional political counterculture of the radical intelligentsia, which espoused the overthrow of the system, emphasized the importance of self-sacrifice for the good of the Russian people, and placed public life over private. Professionals argued that they, too, sacrificed much for the welfare of society. They did not want to overthrow the autocratic system but rather to work within it. Nor did they want to sacrifice their private lives in order to serve. The rise of the professions in Russia did not seem to threaten society as much as did the radical intelligentsia's utopian visions; nevertheless, it undermined the autocratic system in less dramatic ways by offering another vision of a new Russia and of the relationship between state and society.

There were three areas where teachers' professional consciousness conflicted with older and more established values. First, *proizvol*, arbitrary treatment at the hands of government officials, was a widespread problem in imperial Russia. Teachers often felt themselves at the mercy of government officials who had little understanding of education and were interested only in the exercise of power. Second, the government expected teachers to instill the traditional values of loyalty and service to the tsar in their pupils. Instead, teachers had been trained to encourage individualism and autonomy through the use of newer teaching methodologies. This contradiction in teachers' role brought the conflict between the older autocratic society and the new civil society into the classroom, making it difficult for teachers to ignore this conflict. Finally, teachers were angry at the lack of meaningful financial recognition of their work, particularly when compared with that of other professionals and government bureaucrats. These conflicts between city teachers and school administrators brought into sharp relief their respective attitudes and values and helped teachers crystallize their own views. Just as many city teachers' growing professional consciousness grew out of an antigovernment stance in the teacher training programs, their difficulties with school officials heightened this antigovernment feeling in the workplace. Given that school officials were quite ready to fire contentious teachers, teachers' willingness to articulate their concerns was a sign of true courage.

The Problem of *Proizvol* and Teachers' Lack of Legal Rights

One of the major aims of the Great Reforms was to rid Russia of the arbitrary use of power (*proizvol*) by government officials and institute a rule of law (*zakonnost'*). Russians had been subject to the whim of petty tyrants for too long, and the reformers wanted to regularize government authority on all levels. This grand design proved harder to achieve than the reformers had hoped. Because the reforms introduced the rule of law while maintaining an autocratic political structure, the reform legislation created semidemocratic institutions within an autocracy, which resulted in an extremely unstable political situation. As a result, *proizvol* remained a feature of Russian life throughout the nineteenth century.

When they found employment, teachers became a part of this half-reformed bureaucratic structure. A full discussion of the educational bureaucracy is beyond the scope of this study, but a few generalizations can be made. When the Ministry of Education reformed the schools in the mid-nineteenth century, it decided to keep complete control over nonclerical, male secondary education, and to share responsibility for women's education and primary education with local governments.[1] All secondary school officials and men teachers were members of the government civil service and a part of the ministerial bureaucracy. Virtually all of these ministry officials had begun as teachers and had become administrators to further their careers.

In contrast, primary schools and their teachers were administered by both state and local officials. The clumsy division of power between the central and local governments in the primary school system meant that there were many officials who could intervene in a teacher's life. School inspectors, trustees, priests, members of the city duma, and other officials all possessed some legal authority over city classrooms. This authority was poorly defined, however, and led to conflict not only between teachers and officials but also among the officials themselves. The newly professionalized city teachers, proud of their status as experts, resented these officials. In their eyes, many administrators insisted upon exercising their power capriciously and arbitrarily and ignored the advice of the experts. These officials showed little regard for the individuals who were affected by their decisions, and more important, teachers had no legal right to appeal their decisions.

The school trustee provides an example that reflects the uneven relationship between school officials and teachers. Possessing increasingly sophisticated pedagogical training, teachers believed they knew what was best for Russia's school-age population. Yet they felt stymied by the trustees in their efforts to teach effectively. Many of these trustees had no understanding of teaching methodologies. Confronted by officials who attached great importance to their own authority but had no technical training, teachers began to assert their right to control Russia's classrooms.

The School Trustee School trustees had two important duties in the municipal primary schools: they selected the teachers for the school and bore all financial responsibility for the school, except for teachers' salaries. When Moscow and Petersburg officials took control of the municipal schools, however, they set up a different administrative system in each city. In Petersburg, the city council created the Executive Commission on Education, which was composed of all the trustees, who governed the schools collectively. To assist the commission, Petersburg school officials appointed *eksperty* (literally, "experts"): these men were trained educators who dealt specifically with pedagogical issues in the schools. In contrast, individual trustees in Moscow had greater authority. Moscow did not appoint *eksperty* but left pedagogical concerns in the hands of the trustees. This meant that Moscow school trustees were responsible for helping to resolve all pedagogical issues that were raised by the teaching staff.

This last duty particularly irritated Moscow teachers. One teacher described the situation in the Moscow city schools, saying that, from the moment the city administration chose a trustee for a school, "the real manager is no longer the city but the trustee."[2] City officials chose the school trustees from among Moscow's distinguished citizens—wealthy noblemen, merchants, bankers, and industrialists. From the teachers' vantage point, this was a serious problem. Many trustees were appointed because of their financial success or privileged rank, not because of their interest in education. Because trustees were so powerful in Moscow, their relationship to the city administration was doubly important. Those trustees who knew city officials well frequently got what they wanted, while teachers who worked with less influential school trustees had to wait longer for the city administration to deal with their requests.[3] Although some trustees had no formal education themselves, they became the teachers' immediate superiors; this led to the charge that in the more extreme cases barely literate school trustees tried to tell teachers how and what to teach. For example, trustees controlled the ordering of texts for each school and could refuse to order a book they did not approve of. Moscow teachers also resented the trustee's power over the head teacher. Trustees sometimes used the head teacher to find out what the other teachers were doing and to control those teachers' actions. This system created an unwelcome inequality among the teachers in the same school and threatened the sense of community teachers were trying to build.[4]

To city teachers, the power of the Moscow trustees symbolized the problem of arbitrariness (*proizvol*) in Russian life. The Moscow school trustee represented yet another example of an official who, having gained power through influence rather than through education and technical expertise, wielded power according to personal whim. Although trustees needed no pedagogical qualifications for their job, the "experts" in pedagogy—the teachers—had little power to exercise their expertise. Thus, teachers played a key role in the conflict between the emerging professional system and the autocracy.

The conflict between power based on influence and power based on technical competence comes out clearly in Moscow teachers' suggestions for reform of the position of trustee. Teachers wanted to replace the trustee with something similar to the Petersburg *ekspert*. In fact, Petersburg officials chose as the city *eksperty* leading educators who had helped introduce modern pedagogy into Russia.[5] When the *ekspert* criticized the teaching in Petersburg schools, he did so as one educator to another, employing terms which both understood. By using educators as *eksperty*, Petersburg school officials did not violate teachers' growing sense of professional consciousness and self-worth. The professionalization of all educational workers, and not just of teachers, was also what Moscow city teachers wanted—an end to arbitrary behavior by those they considered unable to judge their work competently, combined with the right to be judged by their peers.

Surveillance over Teachers' Personal Lives   The conflict between school authorities and teachers took place not only in the classroom but also in teachers' private lives, which authorities attempted to control. In this respect, teachers suffered more from official interference than did other professionals. The attempts to control teachers' private lives stemmed from the view that teachers were role models for their pupils. Wanting teachers to provide the best example possible, school officials and parents sought to scrutinize their public and private lives. As if this surveillance of private life were not difficult enough, teachers could also be fired for any unseemly behavior. Any person could accuse a teacher of immoral behavior, and the teacher usually lost his or her job as a result. Teachers complained frequently about their constant fear of dismissal and their inability to defend themselves from scurrilous attacks on their private lives. More important from the teachers' perspective, the absence of any right to appeal their dismissal emphasized their lack of legal rights and autonomy (*bespravie*).

Control of teachers' private lives took many forms. A teacher's friends and acquaintances were monitored by the police, and teachers were discouraged from befriending politically suspect individuals. The career path of P. M. Shestakov, one of the leaders of the teachers' professional movement, illustrates the difficulties teachers faced. In 1881 Shestakov graduated from a teachers' seminary near Tula. After teaching in rural primary schools in Moscow and Tula provinces for five years, in 1886 he left his position to enroll in the Petersburg Teachers' Institute. He successfully completed his examinations to qualify as an advanced primary schoolteacher, but quite suddenly, and for unspecified reasons, the Petersburg police declared him politically unreliable. As it turned out, the police had information that Shestakov's wife was associating with politically suspect individuals and believed that this made Shestakov suspect as well. The curator of the Petersburg Educational District sent a circular to all the other curators, advising them not to hire Shestakov, and he was sent to Nizhnii Novgorod.

Nevertheless, Shestakov was determined to pursue his profession. In 1890 the Moscow curator petitioned the Ministry of Education to permit him to hire Shestakov, who had been able to convince the curator of his political reliability. Although permission was initially denied, after excellent references from the Nizhnii Novgorod police and the director of the Petersburg Teachers' Institute, the Ministry of Education gave Shestakov permission to teach in Moscow.[6] Shestakov took up his new position, having received a painful lesson on his lack of legal rights as a teacher.

Shestakov's story and others like it show clearly the mixed messages city teachers were given by school officials. Coming from the best teacher training programs in Russia, the majority of teachers in Moscow and Petersburg were the direct beneficiaries of the government-sponsored professionalization drive. Because they had come to see themselves as professionals through their training, they were increasingly offended by the way they were treated upon graduation. As Shestakov's trouble shows, when teachers sought suitable employment, political reliability mattered more than an excellent academic record. All teachers had to supply a certificate of political reliability. Although political reliability was a prerequisite for all government jobs in Russia, city teachers as well as other professionals found supplying the certificate irksome, for it violated their growing professional consciousness. If they were "experts" and performed a noble mission for all of Russian society, why did they suffer these humiliating experiences at the hands of incompetent bureaucrats? Moreover, the government's attempt to control teachers' lives extended to their families as well, as

Shestakov discovered. Thus, city teachers' experiences violated their sense of self-worth, individualism, and technical expertise. At the same time, these experiences also placed in rather sharp relief the ambiguities and inconsistencies of the government professionalization effort.

Equally irksome was the fact that city teachers who committed any immoral acts, defined as those that violated the laws of the Orthodox Church, were dismissed from their jobs.[7] Because their private lives were subjected to more scrutiny than those of men teachers, women teachers suffered in particular from this type of surveillance. For example, in 1912 the local school board in Chistopol'sk required prospective women teachers to submit not only a certificate of political reliability but also medical proof of their virginity.[8] This policy was an extreme example of a commonly held belief that women had to be politically and sexually pure in order to gain employment as teachers.

This intrusive concern about womens' private lives continued even after they received their teaching positions. Many parents and school administrators felt that teachers should have no social life at all because otherwise they might "corrupt" the children. One Moscow teacher reported that women teachers had an 11 P.M. curfew, which prevented them from attending the theater and late evening lectures. The men teachers at the school had no such curfew. When the women asked why they were being restricted, the officials replied that the female servants at the school were also subject to a curfew and would complain if the women teachers did not have the same hours.[9] This incident shows clearly the attitudes of the school administration toward women teachers. All women in the school, regardless of their position, were considered servants and were treated as such.

Teachers' complaints about surveillance of their private lives illustrate the distinction they were drawing between themselves and the radical intelligentsia. Members of the intelligentsia had argued that those interested in serving the people should give up their private lives and devote themselves completely to their work. City teachers did not agree. They believed that teachers should be allowed to have a private family life, and this family life should not be subject to government surveillance or intervention. It was government interference that was wrong, not family life itself. City teachers were seeking the autonomy that would allow them to have a full, rich, public life devoted to educating Russia's children, and an equally rich private life to enjoy as they saw fit.

The Curriculum and City Teachers' Professionalization

In addition to the difficult relations they had with school officials, teachers grew increasingly more troubled by the city school curriculum. Here again, the conflicting aims of the regime became apparent. To be sure, all schools have a political agenda; governments establish schools, which are intended to provide the society with productive workers and loyal supporters of the status quo. In Russia the conflicts between the autocracy and the emerging civil society, which included the professional city teachers, entered the classroom. Although teachers were trained to encourage their pupils' self-esteem and autonomy, the curriculum in the primary schools continued to foster loyalty and support for the autocracy. The ideas of individualism, autonomy, and self-worth were in fundamental contradiction with the ethos of loyalty and service that the autocratic system demanded. In the secondary schools, teachers discovered that their self-image as specialists ran counter to the rigid curriculum and teaching methods. Both primary and secondary schoolteachers found that the curriculum contradicted their pedagogical principles and professional identity.

The Primary School Curriculum and Teachers Despite the differences in school administration, Moscow and Petersburg school officials had the same educational goals for primary schoolchildren. One teacher expressed these goals best when she wrote that she wanted to teach the children to speak and write Russian correctly and clearly, to teach them to understand literary Russian speech, and to give them, as much as possible according to their age, rules for living in the family and society.[10] To achieve these goals, school officials in both cities embarked on an ambitious expansion of the curriculum introduced by the Ministry of Education. The original primary school curriculum included religion, Church Slavonic, Russian, arithmetic, and singing.[11] School officials in both Petersburg and Moscow added subjects such as art, drawing, manual trades for boys and needlework for girls, history, science, and geography. This program reflected the needs of employers in both cities for an educated, well-trained workforce. In addition to the more vocational subjects, city officials and educators alike believed that workers needed an understanding of Russian history and geography to appreciate Russia's place in the world. Although it is clear that not every school was able to carry out this extended curriculum, school officials instructed teachers to include as many of these subjects as they possibly could.

Nevertheless, the primary schools served a greater purpose than simply conveying the elementary principles of arithmetic and letters to Russia's urban children. One Petersburg *ekspert* expressed the school administration's viewpoint: "The Commission [on Education] strongly upholds the principle that a primary school not only instructs, but also provides a moral education for the children (*vospityvaet detei*), and, perhaps, provides a moral education more than instruction."[12] It was for this purpose that religion and Church Slavonic were taught in the primary schools. By acquainting the children with the prayers and beliefs of the Orthodox faith, city educators aspired to provide the children with a strong Christian morality. In Moscow and St. Petersburg, most religion teachers were priests, but some were laymen who had received a clerical education. These religion teachers were responsible for all religious training and assisted in the study of Church Slavonic.

There were many complaints about the teaching of religion in the municipal primary schools. Teachers complained that the religion teachers arrived unannounced for their lessons, thereby disrupting the teacher's plan for the rest of the day. In addition, teachers felt that the religion teachers spent most of their class time with the third grade pupils to prepare them for their final examinations, and as a result, ignored the other two grades. This complaint was sometimes leveled at teachers themselves.[13]

In 1893 the Petersburg Commission on Education studied the complaints against the religion teachers and offered a series of proposals to remedy the situation. Instead of hiring priests on an hourly basis, the commission created several full-time positions with full pension and salary rights. These newly hired priests would no longer have parish duties, but would serve only as teachers. The commission supported the right of priests to conduct their lessons at their convenience, because each priest was assigned to several schools. A member of the clerical estate was to serve as a permanent observer of the religious curriculum in the city schools, thereby keeping control over religious instruction in the hands of the clergy. To assist in training a better group of religion teachers, school officials insisted that religion teachers attend special meetings to improve their teaching. Finally, in the commission's recommendations, school officials explicitly instructed teachers to instill in their pupils a respectful attitude toward the Orthodox church and its rituals through their own example.[14]

These recommendations did little to improve the situation. Rather than support the teachers' complaints against the religion teachers, Petersburg school officials tried to create a more professional corps of religion teachers. They did this because of the importance school officials placed on religion in the school curriculum as the cornerstone of the children's moral education. Teachers objected to this view because it placed the needs of religion teachers above their own needs. Religion teachers still came unannounced and disrupted the classroom teachers' plans. At the same time, teachers were expected to attend Orthodox services to set a Christian example for their pupils. This angered many teachers, who felt that their religious beliefs should be a private matter and not part of their public, professional lives.[15]

This conflict between religion and classroom teachers reflects the growing conflict in urban Russia between traditional, religious learning and technical scientific knowledge. While city teachers might have been expected to support greater professionalization of religion teachers, in fact they did not. Just as school officials came to represent the excesses of arbitrary power in teachers' eyes, the very figure of the priest dressed in his clerical robes represented traditional Russian attitudes toward knowledge and authority. Religion teachers instructed their pupils in the Orthodox faith by asking the children to memorize prayers and points of dogma. In contrast, the modern methodologies emphasized the children's active participation in their education. One teacher expressed her pedagogical goals: "During the lessons we concentrate on developing the children's sharpness of observation and the skills used in observation. We try to impart a curiosity about the earth's environment in order to expand their horizons, to develop a love of learning and to push them to further their formal education or self-education."[16] These goals were the antithesis of the teaching methodologies of the religion teachers. As one scholar has recently observed, "The existence . . . of a child-centered classroom in a coercive, hierarchical, authoritarian society is a major paradox."[17] By insisting on the importance of religion and religion teachers for the school curriculum, Petersburg officials brought the clash between traditional beliefs and modern views into the classroom.

Curriculum in the Secondary Schools   The Ministry of Education had reformed the curriculum in the secondary schools in the 1860s and 1870s. Intended to prepare gymnasium graduates for government service, the classical training included religion, Russian and Church Slavonic, classical and modern languages, mathematics, physics, history, and geography. The heart of the gymnasium's educational program remained the study of Greek and Latin. In contrast, graduates of the *real'nye uchilishcha* received an education to prepare them for business careers. In the *real'nye uchilishcha*, students received instruction in religion, Russian and Church Slavonic, history, geography, mathematics, the modern languages, and physics. The *real'nye uchilishcha* also had a commercial division where students took classes in commercial arithmetic, which included bookkeeping and other related subjects. Young women were trained to be better wives and mothers. The girls' gymnasiums had their own special curriculum, which included religion, Russian and Church Slavonic, modern languages, mathematics, history and geography, pedagogy, hygiene and first aid, and needlework.[18]

Few were entirely satisfied with the secondary school curricula, but the chief complaints centered around the teaching of Latin and Greek in the boys' gymnasiums. The decision to make classical training a cornerstone of boys' secondary education had been controversial ever since the Ministry of Education adopted the classical curriculum in 1872.[19] At that time the classical curriculum formed the basis of secondary education in Western Europe. If educated Russians were to become part of a larger European world, it was important for them to understand the Greek and Roman civilizations that were the foundation of European culture and thought.

For Russian conservatives, worried about the rising tide of student radicalism, the classical curriculum had tremendous appeal for a less academic reason. The intensive study of Latin and Greek meant that students had very little time to read allegedly subversive authors. Conservatives hoped to keep students so busy parsing and translating classical works that they would have no time for student activism. In fact, over 62 percent of class time in the gymnasiums was spent studying Greek and Latin.[20] In adopting the classical curriculum, the Ministry of Education hoped to establish tight control over the minds of Russia's students, and to provide the government with a corps of well-trained bureaucrats who would be comfortable in any chancellery in Europe.

The emphasis not only in the classics but in all subjects was on factual information, not interpretation. Teachers had no time to explain the significance of works of literature or historical events, and students had little opportunity to ask questions. The study of Russian literature ended with Pushkin, and students were not allowed to read Tolstoy, Dostoevsky, or many other politically suspect writers. Russian history texts provided a sanitized version of events: for example, the assassinations of Emperors Paul I and Alexander II were not mentioned.[21] The Ministry of Education tried to remove all works that could foster a spirit of dissent and political unreliability in secondary school students.

Underlying this method of learning was the ministry's desire to influence the moral character of the students. To do this, the ministry introduced the position of *nastavnik*, or monitor, into Russian secondary schools. The *nastavnik* was a regular classroom teacher who supervised student conduct in a particular grade. While subject teachers were discouraged from becoming personally involved with their students, the *nastavnik* was not. The monitor was to be the link between the students, their families, and teachers. The *nastavnik's* job was to make sure that students did their work and to supervise their conduct in and outside the classroom.[22]

Secondary schoolteachers grew increasingly restive under this rather rigid, pedantic system. In the classroom, their attempts to impart their expertise were thwarted by their inability to answer students' questions. They contended that distrust pervaded teacher/student relationships and that strict discipline and surveillance were excessive. A group of newly professionalized secondary schoolteachers described conditions in the Petersburg schools in most unflattering terms:

At the basis of the Tolstoi System a principle was laid that flowed from the ideal of the police state; it was formulated in the following way: "The school must oppose the development of a materialistic philosophy of life. It must train youth in the spirit of conservative principles. It must confirm the younger generation in obedience to the law and respect for constituted authority." Developed to its ultimate conclusion in . . . the classical gymnasium, the conservative system reduced the whole field of education to slavery. The realschule, the commercial school, the clerical seminary, the girls' gymnasium, and the diocesan school, with all their differences in curricula, incorporated in their basic structure one conforming spirit.[23]

More important, the conservative principles upon which the secondary schools had been reformed ran counter to secondary schoolteachers' training and professional identity. Teachers wanted to replace this conservative educational approach with child-centered pedagogy, which allowed greater freedom to teach according to the needs of the students. The newly professionalized secondary schoolteachers described their goals in terms that show their acceptance of the child-centered approach to pedagogy:

We are confronted by a human subject who is complex and inconstant, whose care demands tact and intellectual and moral imagination. The secondary school takes into its hands a boy scarcely out of childhood and deposits him on the threshold of young adulthood. It is concerned with him in the most critical period of his life, when his character is being formed, when his elementary passions are in conflict with his higher spiritual aspirations, when his awakening mind seeks serious nourishment, when he is at the same time credulous and extremely skeptical, gregarious and excessively individualistic, conscious of his weakness and energetically confident of his personal dignity. It is the duty of the school to equip this complex subject for life's struggle and for independent mental labor in the full command of his own powers.[24]

Teachers wanted greater authority to train these complex individuals for "independent" labor, so that they would continue their education beyond the classroom. The ideas of both teachers' and students' individualism and self-reliance contradicted the Tolstoi system and the autocratic principles upon which it was based.

Government offficials were aware of the problems in the secondary schools. Between 1895 and 1904, the Ministry of Education implemented some curricular reforms and experimented with loosening discipline at some secondary schools.[25] This acknowledgement of the correctness of city teachers' complaints, however, only encouraged teachers to seek greater change. When the ministry stopped short of making serious improvements in the schools and refused to grant teachers greater authority and freedom in their teaching, it made a difficult situation worse: the ministry raised expectations it was unwilling to meet. Just as in the primary schools, the secondary schools became a site of the conflict between the old autocratic system and the emerging civil society.

Salaries

The teacher-professionals criticized not only the nature of authority in imperial Russia but also the problem of status and how it was awarded. Teachers believed that birth and rank were insufficient claims to membership in the social elite. Instead, they argued that, in the new civil society that many teachers were trying to create, individuals who furthered the public welfare should be rewarded for the services they provided. Thus, teachers took older notions of government service and attempted to redefine them. While remaining committed to the service ideal, teachers' notion of service and its rewards were evolving in new and different ways.

Most societies award status and privilege based on the acquisition of wealth and rank. This proved to be problematic for city teachers. Teachers decried the fact that the privileged elite in postreform Russia was still the nobility, who had gained their wealth through the labor of others. At the same time, professionals regarded the other wealthy group in Russia—the merchants and industrialists who were beginning to benefit from the government's industrialization drive, particularly under the leadership of Sergei Witte—as representatives of the despised "bourgeoisie." In the eyes of the professionals, these businessmen also exploited the labor of others and therefore were no better than the nobility. At the same time, the radical intelligentsia provided an alternative model for professionals, by sacrificing any claim to financial gain and personal privilege. They claimed that helping "the people" gain political control of Russia was all the reward they needed.

Unwilling to follow the example of these groups, city teachers attempted to forge a middle path between those who benefited from the labor of others and those who sacrificed everything for the common good. Teachers argued that their professional work did not exploit the common people and that education was a tool in helping the common people gain power and status in society. Because of the essential nature of their work for the betterment of Russia through peaceful means, city teachers argued, they should receive greater financial reward. They were not radicals trying to bring down the state, but serious experts who were providing important services of which both state and society approved.

Unlike the puritanical revolutionary intelligentsia, city teachers needed money. Living in the most expensive cities in the empire, teachers in Petersburg and Moscow needed large salaries to support themselves and their families. Receiving salaries equivalent to those of skilled workers, men primary schoolteachers, like their pupils' parents, struggled to make ends meet. The situation for women teachers was different; it will be discussed in the next chapter. Secondary schoolteachers' financial position was more complex. Although they received higher salaries than their primary school colleagues, their expectations were also higher. Their financial situation reveals better than that of primary schoolteachers the new criteria for social status—education, technical expertise, and work for the public good—that they were trying to establish. Secondary schoolteachers were the sons of the upper and middle classes in Russia and were university graduates. Men secondary schoolteachers were usually the sole financial support for their families. When they discussed their situation, these men emphasized their financial insecurity rather than actual want, for they clearly recognized that there were many people less fortunate than they. They wanted to earn enough money to live as equals among the educated classes. In late nineteenth-century Russia, this meant a comfortable apartment with a servant and money to spend on certain amenities such as books, theater, and travel. They also desired the financial security to have leisure time to spend as they saw fit.

Secondary schoolteachers' dissatisfaction stemmed in part from the two-tiered system that was used to calculate their salaries. The salary for full-time teachers at the Ministry of Education's boys' schools was based on a thirty-hour work week. Teachers were paid 75 rubles each for the first twelve lessons, and 60 rubles each for the next eighteen lessons, bringing their total pay to 1,080 rubles a year. Although teachers' salaries were calculated on a thirty-hour work week, teachers were only guaranteed twelve hours of lessons, and any lessons above that had to be scheduled by the director. Thus, there was a great deal of fluctuation in earnings even among full-time teachers. A teacher could raise his earnings by performing extra duties, such as correcting exercises or acting as a monitor. Beyond these measures, however, teachers could do nothing but wait until the twenty-sixth year of teaching, when they received their pensions.[26] Teachers in the Ministry of Education's girls' schools were paid in a similar manner, but their hourly rate per lesson was lower than that of teachers in the boys' schools.[27] Directors received 2,000 rubles a year plus housing, and inspectors 1,500 rubles per year plus housing. Both inspectors and directors could supplement their salaries by teaching as well.[28]

Secondary schoolteachers were also paid by the hour, a system of payment used by those schools administered by the Department of Institutions of the Empress Maria, the Ministry of Finance, and the Ministry of Education.[29] Because they had no guaranteed hours at all, these teachers suffered even more financial anxiety. As might be expected from such a pay system, there was a great range of salaries within each school. The salaries of the teachers at the Moscow *real'noe uchilishche* for the academic school year 1902–1903 illustrate this point. The director of the school received a salary of 2,000 rubles, plus 480 rubles for teaching eight lessons a week in arithmetic, and 1,190 rubles from his pension, bringing his total income to 3,670 rubles. The school inspector received a salary of 750 rubles (school inspectors for the *real'nye uchilishcha* received less money than their counterparts in the classical gymnasiums), 1,056 rubles for teaching mathematics and drawing, and 850 rubles from his pension, making his total income 2,656 rubles. Of the twenty-seven teachers who taught in the school in 1902–1903, one teacher earned more than 3,000 rubles, six teachers earned between 2,000 and 3,000 rubles, five earned between 1,500 and 2,000 rubles, another five earned between 1,000 and 1,500 rubles, yet another five earned between 500 and 1,000 rubles, and four earned between 100 and 500 rubles. The lowest-paid teacher at the school received 192 rubles for four weekly lessons in drawing. Among these twenty-seven teachers, fourteen were able to supplement their regular salaries with pensions or with work as monitors or as teachers of preparatory classes.[30]

In 1900 the Pedagogical Society of the University of Moscow, an organization of university and secondary schoolteachers, published a report on the financial situation of secondary schoolteachers. The compilers of the report estimated the cost of living for a secondary schoolteacher with no children at 1,800 rubles per year and a teacher with seven or more children at 3,200 rubles annually.[31] Since the statistics on the number of dependents for the teachers of the Moscow *real'noe uchilishche* are not available, it is difficult to say for certain how well those teachers were doing. It appears, however, that while at least twelve of the twenty-seven teachers were able to make ends meet, the rest needed to supplement their income. This hypothesis is further substantiated by a survey of Moscow secondary schoolteachers conducted in 1907 by the educational journal *Vestnik vospitaniia*. According to that poll, the average male teacher received 1,473 rubles a year for twenty-eight hours per week while the average female teacher received 592 rubles for twenty-six lessons.[32] Both these figures are far below the minimum budgets calculated by the Moscow University Pedagogical Society.

One item not included in the Moscow Pedagogical Society's budgets, which was of great concern to secondary schoolteachers, was their children's education. Although secondary schoolteachers were given the right to send their children to secondary schools tuition-free, this privilege was limited. Teachers could send their children only to schools administered by the government agency for which they worked. For example, teachers in the schools of the Department of the Institutions of the Empress Maria had to pay tuition costs to send their children to the Ministry of Education's schools. Teachers also had to pay full tuition to send their children to institutions of higher learning.[33] Their children's educational costs only added to teachers' financial burdens.

A secondary schoolteacher could supplement his income in several ways. A working spouse brought in a second income. Because their idea of respectability required women to remain in the home, most men rejected this solution. One teacher recorded his deep embarrassment when his wife, "a woman from society," worked as a baker to improve the family's finances.[34] Other teachers were able to obtain assistance from relatives. The most common way to supplement income, however, was to give lessons outside the classroom. Some teachers gave private lessons after school or in the evening hours, others preferred to teach during the summer months, and still others, particularly those paid by the hour, chose to teach at more than one school.[35] Teachers complained that their efforts to find other sources of income meant that they either neglected their work or suffered from burnout.[36] Their financial insecurity hurt their pride and sense of self-worth. Teachers felt they should be able to live comfortably on their salaries and not have to worry about other employment.

What upset teachers most was the fact that they earned far less than other professionals of similar backgrounds. According to Nancy Mandelker Frieden, in 1905 90 percent of 12,473 lawyers earned over 2,000 rubles a year, and over a third of these earned over 5,000 rubles. The earnings of government bureaucrats were equally high. Of the 91,204 salaried government officials employed in 1905, 46 percent earned more than 2,000 rubles per year. Among physicians, annual incomes ranged from somewhat under 500 to 3,000 rubles.[37]

Although the Russian government and educated society acknowledged the importance of their mission, teachers believed that their salaries did not reflect the importance of their work. Because salaries were low, the profession had difficulty attracting and keeping talented teachers. As teachers began to complain more loudly about their low salaries, the government acknowledged the need to improve their financial situation but did nothing. The pleas of secondary schoolteachers fell on deaf ears until after the 1905 Revolution.

Salary complaints are a common feature among any occupation that is trying to raise its status in the eyes of society. Frustrated workers argue that management does not value their labor. In Petersburg and Moscow, however, teachers demanded financial remuneration that was greater than what workers could expect. City primary schoolteachers received the same amount of money as skilled workers, and secondary schoolteachers were paid extremely well by working-class standards. But secondary schoolteachers wanted to live like other members of the Russian elite. Men teachers wanted to support their families on one salary, live in comfortable apartments, and not have to scramble to support their families. They believed that their education and their work qualified them to be a part of this privileged world. Instead, they were on the periphery. The high cost of living in Russia's major cities, coupled with the recession of 1899–1900, only served to emphasize the precariousness of their financial position.

The salary issue also illustrates the distinction between professionals, government bureaucrats, and the intelligentsia. City teachers wanted to be paid respectable salaries for the work they performed. They constantly compared themselves to the better-paid government bureaucrats, whose work they did not consider valuable to society. At the same time, professionals did not want to become part of the impoverished intelligentsia in order to serve society. Instead, they proposed a third alternative—meaningful work beneficial to society, coupled with a comfortable standard of living.

All these issues that brought teachers and school authorities into conflict helped city teachers articulate their new professional identity. As a result of their educational preparation, teachers began to view themselves as specialists. When these teachers found employment in Moscow and Petersburg, they found themselves in a difficult situation. Russian primary and secondary schools had only been partly modernized as a result of the reform legislation of the 1860s and 1870s. What had remained unaltered by the reforms were employer/employee relations. These relations were still plagued by the problem of arbitrariness (*proizvol*) and lack of legal rights (*bespravie*), which teachers associated with the long tradition of Russian autocratic rule.

City teachers proposed to replace arbitrariness with a new system of workplace relationships based on respect for the individual, whose training and expertise conferred upon him or her the ability to make independent decisions. This new professional ethos in turn enhanced the development of Russian civil society. In the autocratic system, loyalty and service to the tsar were the paramount virtues. In contrast, city teachers emphasized the importance of the individual. They wanted the government, through its officials, to respect their training and experience, give them a meaningful voice in the classroom, and treat them with dignity, as professionals rather than as servants. Furthermore, city teachers believed in the separation of their public and private lives.

These values of public service, individualism, self-worth, autonomy, and technical expertise made up the city teachers' professional identity. As the nineteenth century drew to a close, teachers faced a sharp dilemma. According to their new pedagogy, the teachers' task was to help their students become self-reliant and autonomous individuals. But how could teachers provide their pupils with such values when they themselves were mired in a system that valued loyalty and service above all and denied them personal and professional autonomy? It was this dilemma that gave a sense of urgency to the city teachers' professional movement.

3 Women Teachers and Professionalization

GENDER HAS PLAYED A PROFOUND ROLE IN PROFESSIONAL DEVELOPment. Most occupations that are considered "true" professions, such as law, medicine, and engineering are dominated by men. Occupations in which women are in the majority, such as teaching, nursing, and social work have been characterized as "semi-professions." In the case of the semi-professions, "their training is shorter, their status is less legitimated, their right to privileged communication less established, there is less of a specialized body of knowledge, and they have less autonomy from supervision or societal control than 'the' professions."[1] At the same time, scholars have assumed that if women could gain access to "the" professions or even the "semi-professions," they would be treated the same as their male colleagues. Men's professional experience has become the universal standard for everyone. Thus, women professionals have remained invisible, either because they are not members of "the" professions or because there is no reason to assume that their experiences differed sharply from that of men professionals.

Recent efforts by women's historians have finally begun to make women professionals and the problems they have faced more visible.[2] Gender and its construction has become a key tool in understanding professional development in both Europe and America.[3] According to this view, gender is not simply a biological category which, when applied to the professions, creates "male" and "female" professions. Instead, male professionals have used gender to define the social value of the work to be performed. Law, engineering, and medicine stress science, reason, and mastery of technical specialties, whereas teaching and nursing emphasize the care of others, which supposedly requires little advanced training. Women's work is devalued while men's professions are given status and power. In the case of law and medicine, women were denied admission to the educational institutions necessary to acquire the specialized knowledge. In teaching, men continued to control and supervise a female majority that occupied the lower ranks of the profession.

Thus, the role of gender in professional development provides an excellent case study in the establishment of hierarchies. The rise of professions marked the attempts of these new social groups to change the patterns of power and privilege in society. Individuals would no longer receive social status because of birth and rank, but rather because they had acquired technical expertise and had used it to serve the public good. Professionalization marked an attempt to democratize status and privilege by allowing entry to previously excluded groups. At the same time, each profession attempted to reintroduce hierarchical power by defining who would lead and who would follow. Education, wealth, and class all played key roles in the development of these professional hierarchies, but so too did gender because it seemed such a "natural" form of distinction.

Such a hierarchy developed in the teaching profession in post-reform Russia. While the newly conscious corps of professional men teachers spoke of democratizing status and privilege in Russia, they also attempted to define an inferior position for women teachers. Men teachers were joined by state and local officials and members of the intelligentsia in their efforts to create a negative image of the woman schoolteacher that would justify preventing women teachers from becoming full-fledged members of the profession. To be sure, these men rarely admitted their desire to keep women in a subordinate position. After the debate about the "woman question" in the 1850s and 1860s, which linked women's liberation to the liberation of all Russia, few men who considered themselves progressive would have publicly opposed the improvement of women's lives. Instead, they couched their concerns about women teachers as a concern for the welfare of Russia's schoolchildren. Men teachers, *intelligenty*, and officials singled out rural women teachers and portrayed them as ineffectual teachers of peasant children, as "outsiders" in the peasant community and as passive instruments of government policies. They argued that women teachers could not be given authority or autonomy in the schools because problems of class and gender prevented them from becoming real members of the peasant community. This image of women teachers affected attitudes toward all women teachers; it has persisted in Russian historiography up to the present.

Women teachers tried to oppose this negative image of themselves. The reform of women's education in the 1850s and 1860s created educational opportunities for upper- and middle-class women, but very few opportunities to use their education in publicly useful ways. Women wanted to take full advantage of their ability to join one of the few professions open to them. In order to prevent their marginalization within the profession, women teachers tried to create a more positive image of themselves and the work they performed.

As a result of their efforts, the image of the woman schoolteacher began to change. In creating a new role for themselves as teachers, Russian women could choose from two traditional gendered models: maternal and religious. According to the traditional gender stereotypes, all women were born to be mothers and it was this "maternal instinct" that made women excellent teachers of small children—they were simply replicating in the classroom their role as mothers. Since teaching also concerned the moral development (*vospitanie*) of children, however, traditional views of religious women also came into play. According to this view, women who divested themselves of their worldly concerns and chose to live a Christian life acquired a certain "authority of holiness." People of all social ranks, including peasants, came to these holy women for advice and counsel because of their perceived moral superiority. Because they often taught peasant children as part of their vocation, religious women served as an important role model for women teachers. The first generation of women teachers combined these two traditional gender roles of mother and saint to create a new one, the woman schoolteacher. Furthermore, these women secularized this image by overlaying elements of populism that emphasized "serving the people" as part of their duties. This image of women teachers as secular "holy women" was extremely powerful because radical and nonradical women fit within its framework.

The concepts of sacrifice and service were important for both groups of women teachers. Nonradicals, having accepted the traditional view of women's role in society, needed both to serve and to sacrifice to fulfill their traditional role. Radical women emphasized their capacity to serve and sacrifice to gain entry into the revolutionary movement. But emphasizing the service ideal also meant seeking acceptance into the teaching profession. As we have seen, teachers were trying to create a new professional service ethic to replace the older intelligentsia ethos. In insisting that they too were "serving the people," women teachers were identifying themselves as members of the new profession.

The image of the woman teacher as a holy woman began to change in the 1890s. As larger numbers of women entered the pedagogical courses and received a more professionalized education, they tried to professionalize their image. These new women were located primarily in the cities and particularly in St. Petersburg. Like their male colleagues, their identity was shaped by their growing professional consciousness. Once they found employment, however, women teachers quickly became aware that they were not treated the same as their male colleagues. No longer willing to see their work as either temporary employment or a vocation, they wanted a professional career. No longer willing to sacrifice everything for the sake of their jobs, these women teachers demanded to be treated as equals. Like their male colleagues, they were trying to establish rich professional and private lives for themselves, except this time they faced hostility not only from government officials but from male colleagues as well. Their story reveals much about the serious divisions that troubled the new teaching profession.

The Image of Women Teachers in Russian Historiography

From the moment women entered the profession, state and local government officials, the intelligentsia, and men teachers alike claimed that women made poor teachers, particularly in the countryside among Russia's patriarchal peasants. One commentator wrote, "The woman graduate of the elite city schools, half estranged from city life, never mind rural life, is sent directly from her student desk to teach in the countryside. That countryside often seems to these young women gymnasium graduates, if not like heaven, then at least like a trip to a summer cottage."[4] According to this view, women teachers were "outsiders" in the Russian village. They did not undertake their work seriously, but looked upon it as a vacation. Even their dress, manners, and customs prevented them from establishing meaningful contacts with peasant children and their parents.

In his recent study of Russian rural schools, Ben Eklof has pointed out that all teachers, regardless of gender, were considered "outsiders" by Russian peasants. Peasants were deeply suspicious of individuals who behaved in accordance with attitudes and values different from their own. Eklof argues that teachers could rid themselves of their status as intruders into the peasant world only by marrying and settling with their families in the village where they taught. Without a hearth, teachers remained outsiders and could not provide peasants with an alternative model of behavior, one governed by more modern and "enlightened" attitudes.[5]

According to this view, women teachers suffered acutely from this peasant prejudice against outsiders. Most women teachers did not come from the peasantry, but rather from the upper and middle classes. According to the Ministry of the Interior, in 1885 73 percent of women teachers were daughters of the gentry and the bureaucracy, while only 43 percent of men came from these same groups.[6] The peasants saw these educated women with their city manners as "ladies" (*baryshnia*), unwilling to participate in village life or perform manual labor. Even if women could overcome these sharp class differences, they were still not trusted by the peasants because few women teachers remained at their posts for very long. Most women taught less than ten years and were transferred frequently from one school to another. When women teachers married, they either left the profession voluntarily or were fired. Because of the high turnover rates, they, more than men teachers, failed to serve as the kind of cultural missionaries that educated Russians wanted them to be.

Many members of Russia's disaffected intelligentsia also hoped that teachers could play a political role in the villlages. Once peasants had become "enlightened," teachers could help them find a political solution to their difficulties. But there, too, women teachers failed to live up to these expectations. Many members of the intelligentsia argued that women teachers, hired for their political passivity, served the Ministry of Education's purposes only too well. Women did not provide an alternative political leadership for Russia's peasants or even try to channel the peasantry's concerns into meaningful political protest. According to Scott J. Seregny, women teachers were so politically passive that they played only a minor role in the rural teachers' professional and political movement during the 1905 Revolution, a movement intended to help teachers improve their status in the village. Moreover, Seregny attributes the reluctance of rural teachers to become involved in professional or political matters after 1905 to the government purge of activist men teachers in 1906–1908 and their replacement by women teachers.[7]

This view of women teachers as eternal and politically ineffective outsiders presents a very bleak picture of the Russian woman schoolteacher. A pawn of tsarist educational policy, she had a limited effect on peasant behavior because she did not fit into the milieu. Her attempts to provide her pupils with a more modern worldview failed because of the peasants' deep suspicion of outsiders, especially of unmarried women.[8] Moreover, because of her political passivity, the woman teacher did not join the newly emerging rural intelligentsia, which might have helped her position. According to this view, Russian women teachers remained unmoved by the political and social turmoil that swept Russia during the early years of the twentieth century.

Hostility toward women teachers was not just a reflection of peasant mistrust, however. Russian society as a whole was deeply patriarchal. Most reports of peasant hostility toward women teachers were not written by peasants themselves but by male administrators, *intelligenty*, and teachers. Why were they so interested in reporting women teachers' difficulties? Why did these men take it upon themselves to discuss these issues?

In order to answer these questions, we need to return to the 1850s when the tsarist government decided, first, to emancipate the serfs, and then to educate them. At first, the Ministry of Education, believing peasants would make better teachers than men from the cities, resolved to employ specially trained peasant men as rural teachers. By 1885 36 percent of men teachers were peasants, and by 1911 this had increased to 62 percent.[9] Ministry officials argued that peasants were accustomed to the isolation and squalor of village life and therefore would not get restless in areas remote from urban life and culture. This policy backfired on the Ministry of Education. Peasant men became teachers as a way of raising their status in the villages. When the ministry failed to treat them as members of a new professional elite, men teachers became increasingly hostile toward the government.[10]

Because of the shortage of teachers, the ministry agreed to hire women in 1871. This change occurred after a long and serious debate on the "woman question" during the late 1850s and 1860s. Influenced by Rousseau and other Western European social philosophers, Russian society acknowledged women's role as the "natural"educators of small children in the family. Because of the continuing teacher shortage due to the expansion of the schools, the government granted women the right to bring their familial role to the classroom. As we saw in chapter 1, women's "natural" abilities, coupled with the pedagogical training they received, meant that they were qualified to serve as teachers. Thus, the government drew upon the gender stereotype of women as "natural teachers," but it also transcended the narrow limits of that stereotype in allowing a more public role for women. Ministry officials were only interested in providing more teachers, not in recasting Russian society; they therefore put severe limitations on women teachers' public role. But here, as in other contexts, government motives were extremely complex. Although the Ministry of Education wanted to advance a public role for women to end the short-term teacher shortage, it was not committed to providing women with a meaningful public life. The goal continued to be a rather circumscribed role for women in education.

For its part, the radical intelligentsia also supported the introduction of women teachers into Russian rural schools, for the *intelligenty* believed that women, too, could serve to radicalize the peasantry. But when the peasants failed to respond to society's attempts to educate and "enlighten" them, the *intelligenty* blamed the women for their lack of involvement in politics, rather than recognizing the limits placed on all teachers' political involvement.

The inclusion of women into the teaching profession could not have been more inauspicious for men teachers, for it put these newly hired, status-conscious men in a difficult position. Just when it appeared that the government had provided peasant men with an opportunity for upward mobility in the villages, the same government decided to fill the positions with women teachers. Exacerbating this problem was the fact that these new women were not peasants like the men, but city women from the traditional service elites. The result was that women from the nobility, the bureaucracy, and the clergy were competing with peasant men for teaching positions, and school boards increasingly preferred women teachers to men because of women's perceived political passivity.

Because of their status anxiety, men teachers responded to the ministry's change in employment policy by criticizing women teachers' ability to teach. If they could show that women did not make good teachers of peasant children, the school boards might hire more men. As a result, men teachers put forward professional arguments and peasant prejudice as a way of articulating their own hostility toward women teachers to keep them in an inferior position within the profession.[11] Because men teachers claimed to be speaking only about peasants' prejudice and not about their own, most scholars have failed to see these claims for what they were—the projection of men teachers' fears about their women colleagues.

One example of men teachers' attitudes toward their women colleagues appeared in an 1883 article published by the teachers' journal *Russkii nachal'nyi uchitel'* (Russian primary schoolteacher), which documented peasant hostility to women teachers in Ukraine. The article asked the question, Did men or women make better teachers of peasant children? Several men and women teachers responded. Although this debate represents a small sample of teachers' opinions, the attitudes expressed corroborate what we already know about men teachers' concerns.

The men teachers who answered this question made many of the same points as peasant men. Women teachers were "ladies"—daughters of landlords, civil servants, and priests. These ladies became teachers not out of love for the work but in order to marry. When these women came to the villages, many had "cut their hair, smoked cigarettes and wore glasses." This was the image most Russians had of radical women during the nineteenth century. By invoking this image, these men were attempting to identify women teachers with a small radical group whom many Russians held in great disdain, and to disparage their effort at enlightenment. Moreover, these "shorn" women lived not in the schoolhouse but with the local priest or landlord. The men teachers claimed that the peasants frequently asked the schoolteacher to read newspapers and discuss local and national news with them. Because they did not want to enter the house of either priests or landlords, however, few peasants would voluntarily approach women teachers, thereby putting the women at a great disadvantage. Men teachers also complained that "lady" teachers would not chat with the peasants or even shake their "calloused hands." Women teachers turned down invitations to eat in peasant homes and found peasant customs incomprehensible. Because most men teachers were from the peasantry, they claimed, they did not have the same handicaps; there was no social gulf between them and the peasantry.[12]

Men teachers' complaints went beyond these class differences. They also raised issues of professional competence. Rejecting the idea that women were "natural" teachers, they suggested that women made poor teachers because of their gender. One man wrote that there was a sharp difference between being a mother and being a teacher and blamed many of his pupils' character flaws on poor mothering. "Women are more emotional than men—this is true, but this same ability to feel, as I have had occasion to notice in a few mothers, does not allow them to relate critically with their pupils. There are many instances of these children growing up with undesirable character flaws."[13] Another teacher argued that, since women excelled at sewing and knitting, they should teach in the girls' primary schools. However, only men could teach young peasant boys gardening, land surveying, and gymnastics. He concluded with a dire and chilling warning to women teachers: "Any woman entering a school must understand that the peasants would consider the smallest mistakes her fault and transfer this opinion to the next woman teacher."[14]

Men teachers were also angry at women teachers for the discrepancies that were emerging in teachers' material conditions. They complained particularly about the discrepancies in salaries. Before the expansion of the Russian schools, men served as teachers only in the winter for very low wages (50–100 rubles); during the summer months they performed physical labor in the villages. With the increased financial outlays to education, teachers' salaries had been raised to approximately 250 rubles by the 1880s. According to one embittered teacher, single women teachers could live quite comfortably on their salaries while married men teachers and their families lived in poverty, even though women teachers were paid less than their male colleagues.[15]

These comments by men teachers in the early 1880s suggest enormous class and gender differences within the teaching profession. Even though they were supposedly members of the "lesser" sex, women teachers were the social superiors of the predominantly peasant men teachers, at least in the traditional social order. To compensate for this, the men emphasized their ability to relate to the peasants by participating in village life. In a sense, they were arguing that they occupied a unique position in Russian society. Because they had been born peasants, these men understood the problems and customs of Russian peasants. But at the same time, these men teachers believed they had become part of a newly emerging rural elite because of their training as teachers and their rejection of traditional peasant mores.

In addition to emphasizing their unique social position as a bridge between town and country, men teachers attempted to use professionalization, with its emphasis on technical skills, as a way of keeping women from gaining power and authority within the profession. Men teachers were willing to concede that women were capable of teaching "morals," but only men could instruct pupils in more modern, technical subjects. Surely city "ladies" could not be expected to teach horticulture to peasants? This work was suitable only for men, and particularly peasant men teachers. Thus, even professionalization was defined in gendered terms. In the public realm of the classroom, women were once again relegated to teaching moral lessons, while men teachers dealt with secular technical issues.

The position of the men teachers was exceedingly complex. On the one hand, they opposed women teachers and the government for advocating the introduction of women colleagues, and continued to resist the ministry's efforts well after the decision was announced. At the same time, however, the government and male teachers worked together to exclude women from any position, either in the government bureaucracy or in the professional organizations, that might enhance women teachers' role in education. They justified this exclusion of women by appealing for the needs of the children. According to this view, peasant men continued to be the best teachers of peasant children.

Women Teachers as "Holy" Women

Women teachers responded to the men's criticisms by actively resisting the circumscribed role their male colleagues had prepared for them. They continued to enter the profession in ever-increasing numbers, and they worked hard to create a positive image of women teachers to counteract the image articulated by the men. In the women teachers' discourse, they used older, traditional images of women to create a new image, which would claim a central role for them within the profession.

Women teachers began by attacking the notion that they made poor teachers of peasant children. Their published diaries are full of images of self-sacrificing women forsaking family and friends to teach peasant children.[16] In the candid exchange of letters in *Russkii nachal'nyi uchitel'*, several women responded to the criticism of their male colleagues by acknowledging the suspicions and sexism of the peasants. One teacher commented that, since Ukrainian peasants looked upon women as men's slaves, what was surprising about their inability to accept a woman teacher?[17] Another woman argued that the real problem was that peasants believed that children should fear their teacher and no peasant man ever feared a women.[18]

After acknowledging the difficulties they faced, the women teachers refuted all the points the men had raised. They claimed that most women teachers did not dress or behave like radical women. Teaching was one of the very few employment options available to respectable women in Russia, and most chose teaching not for political reasons but as a means of supporting themselves. Indeed, given that all teachers, regardless of gender, had to be certified for their political reliability, it does not seem very likely that large numbers of radical women would have been allowed to teach.

Women teachers also responded to the class issues raised by the men teachers. According to one woman teacher, women shook hands with the peasants, talked to the elders without embarrassment, and went to the village administration to discuss school problems.[19] The women also reported that they lived at the schools in cold, nasty quarters like the men. One teacher commented that men teachers also lived outside the school grounds, but, she argued, the issue was not where teachers lived but what duty they had to educate children to be useful to their society.[20] The residence of teachers was a function of the financial situation of each school district, rather than the teacher's gender. If zemstvos could afford to build quarters for the teachers, teachers lived there. By 1911 most teachers had such rent-free lodgings, but in the 1880s, this practice was just beginning. The real problem was class. Women teachers shared lodgings with the local elites, while men teachers lived with the peasants.[21]

Finally, the women teachers revealed why women became teachers. One woman replied that most women teachers were deeply committed to their work, and were not just trying to find a suitable mate for marriage.[22] In fact, many women chose teaching as an alternative to marriage. At a time when arranged marriages were still common in Russia, some women looked to teaching as an escape from an unhappy marriage and as a respected alternative to an idle spinsterhood spent living with their parents.

One women, Natalia Nikiforova, wrote in reply to the rural teacher, S. K. Chaikovskii,

You say that "at the present time a rural teacher's participation is not limited by the school walls." That means the teacher's place is not only in the school, but outside it, in society. What is a teacher's role outside of school? In my opinion, a teacher's present place is only in the school. Here lies before him a rich field of activity—and intellectual and moral influence on his pupils. And who is better suited to fulfill the important task of moral upbringing, if not a woman?[23]

Unlike men teachers, who were seeking to raise their social status through participation in village political life, women teachers, according to Nikiforova and the other women teacher respondents, were not interested in such a role. Because all women were excluded from the political realm in Russia, the smallest political act was of radical import and put them at risk of immediate dismissal from their jobs. Men, on the other hand, could claim a legitimate political role for themselves, even if they could not always exercise it. Clearly, there were many women teachers interested in politics, but they chose to exercise their political authority in ways different from those of their male colleagues. They saw their ability to influence young minds through their classroom studies as a safer and more subtle way of bringing about political change.

Despite women teachers' professed lack of interest in politics, both government officials and men teachers were concerned about their potential for influence and tried to keep women from gaining positions of authority from which they could challenge the political order. When the government finally allowed women to become teachers, it prevented them from advancing in the profession by limiting the schools where they could teach, encouraging the dismissal of married teachers, and barring women from the civil service. All these measures kept women in the lowest echelons of the profession. As we will see in chapters 4 and 5, men teachers, for their part, did little to welcome women teachers into the new professional organizations that were forming in postreform Russia; both the leadership and the rank and file of these organizations were predominately male. These professional groups did not address issues that affected women teachers exclusively. Because women were outsiders in any form of public discourse, they needed a chance to air their grievances, but all these policies conspired to keep women from thinking of themselves as legitimate professionals. The all-male ministry continued to formulate school policy, while teachers' response to that policy was articulated by the overwhelmingly male leadership of the profession.

While this might help to explain men teachers' response to women teachers' potential political influence, it does not address the larger issue of women teachers' inability to overcome their status as outsiders. Once again, it is clear that women were trying to create a different role from that of their male colleagues. According to Nikiforova, women wanted to exert an intellectual and moral influence on their young pupils. This role as moral educator constituted their professional self-image and was also a traditional role granted women in

Russian society. In their own eyes, women teachers were not radicals trying to change Russia, but women attempting to contribute to the betterment of Russian society in accordance with traditional gender roles.

Yet the situation was not quite so simple. Women teachers, like their sisters in Europe and the United States, were using traditional gender roles to establish a new place for women in a profession that had been closed to them until 1871.[24] Women may have been "natural" teachers, but the Russian government did not allow them into the schools until the demand for teachers far exceeded the supply. By becoming professionals, women did not become passive instruments of government educational policy, as some have suggested, but rather participants in a complex process to reshape their society. They might not have been the shorn, bespectacled radical women that men teachers feared, but women teachers were demanding a place for themselves in the public sphere, and this threatened to undermine traditional gender relations both in and outside the home. According to Nikiforova and others, women teachers combined a desire to "serve the people" with a clear sense that they were fulfilling their traditional familial and religious roles through the care of young children. Thus, professional women conformed to a pattern oberved by Barbara Alpern Engel in women of the intelligentsia, who combined radical populism with traditional female notions of selfless service and religious duty.[25]

The influence of women's spirituality on their subsequent social and political development has received little attention from scholars. Some new research is suggestive, however. In her recent work on women's religious communities in imperial Russia, Brenda Meehan-Waters has written about the overlooked but important figure of the *staritsa*, or holy woman. These women lived outside the official religious hierarchy, either as hermits or in unofficial lay communities. They strove to lead exemplary Christian lives. According to Meehan-Waters, the *staritsa's* counsel was often sought by men and women of all social ranks; they believed she could advise them because she had divested herself of the world and was able to overcome the petty concerns of others. In attempting to live by the Christian ideal through deep devotion and asceticism, Meehan-Waters concludes, "the *staritsa* was a revered teacher and model, a teacher often of reading and literacy and Psalms and scripture, a teacher of a lived tradition of asceticism and religious practice, a teacher in the way of holiness."[26] It was the *staritsa's* role as a Christian *teacher* that gave her an "authority of holiness" in Russian society.

This evidence of a connection between women's spirituality and their role as teachers is all the more provocative when one considers peasant views of women teachers. According to N. V. Chekhov, a prominent educational activist and historian, Russian peasants called the first women teachers to appear in Russian village schools *chernichki*, or lay nuns. Unlike the *staritsa*, *chernichki* were unmarried women who lived together in small cells in the village and dedicated themselves to the service of God. They performed a number of religious functions: for example, they prepared bodies for burial and read the Psalter and other types of religious literature. Outside their religious functions, they frequently taught young children to read when no schools were available.[27]

What linked the *staritsa*, the *chernichki*, and women teachers was the rejection of their own sexuality in order to lead good Christian lives and instruct others in moral lessons. According to traditional views, women gave up gratification of their own bodies to serve the corporeal and spiritual needs of others, and in making this sacrifice, they became an example to others. More important, it was only these "sexually and morally pure" women who were permitted to instruct others in moral questions. After 1871, when Russian society acknowledged that women teachers could provide the moral upbringing (*vospitanie*) necessary for small children in the schools, it became essential for them to be sexually pure as well in order to conform to this older religious role. Women's denial of their sexuality was considered a great sacrifice and an act of purification. By giving up the opportunity to fulfill their sexual desires, women became saintly and virginal at the same time, and it was this saintly purity that qualified them as teachers of other people's children.[28] According to this view, both *chernichki* and women teachers denied themselves the prospect of meaningful family life in order to lead holy, Christian lives, which included the tutoring of peasant children. As long as women teachers remained celibate and conducted themselves according to those values associated with women's "authority of holiness," they could claim to be a part of this long religious tradition and thereby gain respect within the traditional peasant community. Thus, women teachers could draw not only on motherhood as a model for their self-definition and self-assertion in the community but also on women's religious roles. Both of the roles had been closely linked to traditional gender stereotypes, but in postreform Russia, women teachers were trying to redefine those roles to include a place for themselves as professionals in public service.

Women Teachers as Professionals

These two images of women teachers, as "outsiders" and as secular, holy women, competed with each other in the public discourse on women teachers until the 1890s, when a more professional image of women teachers began to form. A new generation of women teachers emerged in Russia's city schools and especially in St. Petersburg. These women had graduated from the best women's pedagogical training courses in the country. As we saw in chapter 1, these courses were designed to provide women with a "scientific" approach to pedagogy and to develop in them a keen sense of themselves as professionals.

Women teachers' professional consciousness ran counter to the images most city officials had of them. Some officials expected women to teach only until they married, at which time they would take up their "natural" role as wives and mothers. Other officials anticipated that women teachers would view their work as a semireligious vocation and would sacrifice everything for the sake of the children. City women teachers grew increasingly uncomfortable with these roles and wanted to create a role for women that was equal to that of their male colleagues. They wanted rich, productive lives both in and outside the classroom; they wanted careers and family lives as well.

This conflict over women teachers' role in the classroom and in the profession can be seen most clearly in the discourse concerning Petersburg women teachers. Petersburg city school officials wanted to hire the best teachers, and in doing so, hired the most professionally minded of women teachers. At the same time, city officials treated these women not as competent "experts" but as servants paid to do the bidding of school officials. As if this were not bad enough, school officials enacted a ban on hiring married women as teachers in 1897, in effect making celibacy a requirement for teaching. This policy violated the professional values that these women had acquired through their pedagogical training and classroom experience—their sense of self-worth, individualism, and autonomy. Although Petersburg was the only city to enact a marriage ban, firing women teachers upon marriage was a common event throughout Russia.[29] Most women teachers lived in fear of losing their jobs if they opted for family life and found themselves discriminated against both as women and as teachers.

Although the Petersburg city duma lagged behind other cities in providing municipal services during the second half of the nineteenth century, the city's Executive Commission on Education was guided by a group of liberal members who believed in the importance of public education. The first president of the commission was F. F. Eval'd, a respected liberal. He was succeeded by the well-known editor of *Otechestvennye zapiski*, A. A. Kraevskii. When Kraevskii died in 1889, he was succeeded by M. M. Stasiulevich, who had begun his public life as a professor of history at St. Petersburg University. In 1861 Stasiulevich had resigned his position in protest over government encroachment on professorial autonomy.[30] His second career was as the editor of *Vestnik Evropy*, one of the leading "thick" journals of its day. It was these men and their supporters who helped to shape the city's educational policy.[31]

When Petersburg city officials began creating their own local primary school system, they quickly agreed that they wanted to hire only the best teachers for their schools. The person who helped create the 1882 hiring policy for the city was A. Ia. Gerd, who served in the capacity of *ekspert* for the school system. Gerd believed that only individuals with a higher education could provide a superior education for children. He argued that since the Petersburg Commission on Education, the public body charged with overseeing primary education, could not expect men with a university degree to teach in primary schools, the commission should hire women teachers with a higher education or degrees from teacher training programs to work in the city schools.[32]

Gerd's reasoning reflected the ambivalent attitude of the city school officials toward the teachers. School officials automatically assumed that university-educated men were the best candidates for the teaching positions, but their salary demands were too high. The school authorities preferred to hire women who were young and single, because they needed less money to live on; the school boards could thereby justify paying them lower salaries than men, who were supposed to be the sole financial support for their families. In addition, most city officials believed with Gerd that teaching young children was women's "natural" profession and that it helped prepare women for marriage by encouraging their nurturing instincts.[33] The city hired well-educated women who were seen as docile, complacent temporary workers. School officials presumed that these women teachers could be easily managed by their male supervisors and that they would soon get married and leave.[34]

In 1882 the Commission on Education adopted Gerd's recommendations. From that date, the commission hired only women teachers who had graduated from the women's higher courses or who had received some form of specialized pedagogical education, either by taking courses in pedagogy offered at the women's gymnasiums or by attending the Mariinskaia Gymnasium, which had a special two-year teacher training program. Since most gymnasiums offered an additional year of pedagogical training, virtually any graduate who had completed the pedagogical course could qualify to teach in the Petersburg schools. There were so many qualified candidates that some women waited more than five years to obtain a teaching position in the city schools. As a result of these new hiring regulations, Petersburg became the first city in Russia to hire women teachers exclusively; other school boards soon followed suit.[35]

A few years later, in 1887, the Commission on Education established salaries for its teachers. Teachers received a salary of 600 rubles a year, plus a two- or three-room rent-free apartment with a kitchen. In addition, the commission gave each teacher a 50-ruble Christmas bonus. Teachers continued to receive the same salary until they retired. Sometimes, however, the commission awarded a single grant of 50 to 150 rubles in the case of a death or serious illness in a teacher's family.[36] Even though Petersburg teachers did not receive raises, they were still some of the best-paid primary schoolteachers in Russia. Only teachers in Riga received higher salaries.[37]

All these measures encouraged Petersburg women teachers to think of themselves as respected professionals. Many of these women were graduates of the best teacher training programs for women and were among the highest-paid primary schoolteachers in Russia. On the surface, at least, it appears that Petersburg women teachers were treated as competent professionals, and in many cases, treated better than their male colleagues.

In 1897 the Petersburg Commission on Education revised its hiring policy in an attempt to enhance the professionalization of city teachers. The commission proposed legislation requiring teacher candidates to be between the ages of eighteen and thirty, unmarried or widowed without children, and to be graduates of the Mariinskaia Gymnasium with its revamped three-year course in pedagogy—in effect demanding three years of teacher training rather than one.[38] These new rules did not permit the commission to fire married teachers who were already teaching in the schools. Nevertheless, the intended effect of these new rules was clear—the commission wanted to hire young, single, well-trained women unencumbered by husbands and children. Despite a number of articles condemning the new rules as "draconian," the Petersburg city duma approved them on 8 October 1897.[39] After this new legislation was enacted, the local press derisively referred to the city's teachers as the "vestal virgins" (*vestalki*), once again recalling the older images of women teachers, which emphasized that women's sexual and moral purity were prerequisites for their work.

The city duma approved these new rules without significant debate. The deliberations concerning the ban occurred in the special subcommittee that drew up the legislation, and its record of these discussions has not been published. The few published accounts of the debate suggest that the ban's intent was not to prevent women from marrying, but to raise educational requirements so that Petersburg could continue to preserve the high quality of its teaching personnel.[40]

There is evidence that suggests that the city officials had other reasons for enacting the marriage ban. In 1892, 185 women teachers (72.5 percent) in the Petersburg city schools were single and 10 teachers (4 percent) were widows, while only 60 (23.5 percent) were married.[41] After 1892, however, the number of married women teachers increased dramatically, and in 1897 approximately two-thirds of women teachers were married.[42] It was this dramatic increase that prompted Petersburg school officials to change their employment policy. If these married teachers continued to work until their retirement, which the city officials assumed they would do, the school administration would have to pay them pensions. Although the pension allowances for Petersburg schoolteachers were not especially magnanimous, the city administration was already experiencing financial difficulties in meeting the demands of the rapidly growing population.[43]

Even if city officials did not acknowledge financial reasons for the ban, by 1911 the ban's effect on women teachers was apparent. According to the school census conducted that year, 846 women were teaching in the city's primary schools. Of that number, 738 women (85 percent) were unmarried. The rest were either married or widowed, all hired before 1896. More important, women teachers' length of service in the schools remained low. Their average tenure was only twelve years; more than half of the women teachers (477) employed in 1911 had worked less than ten years in the Petersburg schools.[44] Thus, the ban allowed the city duma to maintain a young and docile labor pool. There was no need to pay higher salaries or pensions to more experienced teachers.

Concern over teachers' qualifications and marital status also came at a time when the Petersburg school officials were beginning to reform the school system. These attempts highlight the contradictory nature of the city's employment policies and school officials' expectations of women teachers. The marriage ban was part of a package that included breaking up the old one-room school, which had been in use since 1877, and building special school buildings that would serve an entire school district rather than a single neighborhood. By placing teachers and pupils in large buildings, school officials hoped to exercise greater control in the classroom.[45]

According to the anonymous author of an article that appeared in *Russkaia shkola,* these reforms had some serious drawbacks. The author complained that teachers in these new schools no longer referred to the school as "theirs" or the pupils as "their children." Because the teachers at these schools no longer lived on the premises, they taught their lessons and left without fully taking part in the life of the school. The children did not receive the specialized attention they were accorded under the old system, and individual teachers were no longer the "master" (*khoziain*) of their schools. This deprived the new schools of their "family" character.[46]

This author's praise for the old one-room schoolhouse shows a shift in attitudes toward education since 1870. At that time the Ministry of Education had allowed women to teach because it was their "natural" profession. Women teachers served as surrogate mothers to their pupils. By 1897, city officials no longer saw this type of schooling as adequate. Now, schools were to become more centralized and uniform. Since most educated Russians believed that all Russians were entitled to some form of education, an efficient way of educating the masses had to be devised. In the cities, the result was the replacement of the rather independent one-room schoolhouse by the larger, more centralized schools. This development was part of a larger Western phenomenon of school consolidation and rationalization.[47]

The effect of these reforms on teachers was complex. The effort to obtain the best-qualified teachers was a recognition on the part of the Petersburg Commission on Education that they wanted teachers with professional training: they wanted to hire the best. Despite the desire to hire professionals, however, the Petersburg officials still wanted the women teachers to remain docile, compliant employees. This is why they wanted the marriage ban—city officials wanted to tell the women how to behave and what to teach. Just as mothers had influence in raising their children in the home, women schoolteachers had influence over their pupils in the more "homey" one-room schoolhouse; the Petersburg city duma wanted to deny women teachers this influence by breaking up the one-room schoolhouse. They wanted women to bring their "natural" mothering skills to teaching, and at the same time, they treated women like servants.

The Petersburg marriage ban was introduced at a time when employers in other nations were adopting them as well. Marriage bans had become commonplace in all Western countries by the first half of the twentieth century.[48] As late as the 1960s most nations of the industrialized world reported that the majority of industries had marriage bans against women employees, and many countries had explicit prohibitions against married women schoolteachers.[49] These bans reflected very deep prejudices against married women as productive white-collar workers and professionals.

In his recent study of the feminization of clerical labor in Great Britain, Samuel Cohn has argued that marriage bans are an example of "synthetic turnover" in the work force. According to Cohn, employers have used marriage as a convenient way of keeping women in the lower levels of an occupation. It is not the act of marriage per se that is the issue; rather, a marriage ban is merely a convenient way to weed out women who would otherwise gain seniority, experience, and expertise. Marriage bans occur at a certain moment, when women begin to dominate a particular field and pose a challenge to men for positions of management and power. Cohn argues that marriage bans occur when several conditions are present. Most bans are in effect in occupations where learning curves peak early, where there is a substantial supply of replacement labor, and where salaries are based on length of service. In addition to these specific situations, marriage bans occur when the climate tolerates overt sex discrimination.[50]

In the Petersburg case, most of these conditions for synthetic turnover were present. As more and more young women graduated from specialized pedagogical courses, they were attracted to teaching jobs in the cities with their rich cultural life. The result was a substantial supply of replacement labor for teaching jobs in cities such as Petersburg.[51] Thus, the Petersburg city duma was able to pass a marriage ban, confident that it could easily employ enough teachers based on the new hiring qualifications. It was also true that school officials preferred to hire young, well-trained, but inexperienced teachers who worked very hard for a few years. The perception was that after eight or ten years a teacher began to complain about working conditions and to feel a growing commitment to "her school" and "her children." By putting a marriage ban on hiring, Petersburg officials could reap the benefits of their young pool of teachers without having to deal with the problems of a more mature workforce. And the Petersburg city duma was able to enact such a policy because such sex discrimination was tolerated in Russian society. Perhaps the only one of Cohn's criteria that did not fit the Petersburg case was the tenure-based salary, for in 1897 all teachers received the same salary, regardless of length of service. However, after 1900 tenure-based salaries were introduced and became an incentive for keeping the marriage ban. It became important financially for the city to encourage women to leave teaching after just a few years, in order to keep down expenditures on salaries and pensions.

These contradictions fed the discontent of the Petersburg women teachers. As a result of their training and the desire of school officials to hire the best, they thought of themselves as talented professionals. In the one-room schoolhouse that predominated in Petersburg until the end of the nineteenth century, they were able to utilize their training to enhance their professional consciousness. Yet school officials continued to thwart women teachers' professionalization by treating them in accordance with the older attitudes expressed in the marriage ban. According to the ban, women could either work as temporary workers until their "real" work of marriage began, or they could remain single and devote their whole lives to the care of small children, thereby making a vocation out of their work. The underlying message of the ban was that women could either teach or marry— they could not do both. In this way, the images of women teachers as outsiders and as saintly women competed with the professional image Petersburg women teachers were trying to create.

These antagonistic expectations of Petersburg school officials thwarted women teachers' professional consciousness and self-worth, and caused them to look for solutions to their difficult situation. To repeal the marriage ban, women teachers would have to become a part of a political process that barely existed in Russia at the end of the nineteenth century. In addition, Petersburg women teachers had to find allies to support them in their struggle against the city officials. Naturally enough, they looked to the newly emerging teachers' professional movement as just such an ally. As we shall see, however, their efforts were in vain.

It is sometimes difficult to remember that teaching was not always seen as women's "natural" profession. Women have come to predominate primary and secondary schoolteaching in Europe and America only in the nineteenth and twentieth centuries. This significant shift resulted from important changes in pedagogical theory. Educators, influenced by the writings of Jean-Jacques Rousseau, perceived women to have innate abilities to educate and care for small children. These "maternal instincts" made women natural teachers. The next step was simply to allow these women to take their natural skills as teachers in the home and apply them in the classroom. Given the expansion of schooling during the nineteenth century, women were a ready source from which school officials could recruit instructors.

Despite this advance, problems remained. The notion of "natural" instincts ran counter to teachers' new professional consciousness. Nature was in direct conflict with the professional ethic, which called for the application of science and reason. To create a more professional corps of women teachers, educators argued, women needed to be sent to special training programs where their natural talents could be regulated and checked by "experts." But these measures did not solve all the problems. Once women entered the classroom, they competed with their male colleagues for power, authority, and status as experts. In order to deal with this issue, other means had to be devised to ensure that women remained in a subordinate position within the educational hierarchy and within the teaching profession.

In Russia, women's struggle to gain acceptance as teachers and men's resistance to their claim were reflected in the discursive strategies used to represent women teachers. Men teachers and administrators claimed that women were "outsiders" both to the peasant village and the profession. Women teachers were described as ineffective teachers and therefore in need of constant supervision by their male colleagues and officials. By extension, this meant that women could not be accepted as full-fledged members of the new profession.

Women teachers countered this negative image by images of their own making. The first generation emphasized the continuation of traditional feminine religious and familial roles in the life of the woman schoolteacher. According to this view, women teachers were not interested in "politics" but only in the shaping of young minds in the classroom (as if this task did not have "political" overtones). They were not radicals who were trying to destroy society, but goodhearted women who wanted to "serve the people" in a more public way. In creating this particular image, women teachers were trying to create a circumscribed place for themselves in society, as teachers and as women. The second generation of women teachers was less circumspect. Having received a more "professional" pedagogical training, these women saw themselves as experts who, as such, deserved the same treatment as their male colleagues. The reality of their professional lives was quite different—they were discriminated against in ways that men teachers were not. Although most men and women teachers believed they were denied legal protection and respect for the important work they performed, women teachers saw that they faced additional discrimination, as both women and teachers. They were the "vestal virgins" condemned to live their lives alone in the service of others. While some women teachers continued to find this image appealing, a growing number of city women did not—they wanted to be treated as professionals.

It is important to stress that the problems women teachers faced stemmed from the complex ways that class, and not just gender, entered into these discursive debates. Women teachers were outsiders because they were city women. Their dress, language, and mores were in sharp contrast to those of their male peasant colleagues. Professionalization offered men a rare chance for social mobility, and they wanted to make sure they did not lose their chance to obtain status and power to their social betters. Women used discursive strategies to try to downplay both class and gender by labeling themselves holy women. Women teachers gave up their right to seek sexual fulfillment; they also gave up their social rank by leaving family and friends behind to work for the people. However, just as they could not neutralize their gender, women teachers continued to bear the mark of the social class in which they were raised.

These concerns about gender and class were not frequently discussed in postreform Russia, and the discussion itself was masked by the various strategies of each side. Most of the literature about teachers in this period emphasized those things that drew teachers together—their shared understanding of their important mission, their pedagogical principles, and their classroom experiences. Those issues that divided teachers, like class and gender, remained muted. In failing to grapple with these issues, however, teachers set a dangerous precedent in their attempts to form a profession. By emphasizing unity and equality over the need for hierarchy within the profession, teachers ignored the serious issues that divided their profession and their society.

The government's attempts to reform the schools and to create a professional teaching corps had complex and ambiguous results. Virtually all the legislation that was enacted consisted of half-measures designed to create new institutions but also to shore up the existing regime. New schools were designed, but only to educate children for their station in life, not to provide any kind of meaningful social mobility. Teaching was no longer a part-time job, but one that required specialized training and conferred social status upon its practitioners; yet teachers continued to be treated as little more than poorly paid civil servants and were frequently subject to the conflicting whims of state and local officials. Even teacher training programs contained elements of the old and new approaches to learning. Trained to be experts in either pedagogy or some other academic specialty, teachers were selected for their political passivity. It was their political obedience that furthered teachers' careers, not their training or devotion to their work. Thus, the government decided to encourage the professionalization of city teachers but was reluctant to complete the process by giving teachers the autonomy in the classroom they craved.

This inability of the government to complete the professionalization process it had initiated made life increasingly difficult for teachers in Moscow and Petersburg. Although many teachers continued to ignore the problems, mostly out of fear of losing their jobs, others could not. Having accepted the responsibility for becoming better teachers, they expected the government to reward them for their efforts. But these expectations were thwarted by the government's reluctance to share its power and authority in the classroom with the new corps of professional teachers. This placed teachers in a difficult situation. Because of their training and experiences in the classroom, city teachers were caught between the old autocratic society and the new civil society that was slowly taking shape around them.

Government resistance to teachers' professionalization efforts made city teachers increasingly eager to join the new civil society. Their professional values of individualism, education, initiative, and enterprise were in harmony with values of other members of the new society. But, aware of their isolation, city teachers began to talk about forming a unified teachers' movement that could represent their interests on the national level and work for those changes necessary to promote their values. In order to do this, city teachers needed to join the other disaffected groups in Russia to work for change. Since most city teachers had been specifically barred from participating in political activities, this was a difficult and dangerous step. As the nineteenth century drew to a close with little improvement in their work environments, more and more city teachers were willing to take this crucial step.

4 Politics and Professionalization, 1860–1905

IN TERMS OF THE GOALS SET BY THE MINISTRY OF EDUCATION, the government-sponsored professionalization of teachers during the 1870s and 1880s was a success. By 1890 there were more well-trained teachers working in the schools: fewer itinerant teachers and more individuals who considered their work to be a profession or a full-time commitment. Most had received their education at government-run teacher training programs, which had introduced them to pedagogical theory and practice. At a time when the number of schools was steadily increasing, more school boards were able to hire these teacher-professionals for the schools. The social composition of the teaching profession also changed during these years. As we saw in chapter 3, men primary teachers were generally peasants who joined the new profession in hope of improving their social status by becoming part of a new rural elite. Secondary teaching continued to provide sons of the upper and middle elites with meaningful employment after graduation from the university. But the greatest change came with the influx of large numbers of well-educated city women into the primary schools all over Russia. City officials hired women almost exclusively, and in the countryside, women constituted an absolute majority of schoolteachers by 1911.[1] Faced with few employment opportunities, increasing numbers of educated women bucked prejudice to teach lower-class children the three R's and introduce them to a more "modern" way of life.

The success of teacher professionalization brought new challenges to city teachers and the Russian government. Having taken the wishes of the government for better schools and teachers seriously, the teacher-professionals quickly saw the need for improvement in classrooms beset with problems. The Great Reform legislation had established that the government would no longer shoulder all responsibility for governing Russia and that ordinary subjects would have to assume some government responsibility; a small but growing group of city teachers rose to the challenge—they attempted to initiate change on their own rather than wait for directives from the central government. It was for this purpose that all the representative councils and administrative educational bodies had been created—to divide responsibility for education between state and local governments. But, because they left no place for the "experts" to advise them, the representative bodies were flawed in the eyes of the teacher-professionals. Although they worked in the schools every day, teachers had little voice in their administration. Thus, the newly professionalized teachers began to seek ways to make their views known to state and local officials and thereby utilize their expertise.

Unfortunately, the Ministry of Education and local government officials thwarted city teachers' efforts to carry out their professional work, by continuing to treat them as public servants rather than well-trained professionals. The host of state and local officials that were charged with overseeing city teachers and their classrooms illustrate the reluctance of these government bodies to share their power with the teachers. City teachers, in turn, believed that these ambiguous and conflicting government policies isolated teachers from one another to keep them in a subordinate position. Believing themselves to be "experts," city teachers were imbued with a strong sense of working for the public good and increasingly sought collective action to reform the schools. In the spring of 1905, a group of Petersburg secondary schoolteachers expressed this view:

Union has a more immediate significance for us, the teachers. The teacher is so forgotten, so alone in the contemporary school system, that at every step he feels the impotence of his individual efforts to vindicate his pedagogical ideals and to resist the pressures of the political system. Organized association must replace this isolation with the awareness of common interests and collective work for the good of the school. It gives the opportunity to each to appeal to a large group of people who think the same way and to find among them moral and material help in the difficult conditions often created for a teacher who does not compromise his convictions.[2]

This need to talk and work with "a large group of people who think the same way" stimulated the development of a city teachers' professional movement in postreform Russia. Organizing first at the local level, teachers saw that the problems they faced were national in scope and could not simply be remedied at individual schools. This realization encouraged them to reach out to other teachers' organizations to create a professional movement powerful enough to effect change. Their efforts to make their voices heard spawned a national teachers' professional movement whose unifying force was the professional ethos they had acquired as a result of their training and common experiences as teachers. Because the prevailing autocratic political culture valued service and loyalty to the tsar above all else, city teachers needed their own organizations to help them publicize and support the values they espoused—public service, autonomy, technical expertise, and individual self-worth.[3]

The government's response to the city teachers' professional movement was riddled with contradictions. On the one hand, the government wanted quasi-professional organizations because they encouraged the emergence of a better-trained corps of government employees. As the economy and bureaucracy grew increasingly complex, Russia needed a pool of more sophisticated, trained experts. At the same time, however, the government wanted to control its employees and their activities so that it alone could continue to shape Russia's modernization effort. Because the government usually defined any independent action as "political" and therefore a threat to autocratic power, government officials and city teachers lived in constant tension.

As a result of these contradictory responses, the development of teachers' professional organizations shows a distinct pattern. During the late 1850s and 1860s, the government permitted teachers to form organizations whose purpose was to further city teachers' pedagogical development. However, some important changes in government attitudes occurred during the 1870s that made life more difficult for teachers' organizations. Those teachers who attended the various meetings found it difficult to limit their discussions only to those subjects that the Ministry of Education defined as "pedagogical." Teachers, like other social groups, saw an interrelationship between the difficulties the schools faced and those confronting the rest of society, and they wanted to discuss this interrelationship in order to devise a coherent plan of educational reform. But, particularly after 1872, when Count Dmitrii Tolstoi became minister of education, the ministry believed that all discussions of educational reform should emanate from its chambers. This event, coupled with the growing activism of a revolutionary underground in Russia, meant that during the 1870s and 1880s teachers' organizations grew very slowly and tried very hard not to draw the attention of ministry officials by discussing controversial issues, for to do so was to risk closure of these organizations by the government. It was only after the famine of 1891 and the resulting scandal over the failure of government relief policies that teachers felt it was imperative for them to establish more teachers' organizations. The teachers in Moscow and Petersburg formed their associations by circumventing many government regulations created to prevent teachers from organizing. Finally, after 1900 there appears to have been the critical mass of teachers' associations necessary for the development of a national teachers' movement. Teachers were in fact one of the last major groups in Russia to form a professional movement, because the Ministry of Education tried harder than other government bodies to prevent teachers from meeting.

To be sure, not all government officials or ministries regarded professional activity as "political" and "antigovernment." Official good will allowed teachers to organize and meet. But attempts to control professional organizations revealed the underlying suspicions of officialdom. The ambiguities within the government convinced many city teachers that Russia's educational problems were inseparably linked to the larger problems facing Russian society. Over the course of the second half of the nineteenth century, educational and social reform became inextricably joined to political reform in the minds of the teacher-professionals. Because government officials saw the teachers' criticism of the educational system as a political statement, every attempt to improve teachers' professional standing became an act of political defiance. Professionalization and politicization had become parallel processes in postreform Russia. As city teachers tried to act according to their professional code, they were thwarted by government attempts to control their professional movement. Despite the rather modest nature of many of these professional organizations and activities, the Russian government blocked teachers' efforts to act independently.

The inability of the Russian government to see the development of a national teachers' professional movement in anything but a negative light gave the movement its character. Teachers in other European countries were also inspired by their professional ethos to seek social and political reform, and also were not looked upon with great favor by their governments. However, most of these teachers worked through already established political organizations and processes to achieve their goals, whereas teachers in Russia had no legitimate political avenue to express their concerns or ideas for reform, except their professional organizations. This gave the professional organizations a political character almost from their inception. Russian teachers were hired for their political reliability, and their professional requests were modest and reformist in nature, but as the government grew more intransigent and refused professional claims for autonomous action, it forced these organizations into more radical positions, politicizing teachers and pushing more of them further away from the government. As we have already seen, experiences in their training programs and in the classroom had fostered an antigovernment attitude among many teachers. Now, their involvement in the professional movement intensified that attitude.

It was not the activities themselves that presented such a threat to the government. Behind these activities lay the new values of individual initiative and autonomy. When teachers asserted their prerogative to take the initiative in these matters, when they insisted on the right to shape their own destiny, they threatened to undermine the basis of autocratic rule. Maintaining that it knew what was best for all of Russia's subjects, the government understood the danger posed by this emerging civil society. While in Western Europe civil society had consolidated sufficiently to permit autonomous organizations, in Russia civil society was just emerging. Tragically, the government failed to appreciate its own role in the creation of civil society and the need to work with it; the government continued to believe it could control the professions.

This dovetailing of the teachers' professional and political movements mirrored the situation of professionals throughout the Russian Empire. Their requests rebuffed by various government agencies, Russian doctors, lawyers, and engineers sought professional and political reform through their professional organizations. In a country where political parties were illegal, professional organizations and meetings became substitutes for them.[4] Moreover, professionals were not the only groups seeking change in Russia. Workers, students, and others were actively organizing and attempting to formulate their own desires for reform and a better life. As these groups became frustrated by contradictory government policies, their discontent began to grow and developed into a major political crisis, which finally burst forth into revolution in 1905.

In order to understand the growing crisis and city teachers' participation in it, we will look at the development of the teachers' movement in the two capitals. Teachers in both cities organized pedagogical and mutual-aid societies to provide a forum for addressing their concerns.

Having established professional organizations, city teachers began to link up with their colleagues in the rural schools and to organize nationally. They did so in two important ways. First, they organized national conferences on topics of concern to teachers and the educated public. Although in the beginning it was very difficult to receive government permission to hold these meetings, through hard work and persistence several such meetings were held during the 1890s and early 1900s, uniting teachers from all over the Russian Empire. The three Technical Congresses, the Moscow District Teachers' Congress, the All-Russian Industrial Exhibition, and the Mutual-Aid Societies' Congress were all key in city teachers' growing involvement in the national teachers' movement. At these congresses, teachers from all levels of the school system were able to air their grievances and discover their shared sense of professional identity. Second, through these meetings teachers encouraged the most activist elements within the profession to create a national teachers' organization to lobby for educational, social, and political reform. These plans were well under way when the revolutionary crisis that had been brewing finally broke out, and in 1905 city teachers joined with other professional and social groups in demanding radical reforms.

It is important to stress that one of the chief goals of the teachers' professional movement had become the unification of the entire profession. As the words of the Petersburg schoolteachers illustrate, teachers' sense of isolation—from students, parents, government, and society, but particularly from one another—was so keen that collective work took on great meaning for them. During the second half of the nineteenth century, teachers talked of the need to unite virtually every time they met. In emphasizing the need for a unified profession, teachers underestimated the forces that divided them. They papered over their differences in the prerevolutionary period in order to become strong enough to fight for reform. Collective action was the only way to counter the government's resistance to change. Teachers had had enough of the radical intelligentsia's grand but futile gestures at revolutionary change. They thought it was time to work together and reform the system from within. Because the autocratic system banned political organizations, it is understandable that teachers would emphasize their common interests and use whatever organization they had to effect political change. But by glossing over their differences in class and gender, teachers were unprepared for the forceful emergence of divisions within their ranks in 1905.

Professional Organizations in Petersburg and Moscow

The first attempt by city teachers to form a quasi-professional organization occurred during the era of the Great Reforms, with the establishment of the Petersburg Pedagogical Society. In 1859 P. G. Redkin, a distinguished lawyer and professor, invited some of Petersburg's young teachers to join him in a club to discuss pedagogical subjects.[5] These meetings formed the nucleus of the Petersburg Pedagogical Society, which was granted a government charter in 1860. Biweekly discussions of reports quickly became a forum for all educators to discuss their general concerns. At the height of its popularity, the society's membership exceeded two hundred and included many of the leading educators of the day.[6] After initially encouraging Petersburg teachers to organize, the Ministry of Education began to have misgivings concerning the group's activities, and in 1879 Minister of Education Dmitrii Tolstoi closed down the Petersburg Pedagogical Society. The pretext was the appearance in a prominent newspaper of an article criticizing Russian secondary education which, it turned out, had originally been read and discussed at a meeting of the society. Officially, the society was closed for "discussing nonpedagogical subjects and for admitting students to its meetings." Thus, the first Russian pedagogical society came to an abrupt end.[7]

The history of the Petersburg Pedagogical Society illustrates well the underlying tension between the Ministry of Education and Petersburg teachers. The ministry was willing to permit teachers their societies as long as they did not discuss matters relating to the formulation of school policy or "political" questions; the ministry was determined to maintain its prerogative as the chief architect of school policy. In this way, it was only following Russian law, by holding associations to a narrowly defined charter that delineated what the society could do; anything not officially approved was forbidden.[8] On the other hand, Petersburg teachers felt that the ministry needed to share its role as chief administrator with them because they had important expertise, which the ministry could ignore only at its peril. This conflict between the ministry and city teachers over educational policy and professional prerogative was part of a larger crisis that occurred in Russia in the late 1870s. An increase in peasant unrest and revolutionary violence caused government officials to reassert autocratic authority in a number of ways, one of which was to exercise greater control over teachers.[9]

The dissolution of the Petersburg Pedagogical Society was a blow to city teachers' organizational efforts. The demise of the society left them with no organization of their own: once in the classroom, many teachers worked in almost total isolation. Rural teachers, who worked alone in schools scattered many miles apart throughout the countryside, certainly faced a particularly difficult form of cultural and professional isolation.[10] For those teachers lucky enough to find work in the two capitals, the situation was not quite so bleak. Despite the government's disapproval of teachers' organizations, during the 1870s and 1880s teachers in Moscow and Petersburg did participate in other organizations, where they met and discussed common problems.

Petersburg and Moscow teachers discussed common problems at teachers' meetings held at individual schools. As part of their official duties, city teachers met formally with school administrators to discuss pertinent educational matters. Secondary schoolteachers in both cities met in the pedagogical councils. Each school had its own council, composed of the entire staff, which met at least once a month to make important decisions. Primary schoolteachers in Moscow met with school trustees to talk about their concerns. From 1881 to 1884 the Petersburg Commission on Education organized periodic meetings for its city teachers, but interference from the Ministry of Education curtailed these meetings. The ministry had wanted to subject these meetings to more rigorous supervision, but the Commission on Education was not willing to allow the ministry more power than it already had in the city schools. In 1893 the director of primary schools for the Petersburg province, V. A. Latyshev, organized meetings for teachers in the Petersburg province, but these were not popular with city teachers.[11]

All these meetings took place in the presence of school administrators. Teachers felt constrained in talking about problems because they believed that such discussions made them appear to be bad teachers. More important, school officials set the agenda for the teachers' meetings; this meant that some of the more intractable problems between officials and teachers, such as official surveillance over teachers' private lives and teachers' lack of legal rights, were not discussed. All these difficulties led city teachers to seek new forums where they would be able to discuss their problems free from official interference.

To overcome the official presence at their meetings, teachers in Petersburg and Moscow joined several organizations that helped to encourage more progressive educational ideas in Russia. This marked their growing professional commitment. One such organization was the Petersburg Froebel Society. Established in 1871 by the same Professor Redkin who had founded the Petersburg Pedagogical Society eleven years earlier, this society was intended to popularize the teachings of the German educator Friedrich Wilhelm Froebel, an advocate of child-centered pedagogy and the founder of the kindergarten system. The Petersburg Froebel Society was very influential in the establishment of kindergartens and summer camps for children; it also established pedagogical courses for kindergarten and primary schoolteachers.[12]

City teachers also participated in the activities of two organizations devoted to the promotion of vocational education in Russia. In Petersburg, teachers belonged to the Imperial Russian Technical Society (founded in 1866), and in Moscow, to the Society for the Dissemination of Technical Knowledge. Both societies advocated including more vocational training in the existing school curriculum and increasing the number of vocational schools in the Russian Empire. Desiring to democratize education, the societies organized schools for workers. Teachers from all levels of the educational system as well as members of the Russian educated public participated in the societies' activities. This gave teachers the opportunity to meet and discuss not just technical education but other educational projects as well.[13]

The most distinguished of the Russian educational societies were the two literacy committees—the Literacy Committee of the Free Economic Society, founded in Petersburg in 1861, and the Literacy Committee of the Moscow Agricultural Society, founded in 1845. Many of Russia's most distinguished public figures, as well as many teachers and educators, participated in the activities of these committees. Their purpose was to provide material assistance to schools (teaching aids such as maps and globes), to publish books for the popular reader, and to collect data on education in Russia. Both committees did a great deal to further Russian cultural life during the second half of the nineteenth century.[14]

These societies presented city teachers with the opportunity to break out of their classroom isolation and develop contacts with other members of Russian educated society. In meetings, teachers could speak openly with other interested individuals about their problems and publicize their ideas for reform. Having discovered the importance of associational activity for fostering a sense of solidarity and collective responsibility, teachers in Petersburg and Moscow wanted their own independent organizations that could address the problems specifically related to their profession. Through professional organizations, city teachers hoped to develop further a sense of corporate identity and professional consciousness. The only type of teachers' organization the Ministry of Education was willing to permit was the mutual-aid society. This type of society allowed teachers to help one another by providing material assistance in the form of pension funds, savings accounts, nurseries for teachers' children, and other forms of monetary assistance. These mutual-aid societies gave teachers their first legal opportunities since the closing of the Petersburg Pedagogical Society to gather and discuss their concerns, and their formation was a critical development in the city teachers' professional movement.[15]

By 1900, there were several mutual-aid societies in the two capitals: the Mutual-Aid Fund for Teachers in the Moscow City Public and Private Schools (founded in 1880); the Mutual-Aid Society for Members of the Teaching Profession in the City of Moscow (founded in 1882); the Moscow Society for the Improvement of Teachers' Living Conditions in the Primary Schools (founded in 1895); the Mutual-Aid Society at the Moscow Teachers' Institute (also founded in 1895); the Society for the Welfare of Women Educators and Teachers in Russia (founded in 1866); the St. Petersburg Mutual-Aid Society (founded in 1890); the Mutual-Aid Society for Former Students of the St. Petersburg Teachers' Institute (also founded in 1890); and the Mutual-Aid Society for Male and Female Primary Schoolteachers in the St. Petersburg Province (founded in 1892). As the names of these organizations indicate, each society had a particular constituency, both regional and functional, that it hoped to assist. In many cases, these functions and constituencies overlapped, and the members of one mutual-aid society were eligible to join others.

Of all these mutual-aid societies, the two that contributed the most to the development of teacher professionalization were the Moscow Society for the Improvement of Teachers' Living Conditions and the Petersburg Mutual-Aid Society. They began as modest mutual-aid societies, but developed into quasi-professional organizations concerned with much more than rendering monetary assistance to teachers. These modest organizations became Tocquevillian "schools of democracy" that trained their members in the principles and practices of associational activity, the give-and-take of self-governing organizations.[16] And these lessons were important, since the members of these mutual-aid societies helped to spearhead a professional movement whose goal was to unite all teachers into a single organization and to promote and defend their shared values.

The Petersburg Mutual-Aid Society The charter of the Petersburg Mutual-Aid Society was approved by the Ministry of Education in December 1890. Because the society was based in Petersburg, it became a legal meeting place for teachers, administrators, and all those interested in education. As was typical of other teachers' organizations, the membership grew slowly but steadily during the 1890s. In 1894 the society had 226 members. By January 1904 that number had reached 660. Of this number, 45 taught at institutions of higher learning, 223 taught in secondary schools, 215 in primary schools, and 34 in military schools. An additional 43 members served as school directors and inspectors, and 41 identified themselves as private teachers: the rest did not list a place of employment.[17] Given the thousands of teachers employed in Petersburg during these years, neither number is particularly high and at no point did the society represent even a simple majority of Petersburg teachers. It is important to remember, however, that it was an act of some political courage to belong to such an organization, since teachers lived in constant fear of losing their jobs if they became involved in "politics." Moreover, the many women teachers in Petersburg must have found it very difficult to even think of joining the society, given the hostility expressed toward "activist" women. Despite these important checks on the membership of the Petersburg Mutual-Aid Society, the society's importance for the city teachers' movement is undeniable. Teachers from all levels of the school system were meeting and discussing problems, often for the first time, and they were meeting legally. And, just as important, all the leaders of the Petersburg teachers' movement in 1904–1905 were members of the society.

For several years, the Petersburg Mutual-Aid Society performed its functions rather quietly, but beginning in 1896 the society took on an increasingly active role. This growing activism was the result of two important events: the famine of 1891–1892, which had a profound impact not just on teachers but on all of society, and the cholera epidemic that accompanied the famine.[18] The teachers, doctors, and statisticians who worked in the countryside all witnessed the peasants' terrible suffering and publicized this tragedy in the press. When government relief efforts appeared inadequate to cope with the famine and its aftermath, many members of civil society, and particularly professionals, sprang into action. They organized their own relief efforts in an attempt to sidestep the bungling bureaucracy. As news of the epidemic spread, peasants panicked and resisted the sanitary measures, which violated age-old customs. Some professionals died from their exposure to the disease; others were attacked in the cholera riots. When the effects of famine and epidemic finally subsided, most professionals better understood the effects of poverty, disease, and ignorance on village life, and by extension, on all of society. These professional men and women became convinced that they had to act to end Russian backwardness. Thus, the 1890s became a period of great activity for civil society. New organizations sprang up to deal with Russia's social ills, and existing organizations entered into an activist phase. One example was the Petersburg Literacy Society. Many members were convinced that the famine could have been avoided had it not been for peasant ignorance of modern agricultural techniques. It was peasant backwardness that had caused the famine, and the only way to prevent such catastrophes in the future was to educate the peasantry.[19] These convictions led the committee to convene a meeting of zemstvo specialists to discuss these and other problems facing Russia. Committee members arranged the meeting, which drew over one thousand people, without obtaining government permission. The Ministry of Education reacted swiftly by revoking the committee's charter and creating a new organization supervised directly by the ministry. As a result of these sweeping restrictions, six hundred members of the Literacy Committee resigned in protest.[20]

The disbanding of the Petersburg Literacy Committee had a radicalizing effect on the Petersburg Mutual-Aid Society. Although it is difficult to ascertain the exact number of teachers who were members of both societies, the governing boards of both organizations had several key members in common.[21] Angered by the actions of the Ministry of Education, these activists set about to transform the Petersburg Mutual-Aid Society from a monetary fund into a professional organization that could provide teachers with the forum to discuss educational reform and publicize grievances. With the demise of the autonomous Literacy Committee, the Petersburg Mutual-Aid Society now became the meeting ground for teachers "who did not compromise their convictions" and "who thought the same way."[22] The teachers' resolve to increase their activities was strengthened by the growing activism of other professional and political groups in Russia during the 1890s.[23]

The first indication of this new spirit was the formation of the Ushinskii Commission, a subcommittee of the mutual-aid society, in 1896. In 1894 the Ministry of Education had issued a new law governing the organization of mutual-aid societies that were forming as a result of the new activist phase among teachers. In accordance with the statute, the ministry limited the mutual-aid societies to providing members with financial assistance and nothing else. These rules were designed to prevent teachers from discussing educational policy.[24] Since the Petersburg Mutual-Aid Society had been chartered in 1890, it was not subject to the new rules. But, in creating the Ushinskii Commission, the society openly defied the new limits set by the Ministry of Education. The city's teacher-activists clearly wanted more than financial assistance from their organization. They were determined to create a public forum to critique government educational policy and to suggest changes based on their expertise and experiences as teachers.

In the published report announcing the creation of the Ushinskii Commission, the members agreed to study the social and material position of teachers, which was after all the goal of the entire society. In thinking about the condition of teachers in Russia, various members of the society raised questions: "Why are there not any new Ushinskiis, Pirogovs, Korfs, Stoiunins? Why are there no talented teachers? Why does pedagogical enthusiasm and creative activity dry up among teachers? Why does contemporary teaching provoke so much justified criticism and complaints?"[25] The members of the commission clearly acknowledged the truth of the complaints against the teaching profession in Russia. At the same time, they wanted to know why these problems had arisen and how they could be solved. In order to get to the root of the problems facing teachers, the Ushinskii Commission hoped to ascertain the true pedagogical, social, and economic position of the contemporary teacher. They wanted to give those teachers who were willing an opportunity to discuss and make recommendations to improve their lives both in and outside the classroom. Petersburg teachers hoped to make the results of their findings available to like-minded colleagues interested in improving professional standards.[26]

In addition to organizing the Ushinskii Commission, maintaining a library for its members, and administering a savings fund, the governing board of the Petersburg Mutual-Aid Society took steps in 1903 to organize a new commission called the Public Education Section. This new section examined questions dealing with primary education and the position of the teachers in the elementary schools. In its first year of existence, the Public Education Section met eleven times and heard various reports on primary education and on the specific problems facing Petersburg teachers. Its members numbered forty-six in 1903–1904, the overwhelming majority of them women primary schoolteachers in the Petersburg city schools.[27]

The Public Education Section of the Petersburg Mutual-Aid Society occupies a special place in the history of the teachers' movement, for it was one of the very few organizations run for and by women teachers. In light of the growing feminization of the teaching profession during this period, its uniqueness is startling, but it shows the difficulty women teachers had gaining acceptance. The prohibition against married women teachers was a symbol of this inability to gain acceptance as full-fledged members of the teaching profession. Not expecting to remain in their jobs for very long, most women did not have much interest in joining organizations to improve their working conditions. Moreover, most positions of authority in imperial Russia were held by men. The government and the Orthodox Church, to give two examples, specifically prohibited women from holding positions within the power structure. Although this notion had been under attack since the middle of the nineteenth century, the underlying assumption of Russian society was that men would control public life and women would be in charge of the home. Despite men teachers' antigovernment stance on most issues dealing with women's professional status, the men teachers were no more inclined to admit women into the power structure of their organizations than was the government. Women were believed to be too immature to be given responsible positions in the professional societies.[28] Of the few women who did emerge as leaders in the teachers' movement, many were married to the movement's male activists. For example, the Vakhterovs and the Popovs were prominent couples in the Moscow teachers' movement. By marrying men who became deeply involved in the professional movement, these women were drawn into the movement and were able to lend their talents in ways that might not have been open to them before their marriages.[29] Despite the feminization of the profession, only in Petersburg did women play a prominent role in the professional movement.

The Petersburg Mutual-Aid Society differed from the other mutual-aid societies that teachers formed in late nineteenth-century Russia. Primarily because of its location, it was able to attract some of the nation's best educators; it also welcomed women teachers. More important, the society defined its purpose more broadly than did most mutual-aid societies. It set out to provide its members with a forum to discuss the serious problems facing the teaching profession.

The Moscow Society for the Improvement of Living Conditions A similar development occurred among the Moscow teachers' mutual-aid societies. Of the city's three teachers' mutual-aid societies, the only one that evolved into a kind of quasi-professional organization was the Society for the Improvement of Teachers' Living Conditions in the Primary Schools in the City of Moscow. At its first general meeting, held in October 1895, the society announced that its aim was to provide financial assistance to its members through periodic or one-time subsidies in cases of illness, death, or other catastrophic events, to provide medical assistance to members and their families, to build a savings fund for teachers, and to assist in the education of teachers' orphaned children. The society also ran a group of inexpensive summer resorts for teachers.[30]

Building libraries and pedagogical museums for use by teachers proved to be the society's most controversial projects. Although these projects might seem innocent enough, the Ministry of Education specifically forbade mutual-aid societies from establishing cultural organizations. In order to circumvent this prohibition, the Moscow society submitted its charter to the Ministry of Internal Affairs rather than to the Ministry of Education. The Ministry of Internal Affairs, for unknown reasons, approved the charter, allowing the society to proceed with the projects.[31]

The Moscow society grew steadily during the first few years of its existence, and by 1901, 670 Moscow primary schoolteachers had become members. The society's success was due to the dedication of a small group of members who took their mission seriously and worked hard to improve the lives of their fellow teachers. In 1898, the society established a Commission for Investigating the Lives of Primary Schoolteachers, and sent out one thousand questionnaires. After many delays, the society was able to open its library for teachers in 1898, when a member donated fourteen hundred rubles for the project.[32]

Like the Petersburg Mutual-Aid Society, the Society for the Improvement of Living Conditions defied the Ministry of Education's restrictions on teachers' mutual-aid societies and offered Moscow teachers a forum to discuss their professional concerns. But the ministry's restrictions still thwarted the organizational efforts of Moscow teachers. Other professions had genuine professional organizations and did not have to use mutual-aid societies as substitutes. For example, the Pirogov Society represented the medical profession. Teachers wanted a comparable organization. Finally, the Ministry of Education relented and chartered the Moscow Pedagogical Society in 1898, as part of its "official thaw in academic formalism."[33]

The Moscow Pedagogical Society The Moscow Pedagogical Society came into existence nineteen years after the demise of the Petersburg Pedagogical Society. The purpose of the new society was similar to that of its predecessor, namely, "to investigate scientifically questions of pedagogy and didactics, their content, application, and history." Unlike the mutual-aid societies, the Moscow Pedagogical Society was permitted to organize lectures, pedagogical museums, and libraries. And like the Petersburg Mutual-Aid Society, the Moscow Pedagogical Society became a meeting place for many education activists and teachers in all the different educational institutions in Moscow.[34]

As a result of broadly defined powers granted in the government charter, the Moscow Pedagogical Society became one of the most important teachers' organizations in Russia. In 1903, it boasted 1,663 members, which made it the single largest teachers' organization. In order to function more effectively, the society organized itself into nine sections, three standing committees, and one temporary committee.[35] As the names of the committees show, the membership involved itself in all aspects of Russian education: religious-cultural education and upbringing (75 members); Russian language and literature (250 members with eight meetings per year); history (150 members with eleven meetings per year); physics and chemistry (98 members); natural sciences (140 members with nine meetings per year); mathematics (106 members with seven meetings per year); modern languages (50 members); geography (12 members); and primary education (390 members with twelve meetings per year).[36] Since the members of these committees represented some of the best educators in Russia, the various reports published by the society were read with great interest by both government officials and the educated public. The society addressed itself to many of Russia's educational problems, especially to problems in the secondary schools and the plight of Russian teachers.

Thus, three societies—the Moscow Pedagogical Society, the St. Petersburg Mutual-Aid Society, and the Moscow Society for the Improvement of Living Conditions—became the main organizational centers for teachers working in the capitals. Because they were not as limited by the Ministry of Education's regulations as were other teachers' associations, these societies had a greater range of activities. Members of all three organizations included some of the most prominent activists in the profession. Motivated by the values that shaped their professional ethos, these men and women were determined to improve the quality of their working lives.

Once teachers in Moscow and Petersburg had gained the right to meet, they wanted to reach out to their colleagues in other Russian cities and villages. City teachers realized they did not have much power when acting as a small group. If they could somehow break out of their isolation and act as a unified profession, they would become a powerful voice, one that the Ministry of Education would have to heed.

Professional Meetings and Congresses

The solution to the problem of isolation lay in the organization of teachers' meetings and congresses that would gather teachers from all over Russia. The government's policy toward teachers' meetings and toward societies had been contradictory. During the early 1870s the Ministry of Education had actually encouraged teachers' congresses as a way to improve the quality of teaching in Russia. The ministry quickly became disillusioned with these meetings, however, when it became clear that the teachers were discussing "politics" as well as pedagogy. In 1875 the Ministry of Education issued more restrictive regulations governing summer pedagogical courses for teachers and at the same time omitted any new regulations for teachers' congresses. Since there were no guidelines to govern them, the legislation effectively barred the convocation of teachers' congresses. There was a brief flurry of teachers' congresses in the early 1880s, but in 1885 the Ministry of Education specifically prohibited their organization. That ban remained in force until 1899.[37]

Despite the Ministry of Education's prohibition against congresses, Russian schoolteachers began to meet together beginning in the early 1890s. The meetings that had the greatest impact on city teachers and their professional movement were three technical congresses as well as the All-Russian Industrial Exhibition, the Moscow District Teachers' Congress, the Mutual-Aid Societies' Congress, and the Congress for Teachers in the Advanced Primary Schools. The importance of these meetings, even for city teachers who worked in close proximity to one another, cannot be stressed enough. The congresses played an important role in allowing the leaders and the rank and file of the professional movement to discover they all shared the same professional identity and values.

The first congress on education was held in Petersburg during Christmas vacation, 1889–1890. The First Congress of Russian Participants in Technical and Vocational Education (hereafter, the First Technical Congress) was sponsored not by the Ministry of Education but by the Ministry of Finance. The Ministry of Finance had a number of schools under its jurisdiction that offered both technical and vocational training and competed with those Ministry of Education schools that offered vocational education. Wanting to demonstrate that it placed greater importance on technical education than did a rival ministry, the Ministry of Finance convened the congress.[38]

The First Technical Congress was a remarkable event. Lasting ten days, it included 1,076 participants, with teachers from all levels of the school system, administrators, and even some industrialists in attendance.[39] Although most participants came from the two capitals, the congress represented the first opportunity for teachers to discuss important issues with others members of educated society at a national congress. The reports read at the First Technical Congress covered all aspects of Russian technical education, from the role of physical education in technical education to techniques and innovations in the teaching of technical subjects in the schools. The published reports contain an excellent description of the state of vocational education in Russia at that time.[40] The congress was such a success that the participants agreed to convene another meeting within a few years.

The Second Technical Congress, held in Moscow from 28 December 1895 to 7 January 1896, was similar to the previous congress in that it attracted a large number of participants, who discussed all aspects of technical and vocational education.[41] What made the Second Technical Congress different was a newly organized series of meetings described under the title "General Questions." In the opening remarks that introduced this new section, addressed to the six thousand participants, the zemstvo educator V. P. Vakhterov explained that the only way to improve Russian technical education was to improve Russian education in general.[42] The participants heard reports on many troubling issues, such as the plight of teachers and the needs of mutual-aid societies. These reports reflected the growing professional commitment among teachers to looking out for one another and not waiting for government intervention. The participants' behavior at the congress also suggests the new confidence of some teachers. After only one meeting, these teachers were willing to speak openly about their problems, an act of some courage given the government's ambivalent policy toward teachers' participation at such meetings. Vakhterov concluded the congress by reminding society of the importance of education for Russia's future: "Life is drawing us with irrepressible power toward the democratization of education, toward the dissemination of knowledge everywhere among the lowest, darkest and most ignorant levels of the population."[43]

The Second Technical Congress marked an important beginning for Russian schoolteachers. As a result of the work in the General Questions Section of the Congress, teachers from all over Russia were able to speak openly for the first time in a public forum about their specific problems, and to offer their views on educational reform. There were reports on universal education, teaching methodologies in factory schools, school administration, teachers' mutual-aid societies, and congresses. Outside the public meetings and reports, teachers discussed their concerns more informally and more candidly. It was an important moment for all the congress participants, who realized that no matter where they taught, Russia's teachers shared similar problems and goals.

The Second Technical Congress was soon followed by another important event for Russian teachers, the Education Exhibition at the All-Russian Industrial Exhibition held in Nizhnii Novgorod in the summer of 1896. Sponsored by the Ministry of Finance, the exhibition was the first mass meeting of urban and rural teachers—over forty-five hundred from eighty provinces, more than half of whom were women. In addition to attending lectures, some teachers organized unofficial meetings in the dormitories, much to the dismay of the local police. At these meetings, Vakhterov, the speaker from the opening session of the Second Technical Congress, encouraged teachers to "consider their professional unification above everything else" and urged them to form local mutual-aid societies. One participant at the Nizhnii Novgorod meetings considered these informal gatherings critical for teachers' professional development: "This congress gave a push toward a general organization of teachers' societies. It was there that the idea of building a real all-Russian teachers' congress and professional organization arose for the first time."[44]

The next meeting of teachers was of a more limited nature than the previous meetings, but, because it was the first teachers' congress allowed by the Ministry of Education since 1885, it was no less important. In 1899 the Ministry of Education lifted its ban against teacher congresses by issuing "temporary" rules governing their convocation. The ministry had clearly failed to prevent teachers from meeting, and there was a softening in attitude among ministry officials, as many came to believe that some sort of educational reform was necessary.[45]

The Moscow District (*Uezd*) Teachers' Congress in August 1900 was the first to convene under the new rules. Of the 224 participants, approximately 200 were women, most of them recent graduates of the various pedagogical courses and schools designed to train women teachers.[46] Their participation at the congress suggests the effectiveness of their professional training: these women saw the congress as an opportunity to continue their pedagogical training so that they would remain effective teachers.

Despite the limits placed on the congress by the ministry's rules, the congress was an enormous success. The participants impressed many observers with their seriousness and their dedication to education. Most of the reports focused on various aspects of school life, from improvements in the curriculum to sanitation, but there were also a few reports about the plight of the teacher. These reports described the lack of civil rights for teachers, especially vis-à-vis the school administration. The participants also spoke of wanting more authority in the classroom and about other ways to improve their material lives. When asked about the impact of the congress, one teacher replied, "So great, so much, I still cannot completely understand all the particulars. I shall go home and there I can think and understand."[47]

By the turn of the century, it was possible to discern the beginnings of a national teachers' professional movement. Mutual-aid societies and other educational organizations had begun not only in Petersburg and Moscow but also in many other provincial towns and villages. In their meetings, teachers began to discuss openly some of the issues troubling them and to offer their own solutions. Both city and rural teachers had been able to meet face-to-face at a few congresses and to discuss ways in which teachers could work together to bring about change.

If the Russian government harbored any hopes that these few concessions to the teachers would satisfy them, it was mistaken. On the contrary, city teachers wanted more meetings and congresses that might lead to direct action rather than just talk. In 1896, at the Nizhnii Novgorod Exhibition, many of the leaders of the teachers' movement discussed the possibility of forming a union to represent the teachers' interests—a union that would unite city and rural teachers from the lowest to the highest levels of the educational system. A united teaching profession became the goal of these teacher-activists.

Against the backdrop of thoughts about a unified teachers' movement, in 1900 the Kaluga Mutual-Aid Society requested assistance from the Moscow Society for the Improvement of Living Conditions to build a sanatorium for sick teachers. Since such a project was beyond the means of either mutual-aid society, the Kaluga Society proposed that all the teachers' mutual-aid societies contribute to the sanatorium. The Moscow society agreed to act as coordinator for the project.[48] In order to determine teachers' needs, the society decided to convene a national meeting of representatives of all the teachers' mutual-aid societies to discuss the sanatorium. The Moscow organizers quickly realized, however, that this was a golden opportunity to discuss other issues as well. In April 1901, the Moscow society petitioned the Ministry of Education for permission to convene such a meeting. After some deliberation, the ministry sanctioned the meeting with certain stipulated conditions. The ministry named the curator of the Moscow Educational District as chief government observer and gave him discretionary powers to close the congress if things got out of hand. In addition, all reports were to be submitted in advance to the executive board of the congress, whose members included several ministry officials. This committee alone had the power to approve reports that were to be read to the entire congress. General sessions were open to the public, but other meetings were for participants only.[49]

Plans were made to convene the First All-Russian Congress of Representatives of Teachers' Mutual-Aid Societies for ten days during the Christmas holidays in December 1902 and January 1903, and invitations were sent out to the seventy-one teacher mutual-aid societies. According to the editors of the congress's published reports, there were 349 participants, of whom 213 were teachers. Yet a government investigation of the congress completed in 1904 claimed that the majority of participants were not teachers at all, but members of other professions, most prominently "Third Element" employees of the zemstvos, whom the Ministry of Education believed to be more radical than the rank-and-file teachers.[50] Although it is difficult to determine the actual number of participants, this disagreement is another example of the Ministry of Education's failure to understand the seriousness of the teachers' movement. The ministry went to great lengths to ensure that only politically reliable individuals became teachers. As the Mutual-Aid Congress demonstrated, however, a significant portion of even these carefully selected teachers were becoming increasingly radicalized by the ministry's contradictory policies, and a significant minority of them were ready to propose sweeping educational reforms. The Ministry of Education chose instead to blame the congress's proposals on the "Third Element" employees. In doing this, it dismissed the Mutual-Aid Congress as the product of "outside agitators" from the radical intelligentsia rather than see it as a serious development among the teachers.[51] The failure of the ministry to recognize the growing popularity and seriousness of the teachers' professional movement was symptomatic of the entire government's inability to recognize the crisis spreading throughout society. At a time when virtually every social and occupational group in Russia was organizing, the government's myopia was all the more perplexing.

Because of the many issues to be discussed at the congress, meetings were divided into four sections—general questions on improving teachers' lives, the material situation of teachers, teachers' self-education and the education of their families, and teachers' organizations and their unification.[52] Within these general sections, individual teachers read reports on specific issues. Virtually all the issues that individual societies had been discussing among themselves were finally given national attention. The reports reflected teachers' professional values by emphasizing their expertise, individual self-worth, and autonomy.

During those ten days in the winter of 1902–1903, the representatives of teachers' mutual-aid societies spoke about the many problems they faced. Delegates placed particular emphasis on the plight of the lowly rural schoolteacher, who worked in much worse conditions than the city teacher. Nevertheless, all agreed that urban and rural teachers shared the same problems. Teachers spoke of their isolation, both cultural and social: "Isolation is the enemy of all that is good."[53] They spoke of their difficult legal status (*pravovoe polozhenie*), that is, their lack of representation on school councils. They decried the unwarranted dismissals of teachers from their jobs, against which they were unable to defend themselves. They talked of inadequate salaries, shabby living conditions, and unfit schoolrooms. And, although some delegates thought it was wrong to complain since many of the teachers' pupils and their families lived in worse conditions, the majority of delegates believed that change had to occur.[54]

Focusing on the problem of isolation and the need for unity, the fourth section of the congress proposed a union of all teachers' mutual-aid societies. N. V. Tulupov, one of the leaders of the teachers' professional movement, proposed a multitiered system for the new union, which would unite teachers in neighboring schools. This was particularly important for rural teachers, who were often separated from one another by many miles. According to the proposal read at the congress, this national organization for teachers' mutual-aid societies would have several functions. It would set up a central information bureau to serve all members and establish a publishing concern to publish books and articles by teachers and by the mutual-aid societies. The national organization was also given the task of organizing a central teachers' museum and building dormitories and sanatoriums for teachers and their families. Most important, the national organization was charged with helping teachers organize new mutual-aid societies, teachers' congresses and congresses on education. The funds for these various projects were to come from dues paid by the members of the national organization, donations from other societies, and fundraising events sponsored by the national union.[55]

This blueprint for the new teachers' organization clearly shows that teachers were not proposing a full-fledged labor union, which would have been illegal, but rather a professional society and information bureau whose duties on the national level were very similar to those performed locally by the mutual-aid societies it would represent. In fact, this step showed teachers' willingness to work within the tsarist system, since the proposed teachers' organization was very similar to the Pirogov Society for doctors founded in 1885.[56] Given the restrictions on free association that existed in late imperial Russia, teachers were not about to propose a more radical, illegal organization, which could be quickly destroyed by the authorities. They did, however, want to establish the kind of national organization that would help foster a sense of corporate identity and unity among all teachers; unifying the mutual-aid societies seemed like an important step in that direction.

Nevertheless, one hotly debated proposal to establish a court of honor (*sud chesti*) in an attempt to set up a peer review board, would have differentiated the new organization from other mutual-aid societies. The court of honor actually began in the military. Officers of a particular regiment gathered to judge alleged violations of personal or family honor by a fellow officer. The court determined the guilt or innocence of the accused and the punishment for the crime. The entire court was extralegal; the military high command knew of the court's existence, but did nothing to stop its proceedings. Eventually this type of trial by equals was adopted by university students and revolutionary groups as well. If the court of honor were to be adopted by teachers, they would be judged and punished by their peers, not by members of the educational hierarchy.[57]

This rather dramatic proposal to establish a court of honor would have made significant changes in the proposed teachers' professional society. The court of honor proposal faced strong opposition at the congress, demonstrating that, at least on some issues, teachers were not united. Less politicized than the leadership, most rank-and-file delegates were unwilling to adopt such a radical measure, which clearly would have antagonized the Ministry of Education. When no consensus could be reached in the limited time available, the delegates agreed to give the Moscow Society for the Improvement of Living Conditions the power to draft a proposal for a court of honor, to be presented at the next congress.[58]

The debate over the court of honor was only part of a larger debate about an issue that lay at the heart of teachers' conflicts with the Ministry of Education: teachers' legal status. To report on these issues, a new commission was organized during the course of the congress. At the penultimate session of the congress, the commission read its findings and its thirty-two proposals for reform to all the participants. The report shocked the Ministry of Education's observers, and they immediately shut down the meeting. The delegates reconvened the next day for the last session, but at the insistence of the government officials who threatened to disband the congress, the proposals on teachers' legal status were not submitted to a vote.[59]

The commission's proposal to improve teachers' legal status not only summarize the chief concerns of the vast majority of Russia's teachers; they also illustrate the dilemma the teachers faced. Teachers wanted to work within the system, but they also wanted a complete restructuring of that system. They offered a new way of organizing school administration so that teachers and local government would take more responsibility from the Ministry of Education. Teachers were to have a voice on all bodies that dealt with matters of public education. Government officials could exercise their authority in pedagogical matters only, and religion teachers, school trustees, and inspectors could no longer supervise teachers' private lives. Teachers were also to be given the right to defend themselves against slander and charges of misconduct. The Ministry of Education was asked to recognize that, as a result of their training and years of experience, teachers were entitled to representation on educational boards. The commission argued that teachers, not government bureaucrats, were the experts needed to keep the schools functioning. In N. V. Chekhov's summary, the proposals were a "declaration of rights of the Russian teacher."[60] This "declaration" shows quite clearly the developing professional ethos among teachers and the intractable nature of their conflict with the Ministry of Education. The proposals amounted to a complete restructuring of public education in Russia. Although teachers were not revolutionaries, they clearly wanted a new Russia.

At almost the same time as the representatives of the mutual-aid societies were meeting in Moscow, another group of city teachers also convened its congress. Two years earlier the Moscow Teachers' Institute had petitioned the Ministry of Education to convene a congress of all advanced primary schoolteachers in the Moscow Educational District. Permission was granted, and the meetings took place from 2 to 11 January 1903. According to the account of one participant, the ministry did everything it could to prevent open discussion of the serious issues facing the advanced primary schools. Ministry officials decreed that the congress could not issue any official recommendations nor publish an official history of the meeting. Strict procedure was to be followed at each session. A previously approved report was to be read, followed by comments from the audience; there was no possibility for debate or rebuttal. The final restriction stipulated that since the congress was "strictly professional" (*chisto-professional'nyi*), no outsiders would be permitted to attend the meetings. There were approximately three hundred participants at the congress, but many became discouraged by these restrictions and failed to attend the sessions. Some teachers met in other rooms while the sessions were going on to discuss impermissibile subjects; not surprisingly, these private conversations tended to stray toward "nonprofessional" topics.[61]

Despite the restrictions on discussion and the lack of interest on the part of some participants, the congress managed to debate some of the issues unique to the advanced primary schools. The participants argued that the schools should be linked to the lower grades, so that the graduates could continue their education at other secondary schools, thereby creating a ladder system of education where one school connected with another. The delegates also believed that the curriculum of the advanced primary schools should be changed from vocational to general, with the addition of several new subjects, including modern languages. Over the issue of how to organize the teaching of the curriculum, the participants split, with older teachers favoring the subject method and younger ones preferring the class method. The congress reached a compromise on this issue, recommending that the pedagogical council choose the teaching method to be used in each school. Echoing the debates of the Mutual-Aid Congress, the advanced primary schoolteachers discussed the role of the pedagogical council and its members and recommended greater roles for themselves and the school doctors on these councils.[62]

The issue that attracted the greatest amount of attention from the participants was the report on the economic plight of the advanced primary schoolteachers. They reviewed their position in comparison with their Western European counterparts and discovered what many of them already knew—that Russian teachers were in an inferior economic position. They made specific recommendations to improve their financial status and help prevent teacher flight from the advanced primary schools.[63]

The Moscow Advanced Primary Schools Congress ended on 11 January, one day early. At least one participant went home with mixed feelings about the results of the first meeting of this group of schoolteachers. His remarks represented the views of many teachers after all these congresses: "Thanks to the congress, many teachers saw their comrades (*tovarishchi*) for the first time after a fifteen- or twenty-year separation; if we parted with heavy feelings of oppression, without hope for the improvement of our material and cultural position in the near future, it is certainly because we are few and we are needy."[64]

The winter of 1902–1903 was a complex and exciting time for city teachers, simultaneously full of promise and failure. Teachers from all over Russia had experienced an unprecedented opportunity to meet and discuss their concerns and hopes for the future. Disagreements about political or educational reform were deemphasized and unity was stressed. Yet all of this activity remained just talk, and nothing concrete was established. The Mutual-Aid Congres and the Congress of Advanced Primary Schoolteachers had been carefully supervised by the Ministry of Education and it was unclear how the ministry would respond to their recommendations. After the Mutual-Aid Congress, both sides had a better understanding of how far apart they were.

Prelude to Revolution

The Mutual-Aid Congress marked a turning point in the city teachers' movement. After the congress, teachers who had previously remained aloof from the professional movement joined the teachers' organizations. As we have seen, by 1904 hundreds of teachers belonged to the Petersburg Mutual-Aid Society and the Moscow Society. The government response was as complicated as ever. While it allowed more organizations and meetings, it still tried to control them by asserting its prerogative to initiate, approve, and disapprove. Meanwhile, a growing number of teachers in Moscow and Petersburg resolved to take the necessary steps, no matter how painful, to achieve their goals. Given the government's reluctance to allow greater professional autonomy and initiative, city teachers felt they had no alternative but to join other opposition groups to press for political change. City teachers participated in a variety of activities, but the most important for the development of their professional movement were the formation of illegal unions, a campaign to end the marriage ban, and the 1904 banquet campaign.

The formation of the illegal Union of Teachers in the winter of 1902–1903 was one expression of this new mood among a portion of Russian schoolteachers. Members of the union declared themselves to be revolutionaries and socialists. Their immediate goal was the overthrow of the autocracy and the eventual establishment of a socialist order.[65] The new union refused to adopt the political platform of any of the illegal political parties, hoping instead to serve as a broad-based coalition of all opposition groups, foreshadowing the position of the national teachers' union in 1905. Despite the nonparty platform, the executive bureau was composed of teachers affiliated with or sympathetic to either the Social Democratic Party or the Social Revolutionary Party.[66] The divided allegiance of the first teachers' union demonstrates clearly the sharp political differences among teachers. They adopted a nonparty status because these teachers, who represented the most politicized of all teachers, could not agree on which platform to adopt. Despite all the calls for unity, there was little agreement on key political issues that faced the teachers' movement.

What is interesting about the party affiliation of the executive bureau's members is the split between city and rural teachers. There were ten members in the bureau. Four members taught in the Moscow city schools, and all aligned themselves with the Social Democratic party. The remaining six board members worked in the rural schools and were members of the Social Revolutionary party. This breakdown by party affiliation shows that the most radical of Russian schoolteachers identified themselves with the people they served, rather than with their fellow teachers or the Union of Liberation. Those who worked among the urban working class gravitated toward the Social Democrats with their Marxist belief in a proletarian revolution. Teachers who worked among the peasantry tended to favor the Social Revolutionaries, who espoused a more broadly based popular movement with strong elements of agrarian socialism. Thus, the leadership of the earliest of the Russian teachers' unions adhered to the Russian tradition of the intelligentsia serving the interests of "the people" and the ideologies that served those interests.

The persistence of intelligentsia values among radical teachers shows the enormously complex, but uneven, transformation that had taken place among teachers. Teachers had clear, well-defined professional goals—they wanted to be free to exercise their expertise in the classroom and free from government meddling. At the same time, these arguments did not lead them to identify with their own class interests, an identification that should have led them to support the Union of Liberation, a political party that formed in 1902 and 1903.[67] The union's members were primarily professionals and zemstvo activists, and its political agenda included strong support for liberal democracy and civil liberties. Because the union was a strong supporter of many of the same values teachers held dear—individual initiative, freedom of speech, rule by law—it is surprising that these radical teachers did not support the union's political program. Instead, radical teachers identified themselves with the "people," rejecting self-interest in favor of the interests of the people they served. Service to the people had become so much a part of their professional identity that they found it difficult to act in their own political self-interest. Given the interconnectedness of the teachers' professional and political involvement, their lack of political unity would cause serious trouble during the 1905 Revolution.

The new Union of Teachers was a short-lived organization. Its main activity was to propagandize among the teachers, primarily through the distribution of illegal literature. Members of the union were active at the teachers' summer courses and congresses. Because most of the teachers who attended these summer courses were rural teachers, the SR literature was the more popular.[68] By the fall of 1903 the police had established the identities of the union's activists and had begun to arrest them. In early 1904, most of the union's leadership had been arrested and the union ceased to exist.[69] Despite the short tenure of the Union of Teachers, however, it proved an important precursor to the All-Russian Teachers' Union of 1905.

While the radical teachers in Moscow were busy organizing an illegal teachers' union, the women who taught in the Petersburg city schools began a campaign of their own, the repeal of the 1897 marriage ban. The ban had been discussed at the 1902–1903 Mutual-Aid Congress, and two teachers read reports on the marriage issue. Nadezhda P. Rumiantseva, a Petersburg schoolteacher and member of the Petersburg Mutual-Aid Society, read a report calling for repeal of the ban. She argued that the marriage ban violated fundamental notions of equality and limited the personal freedom of women teachers.[70] To show that this problem was not limited to Petersburg, another teacher activist from Moscow, Sergei Govorov, delivered a report entitled, "The Marriage Question in A Teacher's Life." Govorov couched his report in terms different from those of Rumiantseva, however. His report addressed itself more to the concerns of teachers who already had families. Although he condemned the practice of firing women teachers, Govorov called for higher salaries and better living arrangements so that teachers could bring up their families in greater comfort, tuition assistance for their children, maternity leaves, and special sickness leaves for women teachers to care for sick children.[71] Govorov's report shows clearly that the male leadership of the teachers' movement failed to take the grievances of women schoolteachers seriously. Rumiantseva spoke of the violation of women's civil rights; Govorov spoke of improved material conditions for teachers and their families. Indeed, he seems to have missed the point that women teachers were being denied the right to have families and remain in the profession. For the men, the women's grievance was just another example of the lack of civil liberty that all teachers faced. As a result, the national teachers' organizations never dealt specifically with the marriage question, even though this question directly affected the lives of hundreds of women teachers. The marriage ban became subsumed under the more general demands for better working and living conditions.

After the Mutual-Aid Congress, Petersburg teachers returned home, determined to press for the repeal of the ban. As a result of their efforts to publicize their plight, a discussion of the marriage question emerged in the press. Supporters of the ban put forward two chief arguments against the employment of married women teachers. The first dealt with the issue of sexual innocence or purity. According to one teacher, school officials complained that if a pregnant woman were allowed to teach, her pupils might begin to wonder about the nature of pregnancy and ask questions about the facts of life.[72] The school administrators feared that the children would be corrupted by such impure thoughts. Therefore, it was important to keep pregnant women out of the classroom, which meant keeping all married women away from the schoolchildren. Supporters of the ban also believed married women were somehow tainted by their sexual life, even within the bonds of marriage, so that they were no longer qualified to be teachers. This was why the press characterized Petersburg teachers as vestal virgins (*vestalki*)—it was sexual purity that qualified them for their jobs. Ironically, those who opposed married women teachers fired them from their jobs so that they could go home and teach their own children.

The second argument was that married women teachers could not devote themselves equally to their families and their work. One teacher commented: "Maternal and school responsibilities are equally great, to combine them without damage to the school is unthinkable."[73] Married teachers were accused of neglecting their pupils in favor of their own children. They often had to stay at home with a child or spouse who was ill, and sometimes neglected their school duties by leaving the classroom before a substitute teacher could be found. Married women needed time off for maternity leaves. The difficulties of breastfeeding a new infant while a mother worked were also mentioned as a drawback to employing married women as teachers. All the inconveniences of childbirth and childrearing were mentioned over and over again as reasons why married women made poor teachers.[74]

Teachers who met the standard set by the marriage ban by remaining single were nonetheless unwilling to accept the assumptions of the ban's proponents. When teachers themselves explained why they had refrained from marrying, other answers emerged. In 1903 Govorov published the results of a survey he had conducted on the marriage question. The survey is important because it represents the voices of the teachers speaking about this important issue.[75] Thirty-five teachers replied that they remained single because of financial insecurity. Twenty-nine did not marry because they feared dismissal. Seven more teachers replied that they were exhausted by their labors and had no time to think about their personal lives, and seven others blamed their closed way of life, which prevented them from meeting educated people and future fiancés.[76] One woman wrote that she had chosen not to marry because she did not like married life. She went on to say that since women were not completely free to choose whom they wanted to marry, they often ended up with unsuitable spouses. And although she had received two marriage proposals, she intended to live her life alone and devote herself to her pupils.[77] Another teacher wrote: "Here is the explanation for the solitude of the majority of women teachers in the primary schools. . . . *They do not need a family.* They have found their family among those whom the Lord called His pupils. As the Lord explained . . . , 'Whoever fulfills the will of my heavenly Father, there is My brother and sister and mother.' "[78]

These replies to Govorov's questionnaire suggest that there were more complex reasons why women chose to remain single than the insistence that marriage and dedication to teaching were incompatible or the simple demand of purity envisioned by the marriage ban's proponents. Despite the emphasis placed on married life in Russian society, many women saw marriage as a road to unhappiness. As single, working women, these teachers could lead independent and fulfilled lives nurturing schoolchildren. Whether they looked upon their teaching as a way of fulfilling their Christian duty or as service to the "people" in the Populist sense, it presented many women with a significant alternative to wedded life.

The vast majority of respondents to Govorov's questionnaire, however, wanted both marriage and employment in order to lead happy and productive lives.[79] They believed not only that married teachers made good teachers but also that married teachers were actually better. One teacher lamented: "Pedantry, dullness and callousness—these are the reproaches which one often hears in relation to old teachers. I am inclined to think that especially we old maids, are not without fault in this because we lack our own family which could warm our hearts."[80]

Some teachers who remained single blamed their physical and emotional problems, such as hysteria, jaundice, neurasthenia, and sluggishness, on their enforced celibacy. "Celibacy has a harmful effect on everything—on health and on character: it causes selfishness, irritability, nervousness, and a formal relationship to the children."[81] These physical and emotional complaints, particularly hysteria and neurasthenia, were frequently associated with unmarried schoolteachers and with other single women in late nineteenth- and twentieth-century Europe and America.[82] Some women overcame these problems by having extramarital liaisons or by keeping their marriages hidden from school authorities. If they were discovered, these teachers were immediately fired for their sexual misconduct. Many teachers remarked that unmarried teachers did not make any allowance for their pupils' inattention or misbehavior in class. Opponents of the ban argued that women understood children better once they had become parents themselves. Furthermore, these opponents struck at one of the fundamental assumptions of their society: they no longer believed that women were born with a "maternal" instinct. Nor did they think that this maternal instinct could be taught in pedagogical courses or acquired in a classroom. The ability to care for and understand children came through the care of one's own children. Women teachers argued that teachers needed to become parents first before they could excel as teachers.

As these comments reveal, many women teachers believed that it was the on-the-job training they received as parents that qualified them as teachers. Their emphasis on nurturing rather than on lesson plans shows that their sense of themselves as professionals was still mitigated by their gender: they believed that their nurturing skills did indeed make them better teachers. They did not see themselves as sexless professionals, but rather as women and teachers.

It did not matter in the end whether married or unmarried women made better teachers; teachers wanted the right to decide for themselves whether or not they should marry. According to Russian law, two individuals had the right to marry freely if they had their parents' permission. There was nothing in teachers' work that should have necessitated government intervention in their private lives. It was this unnecessary meddling that so rankled teachers, and the women wanted an end to this sexual discrimination.

The Petersburg teachers' plight began to receive support outside pedagogical circles. Vasilii V. Rozanov, writing in *Novoe vremia*, condemned the city duma for its discriminatory practices. As a result of the ban, the unmarried teachers suffered from financial hardship. Housing was scarce and expensive in the city, and since the city no longer provided rent-free apartments or a rent subsidy, these teachers had to rent rooms that were usually some distance from the schools. Despite the rigorous qualifications and financial hardship demanded of unmarried schoolteachers, there was no discernible difference between the married and unmarried teachers.

Rozanov ended his article, however, by bringing in a new argument in support of the unmarried teachers, one that differed from those advanced by the teachers themselves. He concluded: "The duma's vestal virgins! How sad and pitiful that sounds. . . . What intelligent woman would give up her right to be a mother? What educated young woman, having known the soul of a small child, would give up the right to bring up her own children and give the motherland useful citizens?!"[83] Rozanov defended married women teachers by arguing they had the right to have a family. The marriage ban violated the fundamental role of women in society—to bear and raise children, the future citizens of Russia. According to this view, the government had no legal right to deny women their "natural" role in Russia. This natural role was maternal, not professional.

The debate over married women teachers was complex. Both sides used arguments about women's nature to support and oppose the ban. The opponents of married women teachers argued that these women should not be allowed to teach because sexually active women had a specific role in Russian society—their place was in the home, not the classroom. If married women were allowed to teach, they would bring domestic problems with them to the workplace, making things difficult for their employers. At the same time, the supporters of married women teachers argued that they should be allowed to teach because they were women. Their skills as parents enhanced their pedagogical training and made them better teachers than single women. Mired as they were in using the existing ideology to justify their view, neither side dealt directly with the issue of women's professional and personal autonomy.

It was the women teachers themselves who tried to express a less traditional view of women in Russian society. Women teachers like Rumiantseva condemned the marriage ban as a violation of women's civil rights. These women wanted the same rights as men teachers— the ability to have a career and family life at the same time. They believed there should be no discriminatory policy against either sex. At the same time, those women teachers who had chosen celibacy defended their choice as a meaningful alternative to wedded life. Although Russian society had never looked with great favor upon spinsters, these women teachers had managed to gain an independent life outside the parental or conjugal home and some respect for the work they performed. Now, they felt their way of life threatened by those women who wanted both career and family. Teaching would no longer be a safe haven for those women who preferred spinsterhood to marriage. Thus, the women themselves spoke of an independent and autonomous life for women teachers, but married and unmarried women defined that life quite differently.

The publicity about the marriage issue and agitation on the part of the Public Education Section of the Petersburg Mutual-Aid Society, coupled with the growth of the Liberation movement and the campaign for civil rights, led some of the Petersburg teachers to seek support for the repeal of the marriage ban. They were determined to seek full professional equality. In November 1903, N. A. Arkhangel'skii introduced a resolution to allow married women to become teachers in the city schools. In support of his resolution, he argued: "This situation weighs heavily upon city teachers and is tantamount to serfdom. Women teachers are primarily poor girls, needing a scrap of bread; the city administration gives them the chance to work and not die of hunger, but under conditions which cripple their natures, condemning them to eternal celibacy."[84] Arkhangel'skii went on to say that it was unfair to discriminate against these young women when teachers hired before 1896 could remain at their jobs and even remarry. This resolution received support from the Petersburg Teachers' Mutual-Aid Society as well as the Khar'kov Society to Aid Working Women. The city duma had no desire to take up this issue, however, and there the matter stood until the spring of 1905.[85]

At the same time that Petersburg women teachers were gathering support for the repeal of the marriage ban, the Petersburg Mutual-Aid Society was beginning to prepare for the Second Congress of Mutual-Aid Societies, scheduled for the winter of 1905–1906. During the First Mutual-Aid Congress, the participants had decided to meet regularly in various towns throughout the empire. They chose Petersburg as the site of their next meeting and charged the Petersburg Mutual-Aid Society with organizing the congress. On 9 May 1903 the society held a general membership meeting to begin preparations for the congress. It decided to set up a special commission composed of representatives of various mutual-aid societies and some of the other Petersburg pedagogical societies.[86]

Because of the summer vacation, the first meeting of the organizing committee for the 1905 Congress took place on 11 October 1903. At that meeting, reports were read on the history, organization, and problems discussed at the First Mutual-Aid Congress. As a result of these discussions, the organizing committee decided it was necessary to expand the program of the new congress and, in particular, to include reports on the organization of secondary schools and the plight of their teachers. At a second meeting held a month later, the committee members decided that the sessions should be organized into six subsections dealing with teachers' legal, economic, and pedagogical problems. The organizers had every intention of promoting discussion of the thorny issues that had almost brought about the dissolution of the First Mutual-Aid Congress.

Having tentatively set up the general outlines of the 1905 Congress, A. S. Famintsyn, president of the Petersburg Mutual-Aid Society, suggested holding a meeting during the 1904 Christmas break with representatives of other mutual-aid societies who were coming to St. Petersburg to attend the Third Technical Congress. These December meetings proved highly successful, and the organizing committee proceeded to petition the government for permission to convene the meeting during the Christmas holidays of 1905–1906.[87]

The Third Technical Congress, held during the Christmas vacation of 1903–1904, was the last big meeting of teachers and educators before the Revolution of 1905. There were 3,198 participants at the meetings, the majority of them teachers.[88] The teachers' movement had become so complex that several members of the Moscow Mutual-Aid Society—N. V. Chekhov, P. M. Shestakov, P. D. Dolgorukov, and others[89]—attended the Technical Congress as well as the meeting of the organizing committee for the 1905 Mutual-Aid Societies' Congress. Their visit to Petersburg also included special meetings organized by the Ushinskii Commission of the St. Petersburg Pedagogical Society.[90] Many delegates to the Technical Congress stayed in the Petersburg city schoolrooms, which were vacant because of the holiday. There they had an opportunity to meet and talk with Petersburg city schoolteachers.[91] In addition, the Ninth Pirogov Congress for doctors and the First Congress of the Union of Liberation were in session in Petersburg at the same time.[92] The leadership of the teachers' movement maximized every opportunity teachers had to meet and synchronized their meetings with those of other professional groups. This careful coordination proved helpful in initiating a process of cross-fertilization of ideas, grievances, and tactics. It demonstrates the increasing sophistication of the emerging leadership.

The Third Technical Congress, which began on 29 December 1903, was divided into ten sections, each dealing with some aspect of technical education. From the outset, the delegates were in a defiant mood. To give an example of the atmosphere that prevailed at the congress, on the evening of 3 January 1904, the Petersburg primary schoolteachers held a supper in the city duma's building in honor of the primary schoolteachers who participated in the congress. Some two hundred diners scraped their plates, eagerly awaiting the guest speaker, N. V. Chekhov, a leader of the teachers' movement. At the end of the meal, Chekhov rose to the podium and began his prepared speech about the development of social consciousness and freedom of speech, two highly charged subjects in the winter of 1904. Suddenly the orchestra began to play, startling everyone, including the speaker. Despite protests from the audience, the orchestra drowned out Chekhov, and the after-dinner speaker was forced to return to his seat. Infuriated by this intimidation, which could only have come from the authorities, the teachers wrote an angry letter of protest to the Petersburg mayor.[93]

In this atmosphere, it was not surprising that the delegates to the Third Technical Congress adopted a very radical set of resolutions. The congress demanded a greater place for teachers in formulating and enacting educational policies. The resolutions called for the introduction of universal education, local control of schools and school boards, classroom instruction in the language of the local population, freedom of action in the schools for teachers and protection of their legal status, and abolition of compulsory examinations, punishments, and rewards.[94] The government was both alarmed and angered by the congress's resolutions. The new minister of internal affairs, Pleve, acted quickly. He disbanded the Third Technical Congress one day short of its official closing for showing "political tendencies"; the Ninth Pirogov Congress suffered a similar fate.[95] The delegates returned home, angered by the government's swift reprisal and determined to keep the pressure on the government to enact reform.[96]

The anger and frustration, however, not just of teachers but of the educated public at large, were defused a few weeks later when Japan attacked Russia (26 January 1904). Except for the radicals, the educated classes believed that it was their duty to support the government in its war with the Japanese. Many rallied to support the government in its war effort.[97] Shortly after the commencement of hostilities, the commander of the Russian land forces, General Kuropatin, telegraphed Prince P. D. Dolgorukov, president of the Moscow Society for the Improvement of Living Conditions, and told him of the army's enormous need for books and other reading material. In the first few months of the war, the Moscow society sent five thousand books and brochures to the front, as well as copies of seventy-seven newspapers and sixteen journals. In addition, the Moscow society contacted other provincial teachers' societies and asked them to help as well.[98] The initial support for the war began to drop off quickly, however, as the Russian forces began to suffer one defeat after another in the Far East. The war was not turning out the way the military had hoped. Society grew more restive and again turned its attention to talk of change.

The focus of the renewed hostility between the government and society was Minister of Internal Affairs Pleve. Since assuming office at the end of 1903, he had done much to thwart the efforts of both radicals and the educated public to transform Russian society. Teachers were especially angry with him for disbanding the Third Technical Congress. By February 1904, Pleve had succeeded in arresting the leadership of the illegal Union of Teachers as well. He was vigorously pursuing all opposition forces in Russia when he was assassinated in July 1904, a target of the SR terrorist campaign.[99] Pleve's successor, Prince Petr Sviatopolk-Mirskii, attempted to restore public confidence and trust in the government by eliminating some of Pleve's more repressive policies.[100] In the fall of 1904, Sviatopolk-Mirskii reached a compromise with some of the zemstvo leaders: they would be permitted to hold a special zemstvo congress without government interference, if they agreed not to meet in a public building. This marked the beginning of the political "spring" of 1904.

In November 1904, the zemstvo representatives met in Petersburg and discussed their ideas about Russia's crisis and its resolution. The results of their discussions were formulated in eleven theses, which called for a healing of the rift between government and society by granting full civil and political rights to all citizens and establishing representative government at both the local and national levels.[101] These eleven theses became a kind of clarion call for Russian educated society to resume its efforts to bring about significant change in the government. Throughout November and December, the educated public joined the opposition movement to bring about these changes.

As an important part of the educated public, schoolteachers participated energetically in the renewed activity. There were no national congresses scheduled for 1904, but many teachers, and especially those who had never before participated, began to join teachers' mutual-aid societies and other pedagogical societies. By January 1905 membership in these societies was at record levels. Encouraged by the new interest in their activities, the societies increased their level of operation.[102]

In addition to increased activity in the various professional organizations, all Russia's professionals were encouraged in their opposition to the government by the Union of Liberation's "banquet campaign," organized in late November 1904 and modeled after the well-known banquet campaign held in France in 1848. The purpose of the campaign was to set up public dinners to celebrate almost any important anniversary the opposition leaders could think of. The speakers criticized the government and discussed the union's political platform. Such banquets were held in many cities throughout Russia, and many professionals, including teachers, attended them.[103] At the banquets the Union of Liberation allied itself with the professions by aiding the development of professional unions. According to one historian, the Doctor's Union, the Academic Union, and the Engineer's Union were organized at various banquets by members of the Union of Liberation.[104]

With these events serving as a backdrop, sometime during the autumn months of 1904 a group of teachers who described themselves as "young and radical" got together in the Rogozhsko-Simonovskii district of Moscow. Unhappy with the moderate leadership of the Society for the Improvement of Living Conditions headed by Prince Pavel D. Dolgorukov, they formed an illegal union called the Moscow City Teachers' Association (*Korporatsiia Moskovskikh gorodskikh uchi-*

telei). Although none of the sources commented on the choice of terms, it is apparent that Moscow teachers intended something by choosing *korporatsiia* rather than the more common *soiuz* ("union") for their organization. No professional group chose *korporatsiia* except the Petersburg city teachers. Moscow teachers used this designation to distinguish themselves from both workers' unions and the secondary schoolteachers' organizations.[105] As we will see in chapter 6, the division between primary and secondary schoolteachers was one of the many fissures that split the teachers' professional movement.

Unlike the earlier Union of Teachers, the Moscow City Teachers' Association was, in fact, a labor union. Its purpose was to represent the interests of teachers in negotiations with the city duma over salary disputes, teacher dismissals, and other issues related to primary education in Moscow city schools.[106] It was a bold step, and one that had frightened the delegates to the Mutual-Aid Society Congress less than two years earlier. But now the formation of a teachers' labor union was consistent with what other professions were doing in Russia in these few months before the outbreak of revolution. The Moscow city schoolteachers had an organization in place whose sole purpose was to defend the interest of the city's teachers when the situation arose. All that was needed was the opportunity to act.

The evolution of the city teachers' professional movement was a remarkable development that demonstrates the dynamism of the new civil society emerging in the wake of the Great Reforms. Having been encouraged by the Ministry of Education to acquaint themselves with pedagogical theory and to imbue their work with a professional spirit, city teachers found their attempts to continue their professionalization through independent action thwarted by the government. City teachers' first professional society was summarily closed by the government in 1879 in a period of reaction following peasant unrest and revolutionary violence. Rather than give up on the idea of a professional organization, teachers began to explore the opportunities that were available to them.

Because of the importance the government placed on city teachers' political reliability—which essentially meant their passivity—teachers did not have as many options open to them to develop their own corporate organizations, as did other professionals. They were limited for the most part to mutual-aid societies whose purpose was to provide a savings bank for the few teachers who had extra money to set aside.

Through various legislative loopholes and administrative manipulation, however, teachers in Petersburg and Moscow managed to make these associations into quasi-professional organizations. These mutual-aid societies tried to further professional development through various cultural and professional programs.

All this local activity whetted city teachers' appetites for more meaningful professional organizations. As teachers looked around and participated in other cultural and educational societies, they began to envision a unified teaching profession and a national organization that would assist teachers in their struggle for educational reform. As city teachers gathered at various meetings and congresses, they began to feel the power of collective work. Given the contradictory nature of government policy during these years, they felt that the government should rely on their expertise, not just on that of the bureaucracy. Teachers, like other professional groups, began to invoke their right to speak as experts and as citizens. In the years preceding 1905, the Ministry of Education and city teachers entered into an elaborate dance, with teachers constantly pushing at the limits of acceptable behavior and the ministry trying, with increasing difficulty, to completely control the professional movement it had helped create.

In the beginning, only a small group of city teachers participated in the new professional movement. These individuals acted in a quiet and circumspect way so that they would not lose their jobs due to their professional involvement. But with the surge of public activism that followed the 1891–1892 famine, city teachers felt emboldened to raise the level of activity and to begin efforts to form a national professional movement. The tempo of the teachers' movement quickened and city teachers began to reach out to teachers all across the Russian Empire to join together in their common cause.

As we have seen, all teachers were not treated equally in the growing professional movement. Women teachers rarely participated in any meaningful way. Gender was not the only problem. At the Mutual-Aid Congress in 1903, the leadership of the teachers' movement was much more radical in its demands than rank-and-file teachers, many of whom had just joined professional organizations and were still hoping that the government would fulfill their demands without much pressure from teachers' organizations. Even within the leadership, important divisions were emerging. There were sharp political differences in the Union of Teachers and the Moscow Teachers' Association. The leaders did not share one political ideology but were divided among the Social Revolutionary Party and the Social Democrats, with a few supporters of the Union of Liberation. Given the extent to which the professional and political movement were intertwined in Russia, this made the call for a unified profession problematic at best.

Nevertheless, as 1904 drew to a close, teachers all over Russia were beginning to believe that if they could only unite themselves into one profession, they could force the government to make the necessary educational and political changes for Russia's survival. The call for an end to teachers' isolation and for collective action proved overwhelmingly appealing. But as the events of the 1905 Revolution would show, teachers faced not only government opposition to their plans but also serious divisions within the teaching profession itself.

5 The Revolution of 1905

AS RUSSIANS WELCOMED IN THE NEW YEAR ON 1 JANUARY 1905, there was little to celebrate. By that time it was clear that Russia was losing the war with Japan. Many zemstvo activists and urban professionals were secretly organizing themselves into illegal unions and publicly demanding a constitutional regime for Russia. The radical movement continued its campaign for the overthrow of autocracy. At the same time, Russian workers were quietly organizing to press for improvements in the factories. It seemed that every group had its own set of grievances against the current political and economic situation. A sense of uneasiness lay over Russian society as nearly everyone waited for the coming political crisis.

The event that triggered that crisis occurred on 9 January 1905—the massacre known as Bloody Sunday. Workers and their families marched through the streets of Petersburg with a petition for the tsar. Instead of being met by government officials, the petitioners encountered bullets and cossack whips. By the time order was restored, over three hundred lay dead or wounded. The response of civil society to this violent confrontation between the government and the workers was immediate. Shocked at the bloodletting, educated Russians believed that the victims of Bloody Sunday were not hardened revolutionaries, but simple workers and their families carrying icons and pictures of the tsar. More and more Russians came to feel that fundamental political changes were necessary to ensure a government that represented all of Russia's citizens, not just the privileged few. Bloody Sunday unleashed all the pent-up frustrations that had been growing for so long. It was the beginning of the 1905 Revolution.[1]

For thirty years, city teachers had worked hard to develop a professional identity and had struggled with the tsarist government to establish professional organizations through which they hoped to improve the quality of the schools and their own lives. At the 1903 Mutual-Aid Congress, teachers endeavored to create a unified teaching profession to end their isolation and raise the status of the profession in Russian society. In 1905 teachers had the opportunity to realize their goals and create a national organization that would further enhance their professionalization.

Yet, as the teachers' movement evolved during 1905, it did not come to represent all teachers, as the leaders had claimed it would. Unresolved conflicts based on class and gender remained within the profession. As we have seen, women's efforts to become teachers were belittled by their male colleagues. Men teachers and particularly those who taught in the countryside derided women teachers as outsiders, and the marriage ban—both the formal one in Petersburg and the informal one that existed virtually everywhere else—ensured that women teachers remained outsiders not only in the villages but in the profession as well. Issues of class division had also emerged in the debate over women teachers. Peasant men teachers resented city women, their social superiors, for encroaching on their jobs and denying them a chance to achieve upward mobility. These men had used traditional peasant arguments of class differentiation against women teachers: besides their gender, what made these women outsiders were their manners, dress, and speech.

Moreover, these same class distinctions divided men teachers. But because of their overarching need to organize a national movement, the men had not addressed these problems earlier. The most public moment of discord broke out at the Mutual-Aid Society Congress when the leadership proposed the controversial resolution concerning the court of honor. At other moments of political division, the formation of the Union of Teachers in 1903 and the Moscow Teachers' Association in 1904, for example, disagreements were less public. These political differences were based in large part on class antagonisms that divided city teachers from rural teachers, and primary from secondary schoolteachers. In this way the teachers' movement in 1905 mirrored the conflicts that were dividing the entire society.

The central difficulty facing Russian society was: what kind of political and social system should replace a weakening autocracy and an anachronistic estate system? Several visions of a new Russia competed with one another in 1905. Business and landed elites pushed for wealth to be the indicator of status and power. The revolutionary intelligentsia, joined by the lower classes, wanted complete social and political equality for everyone. Social justice demanded that the laboring classes, who had been denied status and privilege for so long, receive their due. Finally, professionals argued for a society that rewarded education and technical expertise. This struggle between the restoration of hierarchical power relations based on new criteria, as argued by the new professional and business elites, and the creation of full social and political equality, advocated by the intelligentsia, bedeviled all organizations during the 1905 Revolution and beyond. Because no agreement could be reached on this central issue, the teachers' movement, like the larger revolutionary movement, was shattered in 1905.

To understand this complex problem, we will follow the involvement of city teachers in the 1905 Revolution. Moscow and Petersburg were major centers of revolutionary activity, and the teachers in those cities had ringside seats to the major events. They were also key participants in the effort to create a new social order. During the spring protest movement that grew out of the Bloody Sunday massacre, they sent petitions and organized unions to represent their interests to local and central government authorities. In June city teachers attended the first meeting of the All-Russian Teachers' Union where the social and political antagonisms that divided teachers finally exploded. Realizing that the national union did not represent their political interests, city teachers withdrew from its activities and concentrated on local union activities. In Moscow, primary schoolteachers became embroiled in the Tsvetkov affair while Petersburg teachers campaigned for the repeal of the marriage ban. Teachers in both cities supported the October General Strike, but after the October Manifesto the movement divided among those who wanted to continue the revolution, those who were satisfied with the government concessions, and those who disapproved of any change whatsoever. Despite attempts to reunite the teachers' movement in 1906 and 1907, the movement fizzled out even before the revolution ended in June 1907.

January–February 1905: The Aftermath of Bloody Sunday

City teachers responded immediately to the tragic events of Bloody Sunday. In Petersburg, the principal of a primary school on Vasilevskii Island invited soldiers into the school the day after the massacre and forced the children to serve them (*sluzhit' ikh*). One hundred angry teachers sent a letter of protest to the Petersburg Commission on Education. Twelve days later the Moscow Pedagogical Society met and adopted the first of many resolutions written that year, expressing dissatisfaction with the current state of affairs. In their resolution, the society's members enumerated many of their grievances against the Russian system of education. In particular, they blamed the educational bureaucracy for allowing the situation in the schools to deteriorate to its present condition. The resolution specifically mentioned the inability of teachers to instruct as they saw fit, the use of Russian as the language of instruction in non-Russian areas, the requirement that teaching personnel supervise student activities both in and outside the classroom, and the educational bureaucracy's habit of promulgating circulars, which ran counter to Russian law. The resolution called for the immediate reform of Russian education.[2]

Teachers were not the only ones unhappy with the Russian system of education. Students, too, began to protest conditions in the schools. Although most primary school pupils were too young to initiate strikes and meetings, the secondary school students were quite capable of doing just that, imitating the actions of university students. On 11 January, students at the Larinskii and Vvedenskii gymnasiums in Petersburg held a series of meetings, which ended in a three-week strike protesting the "arbitrary rule of the government" and setting up a fund for the families of the workers killed on Bloody Sunday. This first action taken by Russian secondary schoolchildren was followed by a wave of protests and strikes that affected the secondary schools in most of Russia's major cities.[3]

The unrest in the gymnasiums remained primarily the concern of local officials, who listened to the students' petitions and passed their grievances on to the Ministry of Education. This innocuous but effective way of dealing with student strikes did not continue for very long. On 12 February in the city of Kursk, there occurred what one historian has called "the Bloody Sunday of the schools." On 10 and 11 February, local school officials had allowed students from the town's secondary schools to discuss their concerns at public meetings. The officials assured the students that they would carefully consider their grievances, and on 12 February the students returned to the classroom. At noon, however, the older students at the classical gymnasium left the school and began a procession past the other secondary schools. Many students from these schools joined the march, and by the time the column of students had reached the girls' gymnasium, there were more than a hundred students in the procession. Moreover, police and Black Hundreds had followed the march. According to eyewitness reports, a policeman suddenly signaled and the adults attacked the demonstrators in front of the girls' school. In the end, forty children were injured and six killed.[4]

The public outcry over this event was enormous. Parents in particular were greatly worried about the safety of their children, and for the first time in the history of Russian schools, they organized themselves into committees and denounced the "tyranny of the bureaucracy." In their view, teachers had lost all moral authority among the students because of poor teaching and the teachers' policing role in and outside the classroom. Up until this point, parents had done little to change the schools, but now, since the Ministry of Education could not even guarantee the safety of their children, parents felt it was time to act. In the city of Khar'kov, a parents' meeting proposed several important reforms in the secondary schools: 1) that secondary schools should be open to all students regardless of social origin, nationality, or religion; 2) that responsibility for the fulfillment of religious duties should be left to the parents, not the schools; 3) that surveillance of students should be abolished; and 4) that parents should be given a decisive role in the pedagogical councils.[5]

The Kursk killings also galvanized Russian secondary schoolteachers to express publicly their moral outrage and desire for change. On 13 February, the day after the violence, an article called "Notes of the Moscow Secondary Schoolteachers" appeared in the journal *Pravo*. The authors of the article announced that they could no longer keep silent "when the blood of our children and former students is flowing in the Far East, flowing in the streets of Russian cities." Agreeing with a statement published in January by Russian professors, these Moscow secondary schoolteachers called for the end of the bureaucratic and police regime in the schools. Recognizing the connection between the school system and the political order, they called for the convening of a national assembly of elected representatives to control the actions of the administration. The article was signed by over one hundred members of the Moscow Pedagogical Society.[6]

The Moscow teachers' resolution was just one of many such actions taken by politically active groups in February. Whatever their specific grievances against the government, they all understood that political changes had to come first. In order to respond to these resolutions and curb the growing violence, Nicholas II decided to act. On 18 February he issued an imperial ukaz and a rescript. The ukaz gave Russian citizens the right to petition the throne directly and stipulated that the tsar would turn over the petitioners' proposals to the Council of Ministers for discussion. The rescript ordered Minister of the Interior Bulygin to prepare legislation creating some sort of legislative body to advise the tsar.

Although Nicholas hoped to appease the opposition forces, his concessions to public opinion had quite the opposite effect. The liberation movement interpreted the ukaz as sanction to mobilize. Professional groups throughout the country began to unionize. The already-existing unions publicized their activities, and those groups that did not have unions began to establish them. Rather than calming the ferment, the government's actions only encouraged the revolutionary movement.

March–June 1905: The Creation of the All-Russian Teachers' Union

City teachers launched two simultaneous efforts to organize during the spring months of 1905. City teachers began to establish local teachers' organizations to represent them in their dealings with city officials. They also attempted to create an All-Russian Teachers' Union to represent teachers' interests to the Ministry of Education on a national level. In order for teachers to succeed in their demands for professional autonomy, both types of representative bodies were necessary.

In Moscow radical teachers had already formed the Moscow Teachers' Association in late 1904. At its inception, this union represented only teachers who worked in the schools run by the city of Moscow, the first hint of some division among teachers. According to one of the organizers, Moscow municipal schoolteachers believed they were different from the teachers who worked at the government schools, whom they considered government bureaucrats and therefore a part of the hated bureaucratic regime of the schools. Instead, these primary teachers considered themselves similar to the zemstvo Third Element.[7]

This identification of Moscow's radical teachers with other members of the intelligentsia demonstrates clearly their complex set of identities. While teachers' professional identity was based on new values of autonomy and individual self-worth, in some teachers these values coexisted with older intelligentsia ideas of the importance of service to the people. Both professional and intelligentsia values shaped the choices of these radical teachers in 1905. Moscow teachers felt no solidarity with secondary schoolteachers, the "teacher-bureaucrats," because the primary schoolteachers identified their own interests with those of the working class, not the Russian upper or middle classes. By limiting membership in the association, they prevented these "teacher-bureaucrats" from joining their new union and aligned themselves with the more radical zemstvo activists and the working class. Their service ethic was so strong that in 1905 it prevented them from acting in accord with their fellow professionals.

During the first few months of 1905 the association was unable to attract a large membership. Most of Moscow's schoolteachers were, in the words of an anonymous commentator on the association's activities, "inclined very conservatively."[8] Moreover, because unions were still illegal, it was difficult for the organizers to publicize the association's activities or to attract many new members: a teacher could quickly lose his or her job for participating in an illegal organization. After the February ukaz, the association received a boost. In March the employees of the Moscow city duma, with the approval of the mayor, formed the Union of Municipal Employees. The Union of Municipal Employees was a federation of the different unions representing the workers employed by the Moscow city government. The Moscow Teachers' Association joined in the federation with unions representing school doctors, hospital workers, tram operators, and other employees. Each group had its own charter but elected representatives to a joint council that represented all the unions. This approach to the problem of union representation set the Moscow city teachers apart from the other professional groups that were also forming at that time in Russia. The Moscow Union of Municipal Employees and the teachers' association within that organization resembled a syndicalist union rather than a more traditional labor union.[9] The Moscow city teachers and the other municipal employees joined together to support each other against their common employer, the Moscow city government, rather than organizing strictly by trade or profession.

With the de facto legalization of the Moscow Teachers' Association, membership began to increase. On 13 March an organizational meeting held in a chamber of the Moscow city duma drew approximately eight hundred teachers. According to the proposed charter, the association had two goals: to act in conjunction with the Moscow city administration in the development and improvement of education, and to improve the legal and material position of the teachers. In order to carry out these important functions, the association demanded that all teachers employed by the city administration become members of the organization.[10]

In order to improve conditions for teachers in the Moscow schools, the association's leadership proposed several important reforms. These reforms were intended to solve the problems they faced in the classroom. Teachers asked that the association be given sole responsibility for hiring new teachers, that the firing or transfer of any teacher be a joint decision between the Moscow city administration and the association, and that a court of honor be established to judge any violations of the "principles of professional ethics and union life." These proposals show Moscow teachers' overriding concern about their lack of legal rights. Teachers wanted to end what they considered the arbitrary decisions of the school trustees, who had the power to hire and fire them. They also insisted on the abolition of the position of "head" teacher, who acted as a liaison between the trustees and the rest of the teachers in the schools; instead, the local union would act as their representative with the school trustees. Teachers demanded the power to control their classrooms, and representation on committees that decided educational policy.[11]

In addition to discussing the nature and role of their union, the Moscow teachers who gathered on the evening of 13 March also voted in favor of a resolution supporting the creation of a union to represent the lower level employees of the Moscow city administration. The resolution declared:

Recognizing the great importance of our interests, we primary schoolteachers, in solidarity with the working class, place the interests of the lower level employees side by side with our own interests, and therefore insist on the quick convocation of private and public meetings of lower level workers and their union organization on an equal basis with all the other employees.[12]

Teachers once again asserted their public service ethic by expressing their solidarity with the working class and attempting to break out of what they perceived to be their isolation. As Laura Engelstein has pointed out, "Despite the sharp class divisions in Moscow society, the revolutionary movement of 1905 was in fact a movement of class cooperation. . . . The privileged recognized the social and economic problems of the working class as part of the political dilemma of society as a whole."[13] As their declaration shows, teachers recognized that in order to gain autonomy in their struggle with the Moscow city administration, all other employees had to be autonomous as well. For years teachers had been unsuccessfully waging a lonely struggle to gain more control in the classrooms. Now they hoped that if they acted together with other employees they just might succeed. It was for these reasons that they issued their call for the formation of a stronger Municipal Employees' Union, by insisting on the inclusion of lower-level employees. Through their new unions, they hoped "to take into their own hands the organization of the city's entire economy and administration."[14]

Unlike Moscow teachers, Petersburg teachers had not formed a union in late 1904, but after the events of January and February, they began to organize in earnest. The initiative to form a union came from the Public Education Section of the Petersburg Mutual-Aid Society. On 9 April 1905 the section presented a set of proposals to a meeting of the Petersburg Mutual-Aid Society, calling for the establishment of an association for Petersburg city teachers. These proposals called for a union similar to the Moscow Teachers' Association. The association was to decide such questions as the transfer of teachers and the selection of teacher representatives to the Commission on Education, the school council, and the city duma when these groups were deliberating on matters dealing with educational policy. The teachers' association would also make decisions concerning the educational program used in the schools and would deal with questions of professional ethics. The association argued for freedom for teachers to instruct as they saw fit; freedom in their private and social lives; dismissal only by a civilian court; equalization of teachers' salaries with those of school doctors and religion teachers; and eligibility for pensions to begin after twenty years of service rather than twenty-five. The association proposed several improvements in working conditions for the lower-level employees who worked in the schools.[15]

A lively discussion ensued among the members of the Petersburg Mutual-Aid Society. Many teachers thought they should have their own separate union rather than one so closely linked to the city schools. In the end, the teachers voted to present the proposals to the city duma, not as a petition (*khodataistvo*), which would have required action, but as a recommendation (*predlozhenie*).[16] Because of the alteration in wording, the city duma did not have to respond.

This change in wording suggests that the Petersburg teachers were not quite as confrontational as their Moscow counterparts. Part of the explanation lies in political preference. One Petersburg teacher, a member of the Social Democratic party, attributed her colleagues' timidity to the fact that "among city teachers there could be found both a large section of clearly defined monarchists and people who were completely apolitical."[17] This statement, however, does not take into account the role of gender in teachers' political decisions. Petersburg women teachers had been consistently denied professional and political recognition by Russian society. Women were not welcomed into either realm. Their timidity in the face of such opposition is not surprising. Tsarist educational institutions attempted to train their female graduates for their role in the home rather than the workplace. As we saw in chapter 1, even the pedagogical courses continued to stress the primacy of the maternal role for women. Because of their socialization, women teachers had difficulty overcoming their political hesitancy and confronting the city duma directly, particularly during the early months of the revolution.

At the same time that teachers in Moscow and Petersburg were organizing local unions, they were also attempting to organize a national teachers' union. After the demise of the illegal Union of Teachers in 1904, a group of teachers, encouraged by the Union of Liberation, organized an illegal teachers' club that discussed the possibility of forming a national teachers' union.[18] In December 1904 the members of the Moscow Pedagogical Society had voted for a change in leadership in their organization in electing a group of mostly young, radical teachers that included N. A. Rozhkov as chairman and M. N. Pokrovskii as deputy chairman, both of whom were Social Democrats. This new leadership quickly brought the Moscow Pedagogical Society to the forefront of the burgeoning teachers' movement. In late February, after meetings with Ia. V. Dushechkin from Petersburg, the Moscow society endorsed the idea of establishing a national teachers' union without prior permission from the government (*iavochnym poriadkom*).[19]

On 12 March, after all these clandestine meetings, Petersburg teachers gathered together in the meeting rooms of the Free Economic Society to declare the formation of the All-Russian Union of Teachers and Education Activists (VSU). They voted for a resolution demanding the transformation of the Russian school and society. The Petersburg teachers called for the establishment of a unified school system, the introduction of free universal education, the establishment of a secular school where teachers could instruct as they saw fit and in the language of the local population, and the transfer of control of education into the hands of public institutions with teacher representatives. These reforms could only come about, according to the resolution, with the improvement of conditions for the working class. In addition, the teachers demanded civil liberties: the complete guarantee of personal immunity, the sanctity of the home, and of freedom of conscience, speech, the press, and assembly.[20]

The resolutions passed by this group of Petersburg schoolteachers represented their vision of what Russia should become. They wanted a society where anyone, regardless of race, religion, or sex, could attend the school of his or her choice. The new schools would be run by teachers and elected representatives of the people, not by the Ministry of Education and the ruling elite alone. Just as the schools would be administered by society, so too would society control their curricula. The language of instruction would be determined by the local population, and religion would be relegated to the home and the church, and would not be taught in the classroom. This new Russia would be a place where teachers could instruct as they saw fit without any unnecessary government interference in either their public or personal lives.

This vision of Russia represented much more than a simple claim for professional competence. It was a blueprint for the complete social and political transformation of Russia. The paradox, not just for teachers but for all professionals in 1905, was that to achieve their professional goals, they needed to work for fundamental political change as well. Although teachers were in almost complete agreement about the educational reforms and about some of the political changes necessary to advance their professional interests, they did not agree on the nature and division of power and authority in this new system. It was these issues that came to the forefront of the teachers' movement during the remaining revolutionary months.

Dissident voices were already heard at the very first meeting of the new national teachers' union. One group that did not support the resolution was a certain conservative segment of women schoolteachers who did not want religion to be removed from the school, and therefore did not join the new union.[21] In addition, many secondary schoolteachers were unhappy with the resolutions adopted at the meeting. Although they supported many of the points dealing with educational reform, they objected in particular to the proposal for freedoms of the press, speech, and assembly, a slogan of the Union of Liberation. These teachers did not approve of what they perceived as the radical politics of the Union.[22] They feared that by allowing everyone freedom to speak, the union would strip these teachers of their new status and authority based on their education and professional competence. They had fought hard for this status and did not want to lose it just when they appeared close to victory.

Having voted on their list of demands, the Petersburg teachers went on to elect members of a central bureau for the VSU and to establish the headquarters for the new union in the offices occupied by the Petersburg Mutual-Aid Society. From that moment, the VSU began to publicize its activities and to work toward establishing a national union. As word circulated through the press, teachers from all over Russia began to write to the Petersburg Central Bureau asking for instructions on how to organize union locals.[23]

The month of April proved to be a period of confrontation between city teachers and the government. On 2 April the Moscow *gradonachal'nik* informed the Moscow Pedagogical Society that it was no longer allowed to meet. The Ministry of Education, angered by the society's February resolutions, had suspended its activities in retaliation.[24] The society's closing did not silence teachers, but only further encouraged their defiant behavior. Just eight days later, the Ushinskii Commission of the Petersburg Mutual-Aid Society held a public lecture on the role of women in the proposed Bulygin Duma. At the end of the lecture, the members of the commission approved a statement criticizing the proposed law and called for the creation of a women's political union. In addition, two proposals supporting working women were put forward, one written by a woman worker. The meeting voted to support this woman's proposal, which called for a constituent assembly elected with four-tail suffrage (general, equal, direct, and secret ballot), amnesty for political and religious prisoners, freedom of speech, press, and assembly, paid maternity leave, and a prohibition against using women workers for certain types of work that specifically endangered their health. To show further solidarity with the working class, the meeting voted to attach the demands of the workers who marched on Bloody Sunday to the woman worker's proposal.[25]

Meanwhile, despite the closing of the Moscow Pedagogical Society, Moscow teachers invited members of the VSU to a meeting of union delegates to draft a charter for the new organization. The meeting was held on 11–13 April in Moscow at the nearby estate of V. A. Morozova. Delegates from all over Russia gathered to discuss the goals and functions of the new national teachers' union. After just a few discussions, it quickly became apparent that there was sharp disagreement among the teachers about the nature of the new union. The majority of delegates to the April meeting believed that the new union should be a "professional-political union," meaning that the union would not only represent the professional interests of teachers but would also advocate certain political goals, such as calling for a constituent assembly elected by four-tail suffrage, for freedom of conscience, speech, press, and assembly, and for amnesty for religious and political prisoners. To ensure its political neutrality, the union would not belong to a specific political party. The Social Democrats insisted, however, that if the union were to espouse political goals, it would have to subscribe to their platform, which included resolutions demanding an eight-hour working day and an end to the Russo-Japanese War. When it was clear that the majority of delegates did not want to support these more radical proposals, the Social Democrats insisted that the union would be a strictly professional organization with no political agenda whatsoever. The debate on this issue was long and intense. In the end, the delegates voted ninety-six to twenty-three in favor of a professional-political union, but an agreement was reached to debate the professional versus the professional-political nature of the union at the next meeting of union representatives, which was scheduled for June.[26]

Although notes of discord in the national teachers' movement had been heard at the Moscow meeting, the first real blow to the unity of the movement came a few weeks later. On 1 May 1905 the journal *Pravo* published the Manifesto of the Petersburg Union of Secondary Schoolteachers. The secondary schoolteachers in that city, unhappy with the resolutions of 12 March establishing the VSU, decided to start their own union to represent what they felt were the unique problems of the secondary schools. According to the Petersburg teachers,

We are witnessing the historic moment of the complete breakdown of the state secondary school and the collapse of the mission entrusted to it. Every means was tried to cut it off from life, but life broke into the school and took the pupils, little more than boys, onto the streets under the cossack whips. Planting religious orthodoxy in the school, the government cultivated it in such gross forms that the harvest was religious indifference. Striving to be an instrument of Russification, the school aroused in the border provinces a deep hatred for the Russian language and culture. Supposedly an arena for inculcating obedience to authority, the school taught the young to protest. . . . Teachers became passive tools, devoid of creative possibilities. For when human relations become artificial, the personality of the individual suffers.

Having described the enormous inadequacies of these schools, the secondary schoolteachers issued a plea for unity among all their "teacher comrades . . . to create a new school."[27]

But this call for unity was limited to fellow secondary schoolteachers and did not include the entire profession. Secondary schoolteachers now emphasized the uniqueness of their problems rather than their shared identity with colleagues in the primary schools. The activist primary schoolteachers who were gaining control of the national teachers' union threatened the world of their secondary school colleagues with their radical politics and calls for social justice. Secondary schoolteachers were interested in a reformed Russia where professionalism, not birth or rank, would provide access to status and privilege. These men were influenced less by the intelligentsia service ethic than by economic gain and self-interest. It was they who were most committed to advancing their professional values of individual self-worth and autonomy, because they stood to gain the most from such a system. The best-educated and most experienced secondary schoolteachers could claim a legitimate place for themselves among the social elite, for their expertise guaranteed them such a position. Their dream of a reformed Russia was threatened by the radical ideas of many of the primary schoolteachers. In order to salvage their hopes, secondary schoolteachers decided to separate themselves from these radicals and go their own way.

Despite these challenges to the unity of the teachers' movement, all teachers were greatly looking forward to the first congress of their new union in June. As schools closed for the summer, teachers began to gather in provincial chapters of their union to elect delegates to the congress. For the first time in Russian history, it appeared that schoolteachers were finally to have a public meeting of their union representatives.

The First Congress of the All-Russian Teachers' Union

The First Congress of the All-Russian Teachers' Union was held between 7 and 10 June. Originally, the entire congress was scheduled for St. Petersburg, but after one day of meetings, the delegates moved to Finland to escape police harassment. Over 150 delegates represented a union membership of 4,668 teachers and education activists. For many teachers the congress culminated many years of hard work and struggle.

At the very first day of meetings, the delegates quickly set out to discuss the thorny issue of the nature of the new union. The report on the Moscow meeting was read to the delegates. The delegates unanimously approved the professional goals for the union: the creation of a unified ladder system of education; the introduction of free, universal education; the elimination of the religious element in the school (by this, teachers meant the removal of religion of the school curriculum and the elimination of the position of religion teacher); the freedom to teach as the teachers saw fit and in the language of the local population; the right of any individual or organization to establish an educational institution; and local control of education.[28]

Once the delegates had approved the professional goals for the union, they discussed whether the union should be political in nature. This issue was again hotly debated. The Social Democrats formed a coalition with some Petersburg primary and secondary schoolteachers, which advocated a strictly professional platform. The proposal also called for an eight-hour work day, an end to the war, and a declaration of teacher solidarity with the working class.

This coalition of city teachers resulted from a nexus of several important factors. For their own very different reasons, in 1905 three different political groupings of teachers in Petersburg and Moscow came to support the Social Democrats' view of the teachers' union. One group of primarily older city teachers, that included many secondary schoolteachers, supported the idea of a strictly professional union because they believed that teachers should not concern themselves with political questions. Some scholars have called this view a vestige of the *soslovie* mentality. According to the traditional view of Russian politics, questions of government and politics were left to the tsar and his ruling elite; other members of society were not invited to participate in political life. These more traditionally minded teachers believed that they were not competent to judge matters of political life, and therefore rejected the notion of a professional-political union.[29]

Another group of teachers, strongly influenced by their intelligentsia value of service to the *narod,* supported the Social Democratic proposal because they supported some of the Social Democratic demands. Many of the city teachers lived among the working classes and saw daily reminders of the grim conditions of Russian workers and their families. Throughout the winter and spring months of 1905, Petersburg teachers had passed resolutions supporting workers' demands. Many of them came to believe that life had to improve for all of Russia's citizens, not just for the educated public. These teachers came to support the Social Democratic proposal because it contained many of their own political and social aspirations, even though they did not adopt the entire Social Democratic program. As one historian has noted, "The socialist movement was surprisingly popular, however, among white-collar and professional groups, who often adopted Social Democratic and Social Revolutionary jargon to express their own political goals."[30] These teachers voted for the Social Democratic proposal not only because they favored a strictly professional platform for the union but also because they favored an eight-hour day and an end to the war. For these teachers, though they continued to espouse professional goals that posited the newer values, service to the people was the paramount value that shaped their identity.

The last group that voted in favor of a strictly professional union were those teachers who were already highly politicized in 1905. Political discourse and activities had been going on in the cities for quite a while, especially in Petersburg and Moscow. As the history of the city teachers' movement demonstrates, a significant portion of teachers had participated in professional activities for quite some time, and these professional activities had always been a kind of ongoing critique of the Russian political system. In contrast, most rural teachers began to engage in professional and political activities later and were, as a result, relative newcomers to the political arena. For these political neophytes the professional-political union had enormous appeal. This one union could help rural teachers articulate their professional and political goals.[31]

Nonetheless, many city teachers had already formulated specific political goals for themselves. They clearly recognized that no professional union could possibly represent the range of political opinion that existed in Russia at that time. If they joined a professional-political union, at some point these teachers would be asked to support political views they did not hold. A significant portion of urban activists representing many differing political viewpoints realized that professional unions could not become pseudo-political parties, for in doing so they would cease to represent the interests of *all* their members.[32]

As the debate on the nature of the union continued, Rozhkov, the leader of the Social Democratic teachers, threatened to leave the union if their position was not adopted. Despite this threat, the delegates voted 109 to 40 to adopt the professional-political platform. The Social Democrats, joined by other city teachers in a dramatic display, walked out of the meeting.[33] The majority of delegates expressed their regret over the schism in the teachers' union, but affirmed their belief in the primacy of political goals for the union.[34]

As a result of this schism, the All-Russian Teachers' Union represented primarily the interests of rural teachers. Although some individual city teachers remained members of the VSU, most did not participate actively in the VSU's activities. Some men, like V. I. Charnoluskii and V. A. Gerd, who were drawn from the ranks of city teachers, continued to serve as leaders of the national union, but they did not represent city teachers' interests. The leadership of the VSU passed to a group of teachers who were either members of the left liberal parties or the Social Revolutionary party; most of the rank and file were SRs.[35] Before very long the national teachers' union became associated almost exclusively with the Social Revolutionary party. As one teacher expressed it, "the rural teacher must act as SR, otherwise the peasants will not heed him."[36]

This division between professional and professional-political unions was an issue that affected all professions in 1905; it has been discussed extensively in the historical literature.[37] This historical commentary has focused particularly on the role of the Social Democrats, and particularly the Bolsheviks, in these debates. The Social Democrats did not want to belong to any organization that would ask them to violate their political beliefs and party discipline. More important, they attempted to gain complete control over professional unions through these tactics, and if they did not, they withdrew from these organizations. The Social Democratic and particularly Bolshevik tactics toward professional unions in 1905 showed their deep reluctance to work with other political groups.

But the historiography of "politics" and its place in these unions tends to mask some of the key conflicts that occurred during the revolution. The debates over the nature of professional unions were more significant than those of party affiliation. These debates were also about power and authority in the new society that Russian professionals were trying to construct. City teachers' own professional ethos had led them to expect a leading role in the teachers' union because of their superior education and expertise. Yet they found themselves outnumbered in 1905 by rural teachers, their social and professional inferiors. The motive behind professionalization had been to create new criteria for awarding status. City teachers wanted to replace the old autocratic notion of status with one that rewarded expertise and competence. During the revolution, however, these new professional criteria were being threatened by demands for social justice and equality. In June, the demands for social justice that had been submerged in the effort to professionalize erupted and divided teachers. City teachers left the national teachers' union when they realized that control of the union had passed into the hands of their social inferiors who were, according to their own professional standards, less qualified to lead the union. These city teachers used arguments about political affiliation to mask their efforts to maintain their social superiority. One Moscow teacher reflected on this situation:

There were three discernable strata [among teachers], with distinct moods and *caste* underpinning, but more than that there existed *caste* differences among them. The professors looked down on the secondary schoolteachers, and the secondary schoolteachers looked down on the primary schoolteachers. Moreover, large numbers of secondary schoolteachers were frightened by the clear political and revolutionary mood of members of the Teachers' Union and did not want to join.[38]

For city teachers, class and hierarchy remained important distinctions in attempts to reform Russia. Unlike the radicals, they did not advocate sweeping away all vestiges of status and privilege, but were interested instead in redefining the criteria necessary to achieve them. City teachers, and especially secondary schoolteachers, had more to lose from a radical transformation of Russia. Already well placed in the old system, they wanted to maintain, if not improve, their position in the new one. Paradoxically, these men who came from the upper and middle classes and who taught the children of these classes shared one characteristic with radical teachers—they identified themselves with the people they served. The only exception to this were those city teachers who clung to government service as the paramount duty of all teachers, but these teachers did not play a large role in the teachers' union once it adopted an antigovernment stance. Thus, secondary schoolteachers also had a strong sense of service, but in their case it coincided with their own class interests. In the end, even though teachers shared many of the same values as a result of their professionalization, it was their differing visions of a new Russia that divided them and made a unified teachers' political movement an impossibility.

Moreover, neither city nor rural teachers were particularly sensitive to the specific problems of women teachers. As the union's platform shows, women teachers' complaints were subsumed under the other demands. There was very little room for women teachers, either city or rural, in the union's leadership, or even among the rank and file. In what was rapidly becoming a profession of men and women, only the men had a real voice in the teachers' union. Women's demands for equality and social justice also threatened male dominance in both the new professional hierarchy and in the political system that men teachers were attempting to establish.

Following the June meeting of the VSU, Petersburg secondary schoolteachers made the schism final. Having already rejected the professional-political platform for their organization, these teachers demanded autonomy for their union as a condition for joining the VSU. The VSU delegates vetoed this proposal, claiming that it jeopardized the goals of democratization of the schools and the introduction of a ladder system of education. The Union of Petersburg Secondary Schoolteachers remained separate from the VSU throughout the revolution.[39]

The First Congress of the All-Russian Teachers' Union signaled both the beginning and the end of a unified teachers' movement. Hopelessly divided by political questions, the VSU came to represent only the rural teachers, while city teachers looked to their own local unions to represent their interests. As one teacher described the situation after June 1905: "City primary schoolteachers were weakly drawn into the union (especially in the [two] capitals and in general in the big cities) and [they] did not have any kind of influence on its work. Among the secondary schoolteachers, who had their own union, only individuals participated in the teachers' union (some were members of both unions), and among professors in the higher schools [there was] practically no one."[40] The VSU became a "union of propagandists and organizers. . . . Professional interests were forgotten; they thought about them only so far as they were connected with political work."[41] In the revolutionary atmosphere of 1905, teachers discovered that their professional goals could not overcome their serious political, social, and gender differences.

Because of the city teachers' defeat at the June meeting, teachers in Moscow and Petersburg now devoted themselves to their own local organizations. There was much work to be done in recruiting more members to the local unions. During the summer vacation local union officials prepared to meet the challenges by the beginning of a new school year.

August–September 1905: The Tsvetkov Affair

After the relative calm of the summer, there were signs of increasing unrest in the cities. Beginning in late August and continuing into September, a wave of uncoordinated strikes affected many industries. In Moscow, the strike movement began with the printers and quickly spread to metalworkers, tobacco workers, bakers, and carpenters, to name just the most prominent groups. What gave the September strike movement its impact, according to one historian, was that the strikes took place in the downtown sections of Moscow rather than in the manufacturing zones that surrounded the city. As a result, the strikers suddenly had greater visibility. Many of Moscow's citizens who might otherwise have been unaware of these strikes came to feel that the strikes were a matter of public concern. As a result, the September strike movement was of much more immediate concern to the public at large than the earlier strikes of 1905.[42]

Another event that furthered unrest in the cities during August and September was the beginnning of a new school year, for this meant the return of the university students to the cities after their summer holidays. On 27 August Nicholas II restored autonomy to the universities, which had been rescinded in 1884. In taking this step, the government hoped to pacify students and faculty, but instead the universities became meeting grounds for students, workers, and revolutionaries. Professors stopped lecturing, and students took over the podiums and held continuous meetings without fear of police intervention.[43]

If the workers and students were showing greater militancy, the government too was beginning to take measures to reassert its authority to counter the new wave of unrest. In August the government arrested and imprisoned for one month the leaders of the Union of Unions. In addition to this official attempt to quell the unrest, workers, students, and others believed to be sympathetic to the revolution found themselves targets of attacks by Black Hundreds. Although the Black Hundreds claimed to support the forces of law and order, these lawless gangs only served to raise the level of violence and unrest during the fall months.[44]

It was during this time of increasing tension that the Moscow schoolteachers returned to their jobs following summer vacation. As soon as classes resumed, the Moscow Teachers' Association began to hold district meetings to gather support for the association's charter, which still had not been approved by the Ministry of Internal Affairs. Not unexpectedly, it was the question of the association's political involvement that caused the greatest debate. Those who favored political affiliation were led by I. P. Baltalon, and those who preferred political neutrality were led by I. L. Tsvetkov. The debate was long and heated, just as it had been in June at the VSU meeting. This time the teachers favoring political neutrality won. For a brief period at least, the political role of the association had been settled, and the Moscow Teachers' Association had as its members individuals who represented all of Russia's political factions.[45]

At the same time as the Moscow Teachers' Association was deciding questions of political allegiance, the organization received its first challenge from the Moscow city administration. Despite the fact that the mayor of Moscow had permitted the formation of the Municipal Employees' Union, the city government now perceived this as a mistake. Since its inception, the Municipal Employees' Union had defined its role more broadly than Moscow city officials wanted. The union was determined not only to represent its members in labor disputes with the city government but also to help determine public policy for the city. Both the city duma and local officials were unwilling to share their control with any other organization. As the school year opened, the battle between teachers and school officials for control of the schools began with the firing of two teachers, both of whom were union activists.

The affair began at the Rogozhskoe school named in honor of N. V. Gogol'. The school trustee, with the authorization of the school inspector, had hired I. L. Tsvetkov to fill a vacancy as a classroom teacher at that school for one year. This was the same Tsvetkov who was one of the leaders of the Moscow Teachers' Association and a Social Democrat. In July 1905 the inspector received notification from the Ministry of Internal Affairs stating that Tsvetkov was politically unreliable and therefore should not be permitted to teach. The inspector, wanting further clarification on Tsvetkov's political unreliability, wrote to the Moscow *gradonachal'nik*. He received no answer to his request, and there the matter rested until 22 August, the first day of classes. On that day, when Tsvetkov arrived for work, there was another teacher in the classroom, sent by G. A. Puzyrevskii, the city duma member in charge of education. When Tsvetkov's replacement discovered that no one had fired Tsvetkov, he agreed to relinquish the position of Tsvetkov. Then Tsvetkov went to the head teacher to get textbooks and teaching aids for his class, but the head teacher told him that Puzyrevskii had left explicit instructions not to give Tsvetkov these supplies. There was little Tsvetkov could do except begin teaching his pupils without any textbooks or paper. After class, he sent a union representative to the city school council demanding an explanation. He accused the school inspector and Puzyrevskii of acting unlawfully and arbitrarily.[46] Meanwhile, school authorities also fired A. Il'in, another union organizer and Social Democrat, who worked at the same school.

The firings outraged Moscow teachers. It was just this sort of arbitrary dismissal that they had been fighting against for so many years. The Moscow Teachers' Association began organizing meetings and petitions to reinstate those teachers and to seek guarantees that such dismissals would not recur.[47] The Moscow Teachers' Association's support for the two teachers angered some members, however, and essentially broke the association into two factions. The left supported the two teachers because it was clear that both had been fired for their politics as well as for their union activities. These teachers were angered by the city duma's arbitrary decisions, "which are in complete disagreement with the spirit of the revolution, which had been accepted by the duma."[48] Radical teachers, supporters of the revolution, felt betrayed by city officials. The less radical camp within the association felt they were being manipulated by the radical teachers. In petitions to the mayor, the nonpolitical teachers disassociated themselves from the radical members of the association. They claimed that the radicals, led by Tsvetkov and Il'in, were attempting to bring the Moscow Teacher's Association into the revolutionary camp, while they, the loyal teachers, were working to prevent such a takeover.[49]

For a week in mid-September, the Moscow city duma discussed the case, but in the end both dismissals were upheld. Early in October the Moscow Teachers' Association petitioned the mayor to reverse the decisions, but on 6 October he refused. The association then tried to organize a boycott, whereby any teachers appointed to fill these two vacancies would refuse the positions.[50] But before the Moscow teachers could gather public support for their boycott, public attention was drawn to the Moscow railroad workers and their call for a nationwide strike.

The October General Strike

On 7 October, railroad workers on the Moscow-Kazan line walked off the job and issued a call for a general strike. The strike quickly spread to the other railroad lines radiating from Moscow. From there the strike spread to other cities, as workers from a variety of occupations joined the railroad workers. Within a week the entire country was paralyzed.[51]

In Moscow the first group of workers to join the railroad workers in their strike was the Union of Municipal Employees, which included the Moscow Teachers' Association. On 11 October representatives of the municipal workers met with members of the city duma and presented their case for higher wages and better working conditions, but the city council refused to support their demands. On 13 October the Union of Municipal Employees called for its members to join the strike movement.[52]

At the same time, the Moscow Teachers' Association met to enlist teachers' support for the general strike. The association's membership, badly divided by the Tsvetkov affair, once again formed right and left factions. This time the divisions among teachers were overcome. Moscow teachers voted in favor of the strike because "for the majority it was clear that teachers could not separate themselves from the workers' movement; they could not continue to teach the children while their fathers were out on strike."[53] After the teachers had voted in favor of supporting the general strike, they elected a strike committee composed of thirteen teachers, all of them socialists. The strike committee went about organizing support for the workers. The committee members set up cafeterias in the schools, organized meetings of parents to explain the daily events of the strike, distributed revolutionary literature, and set up first aid stations for the wounded. Each member of the strike committee served as the coordinator for all the activities in his or her district.[54]

In Petersburg, events proceeded a bit differently than in Moscow, for Petersburg did not have an equivalent to the Moscow Union of Municipal Employees. Instead, Petersburg teachers formed a coalition with the Petersburg section of the VSU, the Secondary Teachers' Union, and the Social Democratic Teachers' Union. On 14 October over one thousand teachers gathered in one of the university auditoriums to discuss teachers' support of the general strike. In contrast to the meeting in Moscow, the majority of teachers who came to the assembly were secondary schoolteachers, with only two hundred primary schoolteachers in attendance. These teachers did not share a clear plan of action. Some felt that the schools should remain open to keep the children off the streets, while others felt that the teachers had to show their solidarity with the striking workers. But once again teachers voted in favor of the strike, with only six votes against. Teachers elected a committee to supervise the strike effort and to set up first aid stations. The meeting also urged teachers to write to the Commission on Education to inform board members and school trustees of their decision to strike.[55]

Not a single school opened its doors on the first day of the general strike. In their letters to the Commission on Education, Petersburg primary schoolteachers gave various reasons for discontinuing classes. Some teachers openly expressed their support for the striking workers. Others, fearful of losing their jobs, wrote that they were ill and could not hold classes. Another group of older women teachers discontinued their lessons out of fear of reprisals by the revolutionaries.[56] By the second day of the strike, however, teachers' support began to falter, and only 60 percent of the city's schools were closed. On the third day the proportion of schools still observing the strike had dwindled to 25 percent.[57]

The third day of the strike resulted in significant political change in Russia. After much vacillation, Nicholas II had decided to act. On 17 October the tsar signed an imperial manifesto that promised all of Russia's citizens freedom of conscience, speech, assembly, and association, and called for the creation of a State Duma, to be elected by universal manhood suffrage. With the stroke of a pen, Nicholas appeared to have paved the way for the creation of a constitutional monarchy that would allow Russia's male citizens a voice in their government.

The first effect of the October Manifesto on the city teachers' movement was to encourage those teachers who had not yet formed official organizations to do so. Except for the February statement, teachers in Moscow's secondary schools had remained unorganized throughout the spring and summer. Despite the government's concessions to the revolutionaries, not all government officials acted according to the new rules contained in the manifesto. On 19 October, just one day after the official announcement of the October Manifesto, the curator of the Moscow Educational District, Aleksandr Shvartz, issued a circular demanding that school directors either expel rebellious students or close down the schools.[58] The Moscow teaching community was furious with Shvartz and decided to act. Two days later, 350 secondary schoolteachers gathered together to form the Moscow Union of Secondary Schoolteachers. The next day they issued a proclamation demanding the resignation of Shvartz and the creation of a democratic and autonomous school directly linked to the primary and higher schools.[59]

Another group of teachers that organized in the period immediately following the October Manifesto was the Petersburg city schoolteachers. Although these teachers had declared their intention to form an association in April, the union did not have its first meeting until 29 October. At that time 200 city schoolteachers gathered together to elect their leaders and endorse the association's platform.[60]

If the October Manifesto pushed some professional groups to organize, it also signaled a change of mood among individual professionals. Many who had supported the movement in the spring and summer now began to withdraw from the Liberation movement. The political concessions granted in the manifesto clearly satisfied large numbers of Russians, who had always been uneasy with their involvement in the revolutionary movement. At the very beginning of November several soldiers and sailors stationed at the Kronshtadt naval base were punished for their role in the October General Strike. When the Petersburg Bolsheviks called for a three-day strike to support the condemned men, however, only a quarter of Petersburg schoolteachers honored the call.[61] Similarly, at a late November meeting of the Moscow Teachers' Association, it was apparent that the tensions between the right and left factions were growing stronger and dividing the union.[62] The right faction wanted to end the revolution and to work with the concessions granted in October by the tsar, while the left wanted to pursue their unfulfilled goals of the complete overthrow of the autocracy. And, as the Liberation movement splintered, the government grew stronger.

Despite the growing dissension, the All-Russian Teachers' Union held two important meetings in November to encourage its members and to discuss future plans. The first meeting was held in Moscow with representatives of twelve provinces plus a large Moscow contingent. During these three days of meetings, the teachers heard reports of large numbers of Black Hundred attacks on rural teachers. Although most delegates to the meeting appear to have realized that they were powerless to stop such attacks, they did propose some measures to try and stop this violence toward teachers. Teachers at the Moscow meeting also discussed a possible alliance between the VSU and the Peasants' Union, another indication of the dominance of the rural teachers and their politics in the VSU.[63] The second meeting of the VSU was held in Petersburg and was attended by representatives from all the northern provinces. Delegates discussed the importance of the general strike in helping teachers to achieve their goals. Teachers also discussed ways in which the union could continue the fight for political freedom.[64]

Meanwhile, in Moscow, the struggle between the right and left factions within the teachers' association was finally reaching its climax with the rescheduling of the elections for the association's executive council. According to one source, the right faction, which up to that point had been fairly passive in the association's activities, suddenly came to life. These teachers organized an intensive campaign effort for their candidates; the result was that all the newly elected members of the association's council belonged to the right.[65] This was a real repudiation of the association's leadership, which from the very beginning had been made up of leftists.

Before the Moscow Teachers' Association could assess the impact of its election, however, Moscow teachers were united by another act of mistreatment against a fellow teacher. A teacher at a primary school in the Tver district claimed he was treated "incorrectly and rudely" in front of his pupils by the school inspector, Prince B. Shchetinin. At a general meeting of the association, the teacher brought forward his complaint. The organization passed a resolution criticizing the inspector and demanding that he henceforth refrain from such incorrect behavior in front of the children. When the inspector refused to apologize to the teacher, the Moscow Teachers' Association called for a boycott against him on 4 December.[66]

These actions taken by the Moscow Teachers' Association in the fall of 1905 were quite consistent with city teachers' behavior throughout the revolution.[67] When acting on violations of their professional code, Moscow teachers united and were willing to act to try to force city officials to treat them with respect. It was only when Moscow teachers turned their attention to questions of "politics" that they became divided by their differing visions of Russia's future. City teachers did not lose sight of their professional agenda in 1905, but it was difficult for them to concentrate their efforts on that issue when so much else was at stake. The complexity of the political situation was never more apparent than in December in Moscow when the call for a teachers' boycott was lost in the events that became known as the December Uprising.

The December Uprising

The December Uprising was the culmination of the confrontation between the government and society in the revolutionary year of 1905.[68] The government was disappointed in the results obtained by the October Manifesto. Instead of pacifying the country as Nicholas and his ministers had hoped, the manifesto had only emboldened large segments of society to demand more concessions from the government. Since these concessions had not worked, Nicholas resolved to quell the revolutionary movement. To deal with peasant unrest, he sent special military governors to several of the central Russian provinces to put down the peasant rebellions, which were beginning to pose a serious threat to the nobility. In the cities, the government began a campaign to arrest labor activists; it culminated in the arrest of the leaders of the Petersburg Soviet on 26 November. In addition, the government warned that local and central government employees could not unionize. These actions served only to antagonize the urban opposition, which led workers and professionals to continue their strikes and union activities. In Moscow, the opposition was joined by a rebellion in the Rostov regiment that lasted for several days before the regiment's commanders were able to regain control. This rebellion led many workers to believe that they had allies among the soldiers stationed in Moscow.[69]

The events that precipitated the December Uprising once again involved the Union of Railroad Workers, this time joined by the postal and telegraph workers. The first action was taken by the postal and telegraph workers who went out on strike on 15 November. At that time the railroad workers agreed not to transport the mail, in support of the strike. Late in November, the government arrested several of the railroad labor leaders in the hope that the rank and file would end their support of the postal workers' strike. Instead, the railroad workers called for a general strike to begin on 7 December. The Moscow Soviet reluctantly agreed to support the call for a general strike. On 7 December the vast majority of Moscow workers walked off the job, supported by many white-collar unions as well, including the Union of Municipal Employees.[70] The government's response to this new general strike was to use troops to disperse the crowds that had gathered to listen to revolutionary speeches. As the strike continued, the violence began to increase; the soldiers began firing into the crowds, killing innocent people. Moscow's citizens became enraged at this violation of the October Manifesto, and before long barricades appeared on Moscow streets.

Along with other labor organizations, the Moscow Teachers' Association began to hold meetings for its members to determine how they should respond to this latest crisis. The problem for the association was that the new council consisted entirely of more conservative teachers, while a significant portion of the association's activists were firm supporters of the workers and the strike movement. As a result of this political division in the membership, nothing was accomplished. One participant at this last teachers' meeting before the uprising remembered that the teachers were gathering just as the barricades were going up on Sadovaia, one of the cities' main thoroughfares. At the meeting, there were endless discussions by frightened teachers. Those who supported the strike were angered by the indecision of their colleagues.[71]

Despite the inability of the association to formulate some plan of action, many teachers did come to the workers' aid, but they did so through the old teachers' strike committee that had been organized during the October General Strike and had never really disbanded. This group of leftist teachers began once again to set up cafeterias and first aid stations throughout the city. As conditions worsened, each member of the strike committee operated alone in his or her district as more areas of the city were cut off from the center by the barricades. One strike committee member gave what money he had to the Social Democrats. Another served as the teachers' association representative on the Committee for Self-Defense. These teachers, sympathetic to the workers' cause, did what they could to help the workers in their time of need.[72]

This time the government was able to gain control of the city despite workers' armed resistance. The small bands of men were no match for the soldiers of the tsarist army, who, contrary to the workers' hopes, did remain loyal to the government. The troops quickly gained control over those districts occupied by the workers. One of the last sections of Moscow to be taken was Presnia. A teacher who lived in that part of the city and had been operating a cafeteria remembered the day well: "But then came the morning when we awoke to the sound of nearby shooting, and looking out the window, we saw soldiers, who shot randomly at all sides from the corner of Bol'shaia Gruzinskaia Street. One bullet struck my window. We understood that Presnia had been taken."[73]

With the defeat of the Moscow workers' strike, it was clear that the revolution had suffered a severe setback. In putting down the uprising, the government appeared to be gaining control again and putting the opposition on the defensive. What was not so clear in December was what the next step in the revolution would be. Would this show of force by the government convince the oppositional forces of the futility of further protest, or would these forces continue to demand more reforms? The big question for all of Russia's citizens that Christmas season was: What would happen in 1906? In which direction would the country go?

1906–1907

The change in the political atmosphere following the December Uprising had an immediate effect on the Moscow Teachers' Association. Although the association's council continued to exist, it did not hold meetings or conduct any business at all. As one unhappy member of the association complained, it did not even have a saving fund for members. The leftist faction began meeting again in private circles and attempted to aid those workers and their families who continued to suffer as a result of the uprising. Some of these teachers continued to believe that the workers would rise again—"no later than the spring"—and that the teachers would support them. The workers did not strike in the spring, however, and by the summer of 1906 it was clear that the Moscow Teachers' Association no longer existed.[74]

In Petersburg the teachers' association continued its campaign to change the employment policy for city schoolteachers, for it was the marriage ban that transcended both the political differences and the political timidity of the primary schoolteachers. The protests over the ban allied these teachers with the other disaffected groups in Russian society and drew them into the revolutionary movement. Their demand for equal treatment under the law was similar not only to that of other professionals but to that of workers as well. They were all fighting for respect and human dignity from their government and all its representatives. Some teachers may have been reluctant to advocate violence, but they could no longer wholeheartedly support the forces of order either.

The Petersburg Teachers' Association had organized an active letter writing campaign to ask the support of individual duma members to change the hiring policy. With words expressing supplication rather than revolutionary fervor, one teacher pleaded:

Highly respected P. A.! As god is my witness, it is impossible to remain quiet any longer. In a few days you will be deciding not only the question of marriage for city teachers, but a question of life or death . . . and not of just one person. In your hands is our happiness, our future, all of our life. Oh, feel pity, do not permit the untimely destruction of young life. How many fervent prayers have been offered up to heaven for you.[75]

In late December 1905, the Petersburg city duma began its debate on the repeal of the marriage ban. The timing of the debate was important because it occurred just a few days after the demise of the December Uprising in Moscow. The defeat of the uprising was a clear sign to many that the government was gaining strength vis-à-vis the radicals. This in turn gave greater prestige to all government bodies and put those seeking change on the defensive. Moreover, the debate in the city duma was not between the reactionary forces of darkness and the forces of light. The chief spokesmen for both sides of this issue were all men with distinguished reputations as liberals.

The supporters of the marriage ban were M. M. Stasiulevich and P. A. Potekhin, its original architects. According to one source, the marriage ban had passed in 1897 because of Stasiulevich's reputation as an educational reformer.[76] Now, in 1905, Stasiulevich, the defender of autonomy for professors in 1861, led the opposition against married women teachers. Apparently, Stasiulevich believed that autonomy was important for men but not for women.

He and Potekhin contended that their primary concern was for the Petersburg schoolchildren. Repeating the views of the earlier opponents, they and others argued that the married teachers' role as mothers prevented these women from being effective teachers. They pointed out that women often had difficulty continuing their teaching duties during pregnancy, which meant hiring substitute teachers, with the attendant problems for the children. They also argued that since teachers could not afford to hire wet nurses, either a teacher's child would be deprived of milk while its mother was at work, or the mother would nurse the child during class hours, a practice of which they disapproved.[77]

The women teachers had support from other equally distinguished liberal members of the city duma—V. D. Nabokov, M. I. Petrunkevich, and G. A. Fal'bork, who was active in the national teachers' union. They argued vehemently against the marriage ban with the now familiar arguments: Marriage was a fundamental human right, and it was the duty of the school to uphold the rights not only of pupils but of teachers as well. They also argued that married women with children made better teachers because they understood children better than women who had no children of their own. They insisted that denying women the right to experience "the happiness of family life" undermined their health, which in turn affected their job performance. The supporters of married women teachers pointed to other countries where academic excellence flourished despite the fact that women teachers were permitted to marry. Finally, they stated that in this "battle against the laws of nature" a teacher might very well take "a most dangerous path to evade the regulation."[78]

In essence, the teachers' argument as articulated by their duma supporters emphasized the issue of control over their professional and private lives. They correctly assumed that most members of the Petersburg city duma believed that all women should marry—this was the purpose for which women were created. Therefore, the opponents of the marriage ban argued that women teachers were being denied a fundamental civil and human right; they should be treated as equals under the law. In Russia in 1905 this approach proved very effective, for two reasons. The marriage ban put the city duma in the awkward position of telling women that they could not marry, which everyone saw as an affront to the "natural" female role. At the same time, women teachers were identifying themselves with the larger revolutionary movement, which was also asking for equal treatment under the law and full civil and human rights.

Finally, in February 1906 the Petersburg city duma, by a vote of forty-one to forty, agreed to keep the marriage ban intact.[79] The Petersburg teachers had lost, but by the narrowest of margins. Although the teachers had almost been able to persuade the duma members to accept their position, the city council ultimately decided that the women were asking for something very radical indeed—control over their own lives. The vote put the supporters of the ban in a hypocritical position. Even for a liberal such as Stasiulevich, it turned out that demands for civil rights were outweighed by other considerations. He wanted to ensure that all power to determine school policy lay in the hands of the Commission on Education and the city duma. The teachers were to remain docile servants of the school authorities, even if their civil rights were violated in the process. In taking this position, however, Stasiulevich and the other city duma members were only restating the view of the tsarist government. As guarantor of the national welfare, the government claimed its interests were greater than the individual's right to autonomy and civil liberty. This was, in fact, what the city duma was saying to the teachers. What is most interesting about the city duma's vote is that it shows how much the government position had been undermined during the preceding fifty years. It was being replaced by a different view of politics, one that placed the rights of the individual above government needs. These newer forces were not strong enough in 1905 to defeat the government, but they were growing stronger.

With the women teachers' defeat and the rather rapid demise of the primary teachers' association in Moscow after the December Uprising, the only other local unions left in existence were the unions of secondary schoolteachers. The situation among these teachers had changed since the spring. During the first months of the revolution, parents, teachers, and secondary school students had formed a kind of alliance to help bring about educational reforms, which all considered necessary. After the October General Strike, however, parents wanted their children to return to the normal school routine, and they began to unite with the school administrators who shared the same goal. In November 1905 the Ministry of Education formalized this alliance between parents and school directors with the establishment of parents' committees at all secondary schools. After the Moscow uprising, however, parents began to lose interest in the parents' committees, which had very little control over school administration in any case.[80]

In contrast to their parents, the students had grown quite radical during the revolution. One secondary schoolteacher stated that while the student movement had been "elemental and chaotic" during the spring, with the resumption of classes in the fall of 1905 student actions appeared to be well organized.[81] There were demonstrations, strikes, and boycotts in almost every secondary school in Moscow and Petersburg during 1905.[82] The students demanded representation of all administrative boards as well as the transformation of the existing secondary schools. Like their older brothers and sisters in the universities, the secondary school students appeared radical and uncompromising to the rest of Russian society.

Secondary schoolteachers found themselves in a very difficult position in the fall of 1905. They no longer looked upon the parents of their students as allies, but they also feared the radicalism of their students. Teachers faced the entire educational bureaucracy alone, finding themselves isolated once again. It was for this reason that the Moscow and Petersburg unions began to discuss the possibility of forming a national union of secondary schoolteachers late in 1905. Since they felt so isolated, it was important for all secondary schoolteachers to act together. Despite signs that the government was reestablishing its control over the schools, the Petersburg and Moscow locals called for a national convention to be held in Finland in February 1906.

Between 9 and 11 February, representatives of the secondary schoolteachers met in Imatra to form the All-Russian Union of Secondary Schoolteachers. They adopted as their slogan for the union "the democratic, free, and autonomous school." This slogan encapsulated the hopes and desires of these teachers for the new secondary school. The new school would be open to all regardless of race, religion, sex, or nationality. It would be free from the control of the educational bureaucracy; instead, the pedagogical council would elect its own members, who would decide all matters of policy for the schools. And the secondary school would be part of a ladder system of education that would link the secondary schools to both the primary and higher schools.[83]

Having established the nature of the new secondary school, teachers went on to define the nature of the new union. On this matter, there was less agreement. Once again, issues of power and authority were the cause of the dispute. The Petersburg group wanted a strong central bureau that would make decisions binding for all members. The provincial teachers feared such a strong central bureau, which might prevent them from dealing effectively with their problems; at the same time, these teachers needed a strong national organization to help alleviate teacher isolation. The Moscow teachers proposed a compromise. They suggested a strong national bureau that would determine policy decisions, but left the implementation of those decisions to local organizations.[84] This compromise meant that teachers from both capital cities would control the central bureau, but without totally dominating teachers in the smaller cities.

Another difficult challenge for the teachers was to define their relationship to their students, who were, after all, also fighting to free themselves from the educational bureaucracy. Many teachers strongly believed that they should not ally themselves with the students in any way, nor allow them any voice in school or union affairs. This issue had already caused a schism in the Moscow union in the fall of 1905.[85] The majority of the meeting's participants realized that teachers could not make such a total disavowal of students, particularly since many students were continuing to disrupt classes in 1906. Instead, the teachers' union passed a resolution calling for support and cooperation.[86]

The next congress of the All-Russian Secondary Schoolteachers' Union was held in June 1906 in Petersburg, at the same time as the Third Congress of the VSU. The new State Duma had begun considering educational reform, and the union wanted to make its own proposals in these legislative discussions. The Union of Secondary Schoolteachers decided to call together its representatives so that the congress could put forward the union's views on these issues. In addition, the VSU had begun petitioning the secondary schoolteachers' union to join them as one large union to push for the reforms they all wanted. In order to further these discussions of unification, the delegates to the secondary schoolteachers' congress met in Petersburg while the VSU representatives met in Vyborg.[87]

The teachers who attended the congress had many ideas on how to improve the existing schools. Several proposals for reforming the secondary schools were made and discussed. After much debate, the teachers voted in favor of a plan that would establish a council composed of teachers, parents, and local officials to control the new school.[88] This proposal would end teachers' isolation within the schools and help bring about local control over secondary education. It was this plan that the union hoped to present to the educational committee of the State Duma.

The next order of business was the proposed union between the primary and secondary teachers' organizations. The chief problem was once again politics. The secondary schoolteachers' union had declared itself a strictly professional organization, while the VSU remained fully committed to its political-professional platform. After some discussion between the two groups, the secondary schoolteachers decided they would join the VSU only when it changed its charter to a strictly professional one.[89]

While the secondary schoolteachers were debating this issue, the VSU was once again arguing over its own commitment to the political-professional platform. This debate had begun at the Second Congress of the VSU, held in secret in Finland in late December 1905. Many of the teachers were unhappy with the schism in the teachers' movement and wanted to rid the VSU of its political coloration, but the issue was not resolved at the December meeting. By June 1906 the situation had changed dramatically. Hundreds of rural teachers had been arrested in the intervening months. Some had been dismissed from their jobs and many sent into exile. Due to its own lack of financial resources, the VSU was unable to do much to alleviate the suffering of the purged teachers. The union's membership began dropping precipitously.[90] For these reasons, members of the VSU now began to clamor for a change in the union's platform. They argued that the VSU needed all teachers, both the highly politicized and the politically timid, to become members. Both of these groups, however, stayed away from the VSU: those who were highly politicized because they disagreed with the political stance of the VSU; and the timid because they were frightened by what they perceived to be the VSU's radical politics. In what appears to have been a major policy shift, the majority of delegates to the congress voted to change the platform to a strictly professional one. However, they also added a motion that essentially endorsed the same political objectives they had just taken out of the platform. Despite the so-called changes in the platform, the secondary schoolteachers, correctly understanding that the VSU was still committed to its political role, refused to join the union. Thus ended once and for all many teachers' dreams for a truly united teachers' movement.

A fourth and final congress of VSU delegates convened in June 1907. The delegates agreed to soften the political overtones of the union and return to the original professional goals of the teachers' movement. This action came too late, however. Membership in the VSU had dwindled to just a few hundred. Government repression and a dramatic decline in membership had taken its toll. Even the

THE REVOLUTION OF 1905

All-Russian Secondary Schoolteachers' Union had lapsed into inactivity. But even more important, the tsarist government began to renege on some of the major concessions granted during 1905. On 9 July 1906 Nicholas II dissolved the First State Duma. His action was an enormous blow to revolutionaries and moderates alike, for it showed that the autocracy had regained its confidence and would not hesitate to use its power to maintain its position of authority. Finally, on 17 June 1907, Nicholas II and his minister, Stolypin, arbitrarily changed the election law in order to ensure a new State Duma that would cooperate with the autocracy. The revolution was over.

6 City Teachers After the 1905 Revolution

IN MARCH 1907 A HISTORY OF THE MOSCOW TEACHERS' ASSOCIAtion appeared in the journal *Uchitel'* (The teacher). The author of the article, who chose to remain anonymous, chronicled the rise and fall of the association's activities. The author blamed conservative teachers for the demise of the organization. Even though the executive council continued to exist, it did nothing to help teachers. Radical teachers had once again formed their own organizations, but all they had been able to do was set up a mutual-aid fund. This Moscow teacher, frustrated by the inactivity of the teachers' association, ended the article with this prediction: "Obviously, it is necessary to wait for a new public revival, which will shake the teachers' union again, rally a large circle of teachers and clear a path for professional, associational work."[1]

These words seem remarkably prescient to modern readers, but in 1907 many teachers would have considered them foolhardy. Beginning in the fall of 1905 and continuing until 1907, the government initiated a purge of thousands of professionals who had participated in the revolutionary events in the countryside. Teachers, doctors, and statisticians were arrested or dismissed from their posts.[2] Rural teachers were vulnerable because many had acted as peasant representatives to state and local authorities. When the government did not respond to peasant concerns, their frustrations reached a fever pitch and exploded into a series of jacqueries. The government met violence with violence by using the army to put down the revolts and by arresting anyone suspected of aiding and abetting the peasants. Teachers were easy targets. According to Seregny in his recent history of rural teachers, even though the purge of politically unreliable teachers was over by 1908, "the effects of government repression lingered, affecting the teaching profession's composition, organization and morale."[3] After 1905, rural teachers were reluctant to become involved in any kind of activity that the government could construe as political. This included teachers' professional work and organizations.

The situation was much more complicated for city teachers. Although a complete record of arrests is not available, it appears that there was no significant purge of politically active teachers in either capital following 1905. According to a report for 1906, one teacher in the Moscow region was fired, two teachers in the Petersburg region were dismissed and nineteen arrested; but these figures include the surrounding countryside as well.[4] Tsvetkov, the Moscow teacher fired in September 1905, was never reinstated, but moved to Petersburg where he remained active in teachers' organizations. There were no reports of dismissals among Petersburg city teachers. Until a complete accounting of arrests and dismissals can be made, we must assume that most Moscow and Petersburg teachers kept their jobs, whatever their role in the revolution.

This continuity of personnel had important effects on city teachers' activities after 1905. They were clearly chastened by the revolutionary turmoil that had defeated the national teachers' movement. But unlike their rural colleagues, a significant number of city teachers remained committed to their professional goals. After a brief period of inactivity following the 1905 Revolution, city teachers began to meet and discuss their grievances with renewed vigor during the years preceding World War I.

This persistence of professional activity after city teachers' revolutionary baptism of fire suggests that their professional ethos survived. Despite the loss of their unions, teacher-professionals continued to espouse the replacement of older standards for rewarding status with those that emphasized education and technical expertise. Individual self-worth and initiative underlay their demands for civil liberties and a reformed school. In order to teach children to be independent thinkers as their child-centered pedagogy advocated, teachers themselves had to be free to think and act as individuals. Thus, the values that shaped teachers' activities in postreform and revolutionary Russia continued to influence city teachers' behavior after 1905.

But if city teachers' professional values remained the same, other attitudes changed as a result of the 1905 Revolution. Trying to understand the breakup of the VSU, city teachers came to blame "politics" for the turmoil in the union. According to one teacher, professional concerns had been sacrificed to political work.[5] This conclusion about the failure of the VSU and the splintering of the teachers' movement led city teachers to assume that if they could stay away from "political" questions, by which they meant sectarian affiliation with one political party or another, they could reconstruct a national teachers' movement from the ashes of the old. Now that political parties were legal, in the post-1905 period it was less necessary for professional unions to serve as pseudo-political parties. But the naive assumption that teachers could avoid political questions permeated city teachers' attempts to resurrect a unified national teachers' movement in the interrevolutionary period.

What city teachers failed to recognize was the extent to which "politics" had penetrated the teachers' movement; the 1905 political debates were not simply about party affiliation. The real goal of all professionalization was the redistribution of power and authority to those who were experts. But even professionals, influenced by intelligentsia attitudes toward service, disagreed over whether experts should exercise this authority alone or share it with other unrepresented groups, particularly the lower classes. In the new Russia, should some form of hierarchical social and political relations be introduced, or should there be full equality for all classes? The desire for hierarchy versus the desire for equality had split the teaching profession in 1905. But even after the revolution, city teachers failed to recognize the seriousness of this dilemma. They remained too caught up in their identity as servants for the people, as in the case of the radical teachers, or as civil servants, in the case of the conservatives. There were few teachers who were willing to argue that teachers should serve their *own* interests as members of a newly forming middle class. The intractable and profound inequalities of imperial Russian social relations shaped the nature of the "political" debates before, during, and after 1905. By not attempting to find a workable solution for the problem of hierarchy versus equality, the efforts of city teachers to form a unified profession remained doomed. But this failure simply mirrored the problems of the larger society.

In order to understand city teachers' complex situation in the interrevolutionary period, we will examine their efforts to reestablish a viable teachers' movement. These efforts show a striking similarity to the pre-1905 teachers' movement. Teachers in both cities attempted to wage campaigns for the enactment of their unmet professional goals. In Petersburg, women teachers successfully resumed their efforts to repeal the marriage ban. In Moscow, teachers held their first meeting with school officials in 1912. Feeling isolated from their colleagues in other towns and villages, the teachers in the two capitals tried to reestablish contact with their fellow teachers by building a teachers' house in Moscow and convoking a second mutual-aid society congress in 1914. Although these events demonstrate the persistence of city teachers' concerns, they also show quite clearly their inability or reluctance to deal with the issues directly. Emphasizing unity over a diversity of views, city teachers ignored the fundamental issues facing their profession and their society.

Local Efforts

The response of the Ministry of Education to the 1905 Revolution was complex. Although there has been little historical research on this issue, it appears that the ministry was quite concerned about the turmoil that had engulfed Russian schools during 1905. The ministry's centralizing policies were clearly in danger from all the demands for local control of education. As a result, ministry officials renewed their attempts to improve Russian education and reestablish control over secular primary education, by introducing several bills into the new Russian legislature. These measures included legislation on universal primary education, school subsidies, and new school statutes for primary and secondary education. Of these measures, only the legislation providing government subsidies for primary schools became law in 1908; the other bills languished in the duma until the 1917 Revolution. The 1908 school bill, however, gave the Ministry of Education important financial responsibilities for primary schools and, therefore, indirect control over these same schools.[6]

The response of municipal governments to these school subsidies from the central government was mixed. Local governments in Petersburg and Moscow were certainly willing to accept additional funds to increase their budgetary outlays for education rather than take money away from other municipal services. Nevertheless, accepting funds meant relinquishing local control of the schools. This dilemma encouraged local governments to intensify their involvement in public education. Both Petersburg and Moscow initiated new educational programs to bolster local control of education rather than succumb to the power of the central authorities. In Petersburg local authorities concentrated their efforts on expanding the number of primary schools. In Moscow these initiatives included the introduction of universal primary education, the addition of another year of elementary schooling, the expansion of adult education programs and technical schools, and the opening of a people's university. Moscow citizens and officials prided themselves on the city's leading role in educational affairs.[7]

All these new and expanded programs required teachers' support to succeed. City officials needed well-trained professionals to staff these new schools, but this need presented other problems. School officials had not forgotten city teachers' participation in the October General Strike, nor the formation of local teachers' unions. City authorities were aggrieved by teachers' antagonistic behavior in 1905. At the same time, many teachers believed that the city governments had ignored their petitions for better working conditions, and now they were barred from union activity by a 1906 ban on public employee unions. Thus, local governments' attempts to increase public outlays for education brought the unresolved conflicts between local governments and teachers to the forefront of city politics once again.

The Petersburg Marriage Ban In Petersburg the chief issue that continued to divide school officials and teachers was the marriage ban. If the members of the Petersburg city duma thought that the 1906 vote had ended this debate, they were sorely underestimating the commitment of the teachers to the ban's repeal. After 1906, however, the teachers no longer looked to the teachers' organizations for support. The national teachers' organizations had never been strong supporters of the women teachers and considered the marriage issue of concern only to women. At the same time, it was clear that the national teachers' organizations had been devastated by the government repression following the Revolution of 1905; it could not provide any guidance or support to teachers who were still trying to pursue grievances with local school officials. This lack of support meant that women teachers had to circumvent the ban on public employee unions and find other groups to support their efforts.

Petersburg teachers turned instead to the feminist organizations that had supported them in their earlier efforts to repeal the ban. These feminist groups had been particularly active during the 1905 Revolution. Indeed, Petersburg teachers provided the bulk of the membership for the feminist groups in the capital. Maria Chekhova, one of the founders of the Union of Women's Equality, described the union's membership as "feldshers, doctors, primary schoolteachers, helpers of all sorts who everywhere carried with them the light of education."[8]

Despite the downturn in membership and activities that occurred in all professional and political organizations after 1905, one of the feminist groups, the Russian Women's Mutual Philanthropic Society, pressed the government to allow the organization of a women's congress. After intense lobbying, the government gave its permission for the organization of the All-Russian Women's Congress, which was held in December 1908. One of the resolutions passed by the congress emphasized the right of women teachers to continue to work after marriage.[9]

This resolution was followed by a report on the marriage ban at the Congress on Women's Education held in December 1911. E. A. Chebysheva-Dmitrieva, a veteran Petersburg schoolteacher, spoke about the inequities of the 1897 law. She called upon the Petersburg city council to repeal this ban so that women teachers could continue to instruct Russia's future citizens and take pride in their important work. Following this report, the congress sent a petition to the Petersburg city council calling for a repeal of the marriage ban.[10]

On 20 November 1913 the Petersburg city duma finally voted to repeal the ban. This time, there was only one dissenting vote, cast by P. A. Potekhin, the president of the Petersburg Commission on Education and the last remaining member of the committee that had proposed the ban (Stasiulevich had retired in 1909). The supporters of the teachers insisted that the city council did not have the right to take away the teachers' human right (*chelovecheskoe pravo*) to marry; teachers should have complete freedom in their personal lives. In addition, they argued that it was important for teachers to be "in a cheerful disposition" (*v bodruiu obstanovku*) so that they could be a positive influence on their pupils.[11]

There were other considerations that influenced the city council's vote. The number of Petersburg schools was expanding so rapidly by 1913 and the teaching qualifications were so high that there were not enough teachers to staff the growing school system. In addition, Petersburg schools were losing a significant portion of their highly trained teachers because of the marriage ban; they preferred to work in other primary schools, particularly zemstvo schools. By 1913 the ban was wasting pedagogical talent. More important for the teachers, city officials rather grudgingly acknowledged that married schoolteachers were just as dedicated to their work as unmarried ones.[12] Indeed, it appeared that women were capable of serving both their husbands and school officials.

One other explanation for the repeal of the marriage ban in 1913 was the increasing number of professionals elected to the city council in 1912. Although it is difficult to be precise, at least 25 percent of those elected to the city council in 1912 identified themselves as professionals.[13] As professionals gained greater prominence in Petersburg's political arena, the values that these men espoused—technical expertise, individual self-worth, and autonomy—influenced their actions and voting behavior in the city chambers. The women teachers' demand for professional autonomy furthered the city council members' own goal of replacing the traditional autocratic political culture with a more modern one. The 1913 vote was just one example of the shift that was taking place in the prerevolutionary Russian government, from guarantor of the national welfare to guarantor of individual rights.[14]

The struggle between the Petersburg schoolteachers and the city duma highlights the difficulties women teachers had in gaining acceptance as full members of the teaching profession. Both the city council members and the male leadership of the teachers' movement failed to take women teachers seriously. Petersburg schoolteachers faced a double burden of discrimination—as women and as teachers—but other women teachers throughout Russia experienced this same prejudice. Unlike their rural sisters, however, women teachers in the Russian capital banded together to try to oppose this discrimination. This sense of collective action was important because the national teachers' movement did not deal with the discrimination women teachers experienced as women. The women had to fight this discrimination themselves.

The ban's repeal suggests that the climate of sex discrimination in Russia was beginning to change. What was seen as acceptable treatment of women in 1897 was not acceptable in 1913. If Russia was to become a more just society, women needed to be respected as equal citizens. This shift occurred because a group of determined women resisted the government's encroachment on their desire to exercise control both in their careers and in marriage. It was an important first step if women teachers were to gain acceptance as full and equal members of the profession.

The 1912 Moscow Teachers' Conference In Moscow there was no one single issue that united city teachers, as there was in Petersburg. Moscow teachers had articulated a number of demands during the 1905 Revolution, and none had been resolved. City teachers had demanded a court of honor to judge violations of professional ethics, the abolition of the positions of trustee and head teacher, an end to arbitrary dismissals, and the creation of a pedagogical council at each school composed of teachers and trustees to administer the schools. In the years following the revolution, the city council enacted a number of educational reforms. These included restructuring primary school administration, adding a fourth year to the primary school curriculum, and convening regular teachers' conferences. Certainly, the official published documents of the city duma do not mention any reason for their reforms except the concern of the city fathers for the welfare of Muscovites. In part, these reforms were city officials' attempts to assert local control over the schools to counteract the Ministry of Education's growing financial influence. Until the complete records for the city council are made public, we cannot know for certain the motivations of Moscow officials. Nevertheless, the nature of the some of these reforms suggests that the city duma was trying to win teachers' support.[15]

One of the continual sources of friction between teachers and city officials was the role of the trustees in the administration of the schools. In Petersburg, a single trustee oversaw several schools at once and was also a member of the Commission on Education. It was difficult for these officials to visit their schools very frequently, because of their other official duties and because of the number of schools under their jurisdiction. Instead, the *eksperty*, who held no other official position, visited the schools regularly and advised teachers on their problems. In contrast, each Moscow school had its own trustee, and they played an extremely active role in the daily life of the school.[16] Teachers argued that the trustees were the real administrative power in the primary schools, but most were unable to function well, because of their lack of training. In order to remedy this situation, in 1909 the Moscow city duma created three new positions in school administration, similar to the Petersburg *eksperty*. These assistants, or *pomoshchniki* as they were called, were given various administrative roles, including supervision of teaching.[17] The intent of the new position was to take some of the power away from the trustees and place it in the hands of trained educators. This system had worked very well in Petersburg, and Moscow officials probably hoped that it would ease tensions in their city as well.

When school officials decided to add an additional year to the primary school program, the question arose as to what to teach in the fourth year. A committee of seventy teachers and trustees gathered during the 1909–1910 school year to revise the curriculum. The problem before them was whether to expand the curriculum by adding new subjects, or to maintain the curriculum as it existed. After "heated debates," a compromise was reached. Rather than include history, geography, and natural science as separate subjects, teachers could include these topics in the existing curriculum *however they saw fit*. For example, teachers could select texts on historical subjects to use in their reading classes.[18] The most important change for teachers was that they, not the trustees, would be the ones to determine how to incorporate these subjects into their curriculum.

Both the curricular reform and the introduction of *pomoshchniki* into the Moscow school hierarchy show clearly how the teachers' professional values informed their actions. These reforms placed technical competence above all other considerations as a way of improving primary education in Moscow. The adoption of these measures suggests that technical expertise was not just important for professionals, but was beginning to gain wider acceptance in Russian urban society at large.

The final reform enacted by the Moscow city duma before World War I was the calling of a citywide teachers' meeting in January 1912. School administrators had called special meetings concerning the teaching of penmanship in the city's schools and had recognized the need to have such meetings on a regular basis. Instead of continuing these specialized meetings, the city decided to have a general meeting of teachers who could then inform the city council of the schools' needs.[19] If the previous two reforms demonstrated the acceptance of some aspects of teachers' professional culture, this meeting shows the limitations of that acceptance.

The congress began on 29 January and continued until 8 February. Over two thousand people registered, making it one of the largest teachers' meetings ever held in Russia. The participants included city duma members, trustees, and representatives of various associations concerned with public education. But the vast majority of delegates, over fourteen hundred, were teachers. The congress's program bore a sharp resemblance to many of those congresses held before 1905. In addition to reports on pedagogical subjects,[20] the program included sections on the organization of the school, and on teachers' legal and material situation. One teacher commented that the program was quite similar to the Zemstvo Education Congress that had convened just a few months earlier. Another commentator remarked that he was disappointed that at such a large congress there were only sixty-five reports.[21]

One change between the 1912 Congress and other earlier meetings was the number of women teachers who read reports at the Moscow meeting. Of the thirty-two speakers listed in a newspaper report, twelve were women.[22] Even more telling, at the session devoted to teachers' legal and material position, three women and two men teachers spoke on these important issues.[23] The strong presence of women teachers at the 1912 Congress suggests the growing numerical superiority of women in Moscow city schools. In 1905 the ratio of men to women teachers was 1:7; by 1915 the ratio was 1:10.[24] The reports by women teachers on professional issues also suggest an acceptance of women as professionals by school officials and men teachers alike. In 1905 and earlier, key speeches on professional issues at teachers' congresses had almost always been given by men teachers, but now in 1912 men and women sat on the podium together.

The congress opened with a speech by Puzyrevskii, the Moscow official charged with overseeing education for the city duma, and the same man who had fired Tsvetkov from his position in 1905. His speech recounted the events leading up to the convening of the meeting. According to one police report, Puzyrevskii's speech was met with many "ironic smiles" because he gave the city duma full credit for suggesting the meeting.[25] In fact, a group of school trustees had first proposed a congress in 1901, but the meeting, scheduled for 1904, had never taken place. With the decision to introduce universal primary education in 1910, another group of trustees asked again for the meeting, to discuss the changes necessitated by the reform. This time the city duma agreed.[26]

Both an official observer and a police agent commented on a "sharp antagonism" between teachers and city officials at the congress. Before it was convened, some Moscow teachers decided to boycott the entire congress, some abstained from presenting reports, and others withdrew their reports. The agent described teachers' reaction to the congress as cold.[27] Much of this antagonism stemmed from the issues left unresolved in 1905.

Although teachers might have acted coldly toward the congress, there were nevertheless moments of heated debate. These came when the congress discussed those reports dealing with teachers' status in the schools. On the third day of the congress, the participants discussed the issue of who should control the classroom. It was here that the antagonism between teachers and school administrators fully emerged. After debates that lasted all day, more than fifteen hundred teachers approved a resolution that called for the elimination of individual school trustees and their replacement by a school council composed of elected representatives of teachers, trustees, and parents. Teachers also wanted to organize district teachers' meetings that would then represent teachers' interests to the city administration. All questions concerning the hiring, firing, and transfer of teachers were to be dealt with by a new commission composed of city duma officials, representatives of the district teachers' councils and of the Moscow city administration. Many of the reports called for teachers to have "complete independence" and a "deciding voice" in Moscow school administration.[28]

What is so striking about the 1912 meeting is that Moscow teachers took this opportunity to restate their unmet demands from 1905. At this first opportunity to meet publicly since the 1905 Revolution, Moscow teachers reminded city officials that they had not forgotten their professional concerns and would continue to press the city duma to act on their demands. One commentator observed that teachers were reluctant to demand a teachers' "association" because of this word's connection with teachers' union in 1905. Instead, they insisted upon teachers' "meetings" (*sobranie*), which they hoped would sound less provocative to city officials.[29] Despite the change of wording, however, Moscow teachers wanted representation on school councils and they wanted administrators to listen to their advice and take it seriously. If the wording had changed since 1905, the message had not.

All the goals stated in the 1912 resolution emphasized the persistence of the values contained in Moscow teachers' professional ethos. Moscow teachers wanted to be independent of the incompetent school trustees. They wanted others to listen to their advice because it was based on technical expertise and not political patronage. As further evidence of their professional consciousness, a police agent reported that, although there were no reports on establishing courts of honor for teachers, this was already a moot point. Courts of honor were already operating in Moscow and were disciplining teachers who did not meet teachers' own standards of professional conduct.[30] Thus, Moscow teachers had taken violations of their professional code of ethics into their own hands.

The meeting concluded with two speeches, one by a teacher and one by the mayor of Moscow. The speeches attempted to conclude the meeting on a note of cooperation. The Moscow teacher remarked that this congress marked the first face-to-face meeting between teachers and city officials to decide questions of educational reform. As such, it marked an important beginning. The mayor of Moscow seconded these remarks and commented on the need for all involved in education to contribute to the improvement of the Moscow schools. The congress closed with a resolution calling for a second congress within three years.[31] That meeting was never held.

The Moscow school officials present at the meeting were stunned by the militancy of the teachers and their demands. Puzyrevskii told some teachers in private that they had gone too far and their demands would never be approved by the city administration.[32] While city officials might concede some issues to teachers, they were not going to give teachers any real power. This was the issue that continued to divide not just Moscow teachers but all teachers after 1905. One year later, a Moscow teacher published anonymously a progress report on the 1912 Congress. The author found that none of the teachers' demands had been acted upon by the city government. City officials had even thwarted teachers' attempts to publish the congress's proceedings. Moscow teachers realized that they alone would have to work for their professional goals; school officials were not interested in improving teachers' lives.[33] Having reached this impasse at the local level, teachers turned once again to rebuilding professional organizations that could support them in their call for educational reform.

Teachers' Professional Organizations and Meetings

The mutual-aid societies, which served as the vehicle for teachers' professional goals, suffered a decline throughout Russia after the 1905 Revolution. The total number of societies declined, as did the membership in the remaining organizations. The mutual-aid societies in Moscow and Petersburg were no exception. In 1908 the Petersburg Mutual-Aid Society had only 262 dues paying members; the Moscow society had 528. The annual reports of these societies convey a sense of concern over how to attract old and new members to the societies, so that they could once more represent city teachers' interests.[34]

Despite the downturn in membership, a significant minority of city teachers remained committed to their goal of a united teaching profession. In 1908 the Petersburg Mutual-Aid Society considered disbanding their organization because so many city teachers had not joined. Nevertheless, they decided that there were enough teachers dedicated to the society's goals to continue their work. Rather than disband, they asked themselves how they could best achieve their goal.[35] In their deliberations on how to invigorate the teachers' professional movement, city teachers were directly influenced by their experiences in 1905. The result was a second flowering of teachers' congresses and new, redefined mutual-aid societies.

In 1912 P. Zhulev, a writer and leader of the post-1905 teachers' movement, published an article in the influential journal *Russkaia shkola* on teachers' mutual-aid societies. His study of these societies before and after 1905 led him to some important conclusions on how to improve them. One reason for mutual-aid societies' lack of success was their limited function. Because most mutual-aid societies were restricted by their government charters to providing only financial assistance, a paradoxical situation had arisen. How could mutual-aid societies hope to provide financial assistance to their members when most teachers could not afford the annual dues to join the societies? Zhulev argued that mutual-aid societies had to define their purpose more broadly to include both financial and "spiritual" assistance. In order to raise teachers' financial status, teachers' professional consciousness had first to be nurtured through "spiritual" assistance, the code word for greater access to reading materials, special teachers' meetings, and training courses.[36] Spiritual assistance was needed to develop the professional attitudes and values among all teachers.

The other reason that Zhulev saw for the decline of mutual-aid societies after 1905 was their involvement in the political movement during the revolution. Zhulev, like many city teachers, blamed the VSU in particular for this development. He clearly believed that mutual-aid societies should stay out of politics, which distracted teachers from their professional work. Politics divided the teachers' movement and prevented them from achieving goals.[37]

What is remarkable about Zhulev's article is how it reflects teachers' experiences in Moscow and Petersburg. Unlike the rural mutual-aid societies, those in the two capitals had not been restricted to material assistance before 1905, but had provided both material and spiritual assistance from their inception. The teachers had shaped these societies to serve their professional interests. City teachers contended that the new provincial organizations should model themselves after the mutual-aid societies in the two capitals. By following the urban model for professional societies, rural teachers could avoid the mistakes of the past. In repeating the argument against political involvement, Zhulev was reiterating city teachers' objections to a movement that combined professional and political goals. That movement had failed in 1905 and now it was all the more imperative to prevent such a defeat again, by leaving political demands out of teachers' professional work.

These conclusions clearly informed city teachers' professional work after 1907. A number of articles written by leaders of the teachers' movement appeared in major education journals between 1908 and 1913, encouraging teachers throughout Russia to form mutual-aid societies. Some of these articles included specific guidelines for organizing such groups. The authors placed great emphasis on the need for "solidarity" and a "unified teaching profession."[38] In addition to encouraging rural teachers to form mutual-aid societies, teachers in Moscow and Petersburg attempted to revitalize their own societies. In each case, they chose a project that would bring national attention to the plight of the schoolteacher.

The Moscow Teachers' House

The project that captured the imagination of Moscow's activist teachers was the building of a teachers' house (*uchitel'skii dom*). The idea had first been discussed in 1896 at the Nizhnii Novgorod Industrial Exhibition, and came up again at the 1903 Mutual-Aid Congress. At that time two teachers reported on the need for a teachers' house in Russia. They argued that it would help them unite and would aid them in their professional work. Teachers' houses had become quite common in the Western European professional movements. Inspired by the idea, teachers from the Moscow Society for the Improvement of Living Conditions worked toward providing such a building in Moscow. The end result of that society's initiatives was not a teachers' house, however, but a portrait gallery of writers and social activists.[39]

Following the 1905 Revolution, the idea of building a teachers' house reemerged among a group of teachers in the Moscow Teachers' Institute Mutual-Aid Society. N. V. Tulupov, a member of the society and one of the leaders of the pre-1905 teachers' movement, asked the society to consider organizing a building campaign for the project. The society enthusiastically supported the plan. Tulupov then took his idea to the 1909 Congress for Advanced Primary Schoolteachers. There he read a report outlining his plans for the project and the construction costs. Tulupov argued that the house would provide a place for teachers to fulfill their professional goals and discuss plans for educational reform. Once the teachers' house had been built, the building could house a library for teachers and pupils, provide lecture rooms for pedagogical courses and other educational courses, and accommodate visiting teachers in inexpensive lodgings. The congress delegates heartily approved of the plan; even the Petersburg mayor, N. A. Reztsov, argued that teachers' houses should be built all over Russia, not just in Moscow.[40]

With the overwhelming support of the congress, Tulupov and his fellow Moscow teachers began their building campaign in earnest. They found an inexpensive plot of land in the Zamoskvorech'e section of the city. The teachers hired A. U. Zelenko, a civil engineer and educational activist, to design and construct the building. The Moscow teachers' greatest success was their financial campaign. Usually, such an expensive project would have been beyond the means of any teachers' mutual-aid society. The Moscow teachers, however, received two important financial gifts from I. D. Sytin and A. S. Bairak, both honorary members of the society. These two men contributed sixty-five thousand rubles which, together with the society's money and contributions from ordinary teachers, gave the society enough money to begin construction immediately. Work commenced in the spring of 1910 and ended in 1911. The society dedicated the building in December 1911 and hung a portrait of Tulupov in the entryway, honoring him for his work.[41]

The Moscow Teachers' House became a tangible monument to the city teachers' professional movement. A group of teachers, through their own initiative and with the help of private funding, built a refuge for teachers to help improve their material and "spiritual" conditions. Within the walls of the teachers' house, men and women from Moscow and all across the rest of Russia could improve their professional training through lectures, reading, and formal coursework. Teachers could also visit the "museum" of instructional aids to learn about the latest techniques for improving the learning capabilities of their pupils. The real emphasis of the teachers' house was to improve teachers' pedagogical preparation and instill in them a sense of themselves as competent professionals. As one teacher described the Moscow Teachers' House, it would be "the center and symbol of unity among the dispersed teaching masses."[42] Even the tsarist police recognized the importance of the Moscow Teachers' House. An agent concluded that "the teachers' house has enormous significance, because it appears as a link for all teachers in Russia and because it is under the auspices of a completely legal society."[43] After years of struggle, the Moscow teachers had literally built a monument to their growing professional consciousness, and more important, had done so on their own without any help from the tsarist government.

The Second Congress of Mutual-Aid Societies

While Moscow teachers were busy with the construction of the teachers' house, teachers in Petersburg were concerned with their own project to organize a second mutual-aid congress. This congress had originally been scheduled for the 1905 Christmas vacation. One week before the congress was to convene, the Ministries of Education and Internal Affairs gave their permission to convene the meeting, but only on the condition that the congress be held somewhere other than Petersburg. There was simply no way teachers could relocate the meeting given the short notice, so the entire congress was canceled.[44]

After 1908, however, a congress "mania" seemed to affect educated Russians. Innumerable congresses and meetings were held on all sorts of serious and not so serious subjects between 1908 and 1914.[45] Despite the government purge of their ranks, teachers continued to organize meetings to discuss problems facing the educational system. There were meetings of the advanced primary schoolteachers and of classical language teachers, and congresses on women's education, zemstvo schools, experimental psychology, and family education, to name just a few.

As a result of all this organizational activity, the Petersburg Mutual-Aid Society resurrected its plans to organize a meeting of representatives of teachers' mutual-aid societies from all across Russia. Society members sent out questionnaires to other teachers' mutual-aid societies, asking them if they desired such a meeting. The Petersburg society received enough support that in October 1908 it requested permission from the Ministry of Internal Affairs to convene such a congress during the 1908–1909 Christmas vacation. In February 1909, two months after the congress was to meet, the ministry refused to grant its permission unless certain conditions were met— no Jews would be permitted to attend the meeting and the meeting would have to limit itself to only those teachers living in Petersburg. The Petersburg society refused to meet these requirements, but resubmitted its original request in June 1909. This time the society received no answer at all.[46]

Finally, in December 1911 the executive committee of the Petersburg Mutual-Aid Society received a request from the Moscow Society for the Improvement of Living Conditions and two other provincial mutual-aid societies to organize a second mutual-aid congress. This time, the Petersburg teachers had the moral and financial support of other teachers' organizations in both capital cities. They submitted a new request to the Ministry of Internal Affairs in January 1913 and received permission in October of the same year.[47] Just as the congress organizers received permission, the Moscow society requested they postpone the meeting because the First All-Russian Public Education Congress had been scheduled in Petersburg at the same time. Afraid of losing government permission for the mutual-aid congress, the Petersburg society refused to reschedule, a move that irritated some teachers.[48]

On 30 December 1913 two hundred and twenty-one delegates representing one hundred teachers' mutual-aid societies, met in the auditorium of the People's House in Petersburg to begin seven days of meetings on the state of the Russian teaching profession. The delegates dedicated their congress to the memory of K. D. Ushinskii for his work in promoting a national Russian school. After eleven years of frustration, representatives of teachers' professional organizations were finally allowed to meet again. Some teachers present had been at the 1903 Congress and remembered it well. Teachers like N. V. Chekhov, N. P. Rumiantseva, and I. L. Tsvetkov provided continuity between the two meetings. They were joined by new faces, and together all these teachers set about establishing the agenda for teachers' professional activity for years to come.[49]

In his opening speech to the congress, S. Zolotarev announced the meetings' purpose: "The congress will show not only at what level stand a few individual Russian teachers, but also how much a professional teachers' consciousness has risen among workers in primary and secondary schools."[50] To accomplish this goal, the congress divided its work into many different categories, a practice that bore a strong resemblance to the 1903 Congress. The program included sections on improvements in teachers' living conditions, teachers' participation in the organization and administration of the schools, teachers' material position, material and legal help for teachers, and the organization of teachers' mutual-aid societies.[51] The only new section was a group of reports dealing with teachers' activities outside the classroom.[52]

The 1914 Congress showed striking continuities with the pre-1905 teachers' movement. The delegates argued that all teachers needed better wages and living conditions. Teachers demanded representation on local school boards and greater participation in decisions concerning their hiring, firing, and transfer to another school. Teachers wanted the opportunity to improve their pedagogical training through better pedagogical courses, self-help programs, and travel. They believed that better educational opportunities for their children should be provided through scholarships and tuition assistance. Finally, teachers desired more professional organizations and greater unity among existing ones. To that end, the delegates proposed building an All-Russian Teachers' House modeled after the one in Moscow. This would give all teachers a professional home in Russia, regardless of where they lived and worked.[53]

All these issues clearly demonstrate teachers' continuing commitment to the values that shaped their sense of professionalism and their self-image. These delegates insisted that only those teachers who had received adequate pedagogical training should be allowed to teach, and even these teachers would have to commit themselves to a continuing program of self-education. More important, if the Ministry of Education was not willing to encourage better teacher training and refresher courses, then teachers would have to take the initiative and sponsor better pedagogical training themselves. Once teachers had acquired their technical expertise, they insisted, they should be given the respect other professionals received from society. The many discussions about improving teachers' legal and material position in Russian society underline their continuing search for professional recognition and dignity. All the values that had informed city teachers' professional quest from the beginning remained constant even after the divisive battles within the teachers' movement in 1905.

There were some important differences between the two mutual-aid congresses, and these differences also show how city teachers' commitment to their profession had strengthened in the interrevolutionary period. One key difference between 1903 and 1914 was the role of women teachers at the meetings. Women teachers were much more visible in 1914. The delegates elected Nadezhda Rumiantseva, the leader of Petersburg women teachers, as chairperson of the entire second section of the congress. Out of a total of 221 delegates, 52 women teachers served, representing mutual-aid societies from all over Russia.[54] At this meeting, unlike the 1903 Congress, delegates passed a resolution protesting marriage bans wherever they existed in Russia.[55] The leadership of the entire profession finally acknowledged a problem that only women teachers faced. At a time when more women than men were entering the teaching profession, however, this was only a first step on the part of the male leadership in acknowledging women's role in the profession.

Another important change was in the tone of the 1914 Congress. In 1903 the Ministry of Education considered teachers' professional views seditious. In 1914 teachers not only articulated these same opinions, but now spoke with greater authority and did not fear government reprisals. As Zolotarev observed, "The second congress categorically stated that a teacher must be free to select the best method of teaching . . . must never be persecuted for political and religious beliefs and for participation in organizations not mentioned in the criminal code. The legal section of the first congress dared not to speak in such language."[56] Delegates to the second congress spoke more boldly, and more important, the Ministry of Internal Affairs did not shut down the meeting prematurely. What had been radical in 1903 was no longer so in 1914. For its part, the tsarist government was willing at least to allow teachers to express their professional concerns. This interest in teachers' concerns, however, did not mean that the government had any intention of handing over any meaningful power to teachers, as the Moscow city teachers had already discovered in 1912.

When the congress delegates left Petersburg in January 1914, they had much work ahead of them. The delegates had agreed to begin work on several projects to unify the Russian teaching profession. In addition to organizing a third mutual-aid congress, the delegates began to work on a "Yearbook of Teachers' Societies" and to establish a central information office and an All-Russian Pedagogical Society.[57] Through these activities, the delegates hoped to unite all Russian teachers in a common sense of purpose and identity. As part of a unified profession teachers could then seek the transformation of the Russian school.

What is so striking about the Second Mutual-Aid Congress is the complete lack of discussion of those issues that had divided teachers in 1905. There were no reports devoted to the organizational issues of the teaching profession. There was no discussion of the hierarchical relationships within the profession. Despite the seriousness of the class and gender issues that continued to divide teachers, no one spoke about them. A unified profession remained the goal of the leaders of the profession, but how teachers were to achieve this unity remained elusive. Rather than redefining their goal and accepting the need for hierarchical relations, teachers naively asserted that they were all equal as teachers. More important, a professional hierarchy already existed but went unacknowledged. Most teacher-professionals agreed that certain educational reforms were necessary—local control of the schools, greater participation by teachers and parents in the life of the school, and better salaries and more job security for teachers. But beyond these concrete measures, professional unity evaporated.

The inability of the congress delegates to deal with these issues demonstrates the profound dilemma teachers faced. Teachers' professional values posited that social status should be granted to those who used their professional expertise and education for the benefit of society. An individual's position in the old social system was no longer a guarantee of privilege in the new civil society that teachers were trying to create. Instead, individual merit would determine social standing, and this merit was based on the acquisition of specialized skills and their application to public service. According to this system, any person could rise to the top of society through hard work and accomplishment. This professional ideal, however, masked the reality of life under such a system. Not all Russians had or would have access to the kind of educational institutions that trained professionals, or to jobs that would provide quick professional advancement. All that the professional society would do was replace one kind of hierarchical system—the autocratic—with another—the professional.

But many Russian teachers, and especially the most activist, did not want to create a professional system based on hierarchical relations. This strong egalitarian impulse had a profound impact on their professional consciousness. Teachers' professional ethic was tied up completely with the ideal of public service: they were first and foremost public servants. And, while other European professionals also saw themselves as public servants, this notion had a different meaning for Russian teachers. For Russian teachers public service was overlaid with the older intelligentsia ideal of the abnegation of self. This deference to the will of the people made it difficult for teachers to act in a consciously self-serving way, and made it difficult for them to advocate the introduction of hierarchical relations into the teaching profession. The new teaching profession was to be a place where all teachers could be free *and* equal, regardless of their position within the educational system or the type of training they received. And yet, this egalitarian notion contradicted the very professional ideal they were trying to achieve. Teachers' ideal of public service conflicted with the other values of individual initiative, self-worth, autonomy, and expertise. In order to really achieve the professional ideal they sought, teachers needed to sacrifice their image of themselves as public servants, and this was something they refused to do. They remained wedded to the image of themselves as servants of the people. In the end, their commitment to public service defined in this way meant that they were not members of a nascent middle class, but participants in a new social group that combined old and new social values, a professional intelligentsia.

Conclusion: Pedagogy, Professionalization, and Politics

A REMARKABLE ASPECT OF NINETEENTH-CENTURY RUSSIAN HISTORY is the extent to which government and society worked, sometimes together but more often separately, to create a new Russia. Even before the Crimean War debacle, government bureaucrats, writers, and members of the revolutionary intelligentsia discussed among themselves and with one another ways to reform Russia into a more modern nation.[1] Each group had its own social, economic, and political plans for the transformation of the Russian Empire. These competing visions left behind a complex historical legacy for scholars to unravel.

The government revealed its plans for a new Russia with the proclamation of the Great Reforms at midcentury. Beginning in 1861 with the emancipation of the serfs, the regime instituted a series of sweeping reforms intended to transform the judicial, educational, and economic systems. The purpose of these reforms was the creation of a reformed autocratic state—a state that could achieve great power status through a modern military, legal, industrial, and agricultural infrastructure. To support this infrastructure, the government set out to create a corps of better-educated, well-trained workers, industrialists, lawyers, engineers, doctors, and teachers. For if its plans were to succeed, the government needed the support and dedication of its subjects.

The only structure that remained essentially untouched by the Great Reforms was the autocracy itself. Alexander II and his ministers intended to create their new modern state within the existing political framework. Although institutions for local government were strengthened by the reform legislation, much of the "meat" of this legislation was removed during the counterreforms of the 1880s and 1890s. Power sharing between state and local officials was poorly defined and hotly contested in postreform Russia. In essence, the government sought the transformation of Russian economic life without any meaningful change in the political life of the country.

The revolutionary intelligentsia had a more radical and utopian vision of Russia.[2] Strongly influenced by Western European socialist thinkers, these men and women argued for the destruction of the old autocratic Russia through revolution. In its place, a new socialist state would emerge. Assisted by the intelligentsia, the lower classes would claim the economic, social, and political power they had long been denied. The utopians were divided among themselves as to which economic system should prevail in the new revolutionary Russia. Populists dreamed of the establishment of agrarian socialism, and Marxists envisioned a socialist state where industrial workers would lead the rest of the nation to communism. Despite these serious differences, the revolutionaries looked forward to freedom, justice, and equality for all Russians in the new socialist state.

Another competing vision of a new Russia emerged much later than the utopian vision of the revolutionary intelligentsia and, in some ways, as a response to it. This vision belonged to the emerging entrepreneurial elite in Russia, which grew up in the wake of the government's industrialization drive of the 1880s and 1890s.[3] These men, who began to articulate their views only during and after the 1905 Revolution, sang the praises of the business class and of a capitalist revolution. Their Russia would encourage sustained industrial development, the introduction of the market, democratic institutions, and the self-made man. Rather than viewing capitalist development as a necessary evil on the road to the proletarian revolution, as the Marxists had done, these entrepreneurs argued that capitalism could bring prosperity and security to Russia and make her a major world power.

Finally, there was the new Russia envisioned by the professionals. Much like their intelligentsia counterparts, they were imbued with a deep distaste for merchants and capitalism. At the same time, unlike the revolutionaries, they were not willing to make enormous personal sacrifices for the sake of the people. Instead, they tried to create another path, one that emphasized public service. Rather than faithfully serving the government by becoming state servants or bureaucrats, they wanted to make themselves public servants. They yearned to abolish the old autocratic system of social status and privilege and supplant it with one that rewarded education, expertise, and public service. Their goal was to replace the autocratic, revolutionary, and entrepreneurial ideals with a professional ideal. This professional ideal would democratize status and privilege to allow access to previously excluded groups and thereby make Russia a freer, more democratic nation.

CONCLUSION

The government's response to the other competing visions was negative, even though it had helped to foster the development of the entrepreneurial and professional classes in Russia. The government, in the words of one scholar, "tended to be chary, and at worst even hostile . . . to any social formation of potentially national scope outside its own direct sponsorship and control."[4] Rather than work with the newly emerging civil society, the government treated it with suspicion and mistrust. The central, guiding principle of the autocracy was its belief that it knew what was best for Russia and her subjects. Because it held this principle to be sacred, the government grew increasingly confrontational toward a civil society composed of entrepreneurs and professionals. Like a parent with a rebellious adolescent, the government insisted that it knew best for the child to whom it had given life, while the new civil society, in the role of the adolescent, was determined to make its own decisions. This book has been a case study of one aspect of this troubled relationship: the development of a professional movement among city teachers and the government's response to it.

City teachers' professionalization was a direct result of state intervention. The tsarist government's attempt to reform the educational system during the 1860s and 1870s had serious and far-reaching effects on teachers. In order to create better-educated subjects, the Ministry of Education expanded the number of schools and attempted to regularize classroom instruction. The success of this expansion of educational opportunity, however, depended on the simultaneous creation of a corps of well-trained teachers who could instruct their pupils according to the new educational program.

Government interest in more professional teachers led to a moderate reformation of teacher training programs. Instructors at the women's pedagogical courses and the teachers' institutes advised their students to teach according to the child-centered pedagogy developed in Europe in the first half of the nineteenth century. Child-centered pedagogy emphasized the importance of letting the child's interests guide the learning process. Teachers were training children to teach themselves by observation and study. Through this democratic learning process, children would become independent and self-sufficient thinkers. At the secondary level, teacher training did not place such an emphasis on pedagogy. Instead, students were trained as specialists in their chosen field of study. They were encouraged to become contributing members of their academic specialty, and through their work as specialists they could better teach the essentials of their field to their pupils. However unscientific or nontechnical this knowledge might appear, city teachers believed that it set them apart from other Russians concerned about the future of Russian education, and qualified them as experts.

City teachers' training was severely tested when these men and women entered the classroom. Despite all the emphasis in the schools on pedagogical training, they faced serious obstacles in fulfilling their professional objectives. Many primary schoolchildren came to school hungry, sick, and cold. Teachers constantly had to minister to their pupils' physical needs before they could begin to instruct them. Teachers in the secondary schools entered an oppressive atmosphere with great distrust felt on all sides—between students and teachers, teachers and parents, and teachers and administrators. In such an environment, which discouraged positive and intellectually stimulating interactions between teachers and students, teachers could not convey much beyond the basics of their discipline, and were supposed to avoid any subject that was seen as politically suspect.

In addition to these serious problems, school officials valued primary and secondary schoolteachers' submissiveness to the school authorities more than any other quality. Teachers were not treated as respected, trained experts, but as employees paid to do the bidding of school officials. It was this discrepancy between teachers' anticipation of their work experience and the reality of life in city classrooms that encouraged them to articulate their own professional values and attitudes. Teachers felt they were subjected to undue interference from petty officials in their professional and private lives. These officials had not achieved their position of authority through the acquisition of technical expertise, but through influence and wealth. More important, teachers had no legal means of appealing those officials' decisions. Teachers could be fired from their jobs arbitrarily without any chance to defend their names.

Teachers' experiences in the classroom heightened the conflict between the old autocratic system of service and the newer professional service ideal. The autocratic ideal for government employees posited loyal service to the will of the tsar. But city teachers argued that such loyal service frequently ran counter to their own pedagogical training. They believed they needed to be free to follow the dictates of their training to do what was best for Russia's schoolchildren. At the same time that teachers argued against the autocratic ideal, they were also attempting to redefine the intelligentsia's attitude of selfless service to the "people." City teachers did not want to live in abject poverty and forgo any sort of private life in order to serve the public good, as did many members of the intelligentsia. Instead, they wanted to perform their socially valuable service to the people, and to live in relative comfort with their families. They wanted both a private and a public life, as well as social recognition for their work. This redefinition of both autocratic and intelligentsia attitudes toward service made city teachers' professional ethos potentially threatening to Russian society. Given the government's hostility to city teachers' demands, it was clear it understood the nature of their challenge.

The government's ambivalent attitude toward teachers—encouraging some aspects of professional development but not others—gave the movement an increasingly antigovernment focus. One of the legacies of secondary and higher education in Russia was the antiauthoritarian attitude adopted by a large proportion of students. The student memoir literature is filled with references to how students tried to circumvent school rules by reading "forbidden" literature, gambling and drinking, and harassing fellow students and teachers. Students' behavior at the teacher training programs was no exception to this pattern. The worst situation was found in the teachers' institutes, but even at the women's pedagogical courses, where strict discipline was the rule, rebellious students attempted to break free of the harsh regime. If the graduates of these programs hoped to escape this oppressive atmosphere by becoming teachers, they found instead a host of authorities who attempted to monitor every aspect of a teacher's public and private life. This concern for moral and political rectitude among teachers forced many to leave the profession and others to demand legal measures to protect themselves from overzealous school officials. These experiences of excessive surveillance and strict discipline imposed by governmental authority in teacher training programs and in the schools contributed to teachers' desire to have their own professional, and therefore nongovernment, organizations to protect them against such abuses.

If city teachers thought they understood the obstacles to their professional development, they assumed a unanimity of opinion that did not exist. In asserting the commonality of teachers' experiences and identity, they underestimated the forces that divided them. The teaching profession was a diverse occupation that included teachers from the isolated hamlets that dotted the Russian countryside as well as teachers at the most elite educational institutions in the country. Government recruitment of teachers created several distinct groups within the profession. Secondary schoolteachers were drawn from the middle and upper ranks of urban Russia. City women, also from the upper and middle ranks, and peasant men were recruited for the primary schools. These class and gender distinctions among teachers caused some key fissures to develop within the profession—between secondary and primary schoolteachers, between urban and rural teachers, and between men and women.

The problems women faced in gaining acceptance in the profession illustrate well the serious class and gender issues that divided teachers. Influenced by Western European social and educational thinkers, Russian educators in the mid-nineteenth century began to define teaching as "women's work." Women were the "natural" educators in the home, and as such they represented an untouched supply of teachers for the primary schools. When the government granted women permission to teach in the primary grades in 1871, they quickly flocked to the profession. Men teachers' response to this change in policy was to try to limit women's access to the profession by developing a number of discursive strategies. First, educators determined that though women might be "natural" teachers, their natural talent would have to be regularized and checked by scientific principles through pedagogical training. Women's "natural" abilities threatened the professional ideal teachers were trying to establish. In addition, women could teach only in the primary grades because they allegedly could not handle the more difficult and technical subjects taught in the higher grades. Women could teach the three R's and "morals" but not science. The second discursive strategy was developed by peasant men teachers whose jobs were directly affected by the rising numbers of women teachers, and by government officials who wanted to maintain their position in the educational hierarchy. They argued that women were "outsiders" to the village and therefore did not make effective teachers of peasant children. Because most women teachers were city women, they could not relate to peasant children or their parents. Only peasant men teachers could work in village schools, because only they truly understood the traditional way of life. In this way, women teachers remained outsiders to the profession for which they had trained themselves because of their gender *and* their class.

Finally, although some women thought they could overcome their outsider status, most school officials dismissed women from their jobs upon marriage, arguing that women's family obligations prevented them from devoting themselves to their work. These marriage bans continued women teachers' status as outsiders by making it difficult for them to have a normal private life and practice their profession at the same time. They could teach or they could marry—they could not do both. As these arguments make clear, professionalization was seen in gendered terms, creating different expectations and career paths for men and women.

Women teachers responded to these discursive strategies by creating their own images of the woman schoolteacher. The first generation of women teachers tried to imbue their status as outsiders with more positive connotations. They did so by calling upon traditional ideas not just of Russian women in general but specifically of Russian holy women and *intelligentki*. Both these groups rejected their families and their values to live a solitary life serving others. Women teachers identified themselves with this older tradition of female self-sacrifice and tried to redefine it in terms of public service. According to this view, women teachers were not saintly women or radicals trying to overthrow the state, but public servants trying to bring literacy and enlightenment to the lower classes.

However important this image of women as saintly public servants was to them, it did not advance women teachers' position within the profession. They still remained outsiders because of their inability to have a long, professional career like their male colleagues. In order to overcome this problem, women teachers in Petersburg began a campaign to overturn a marriage ban that had been enacted in 1897. To further their effort, they created a new image of the woman schoolteacher—the professional. They portrayed themselves as highly trained professionals who were suffering from gross interference in their private lives. No longer willing to sacrifice their private lives for their work as did the previous generation of women teachers, they demanded full civil and professional rights, the same rights as their male colleagues.

Women teachers' demands for equal treatment reveal the inherent contradiction in the teachers' movement as it developed in Russia. The declared aim of the movement was the reformation of the school and the creation of a profession that united all teachers under one national organization. To accomplish this, the teachers' movement increasingly became both a professional and a political movement. The government's unwillingness to grant even moderate measures of professional autonomy forced teachers into the political Liberation movement that was taking shape in the late 1890s and 1900s. But this fusing of professional and political movements created problems. Teachers desired unity and cooperation so that they could break out of their isolation in the school system. Strongly influenced by the moderate democratic socialist ideals many of them held dear, they distrusted hierarchial relations, which they saw as the source of their misery, and claimed to believe in the full equality of all members of the profession. But in fact, teachers were not all treated as equal members of the profession, as the Petersburg women teachers' situation made clear. Indeed, the professional ideal that teachers advocated was not that of full civil and political equality, but of the opening of status and privilege to new groups that had been previously excluded. Thus, teachers' professional goal contradicted their political objective because changing the criteria for acquiring status did not mean that hierarchial relations had disappeared, but simply that they had been restructured. This dilemma put teachers in a difficult position—how to resolve the inherent contradiction in their goals? Rather than arguing that hierarchical relations were a necessary part of professional development, teachers chose to ignore this fundamental issue and continued to call for professional unity and political reform. The Petersburg women teachers' challenge to the concept of professional unity was shoved aside. It remained a "woman's" problem and as such did not concern the men of the profession. They viewed it merely as an example of the oppression they all faced as teachers.

This internal contradiction within the profession could not remain suppressed indefinitely. It exploded with full force in the "professional and political" debates that embroiled the newly created teachers' union (VSU) during the spring of 1905. In April and in June representatives of the various teachers' organizations gathered together to form a national union that would serve as *the* professional organization for all Russia's teachers. Although there was complete agreement on the need for a radical transformation of the Russian school and teachers' role within it, rancorous debate broke out among the teachers concerning the nature of the new union: should the union remain a strictly professional organization or should it adopt a political platform as well? In the ensuing debate, the fissures within the teachers' movement emerged sharply. Rural teachers endorsed the professional-political platform while city teachers remained opposed. In the end, the rural teachers' views held sway and city teachers withdrew from the union completely.

The central issue in the political debate in the VSU was: which political party best represented teachers' interests? These debates involved the Social Democrats and Social Revolutionaries; they have been discussed in the historical literature.[5] What has been less well analyzed is the deeper problem that underlay these discussions. The conflicts among teachers centered on two important issues. First, the serious social inequalities of postreform Russia prevented teachers from seeing one another as equals. Primary schoolteachers disliked the secondary teachers, calling them "teacher-bureaucrats." Secondary schoolteachers looked down on teachers in the lower grades. Women teachers were viewed as outsiders. Eventually, secondary schoolteachers completely disassociated themselves from the rest of the profession by forming their own union. As one teacher commented, the division of the profession into castes proved impossible to overcome.[6] Second, at the same time that these existing social inequalities made relations within the profession difficult, the democratic impulse of many teachers conflicted with the professional ideal of others. The hidden agenda in the union's political debate was: who would control power and authority in the new union? City teachers assumed that they, as the best educated and most professional of teachers, would control the platform and actions of the VSU. This is what professionalization meant to many of them—the advancement of individuals with education and expertise into positions of power. Rural teachers, on the other hand, were more concerned about full equality of all teachers within the profession. Many rural teachers had just joined the teachers' movement in 1904–1905 and did not want to lose power to their social superiors, city teachers.

The inability of the teachers' movement to resolve the dilemma between professionalism and equality prevented teachers from achieving any of their goals—political or professional. City teachers left the VSU and tried to achieve their professional program through local teachers' unions, but they were not strong enough to support teachers when state and local governments reasserted their authority in the fall and winter months of 1905–1906. Virtually all teachers' organizations suffered defeat in the last months of the 1905 Revolution.

Ironically, the only group of teachers who were able to achieve any of their demands were the Petersburg women schoolteachers in their campaign to repeal the marriage ban. The first vote for repeal in 1906 ended in defeat by one vote. Gaining strength from their near victory, the women teachers continued their struggle. This time they sought and received support from the various feminist organizations in the capital, and emphasized the discriminatory nature of the ban: the "vestal virgins" were discriminated against as women and as teachers. They insisted that they were being denied their civil rights, and in 1913 the ban was repealed.

What is remarkable about the Petersburg women teachers' successful campaign to repeal the marriage ban is that it is the only example from those years of city teachers' political actions being motivated by clear self-interest. The Russian government tried to select politically passive individuals to serve in the schools, and many city teachers continued their passive role throughout the 1905 Revolution, if for no other reason than that they were afraid of losing their jobs. Other teachers refused to support any political party, believing firmly in the autocracy's political mandate to rule Russia. But even among the most politically active of city teachers, many were affiliated with the Social Democrats. Just as rural teachers supported the Social Revolutionary party and its agrarian socialist program, city teachers sympathized with the more urban, socialist vision of the Social Democrats. Thus, each group of teachers supported the political party that claimed to represent the interests of the class they served. To date, there is very little evidence that city teachers were supporters of the Union of Liberation; this is surprising given the party's emphasis on political and civil rights, which were essential if teachers were to achieve their professional goals. Instead, city teachers couched their political statements in language borrowed from and expressing sympathy with the lower classes. City and rural teachers alike, at several key moments in the revolution, failed to articulate clearly their political self-interest.

The lessons that city teachers learned from the 1905 Revolution had far-reaching consequences. Rather than learn from the example of the women teachers whose political activism finally helped them achieve their professional goal, the leaders of the teachers' movement concluded that teachers should not become involved in any kind of political activity. Politics had divided the movement in 1905, and this emphasis on the differences among teachers was antithetical to the whole tenor of the movement. They rejected explicit political involvement in favor of a total commitment to professional public service. Their rejection of political activism stemmed in part from the government's continued persecution of teachers who became active in Russian political life. But at the same time, city teachers' reluctance to embrace political activity as a legitimate means of accomplishing their professional goals came from within the movement itself. In early 1914 the leaders of the teachers' movement reaffirmed their commitment to establishing a unified profession among *all* teachers.

In recent years a number of scholars have attempted to analyze the middle groups in Russian society. Studies of merchants, professors, physicians, artists, and writers have examined the nature of their social identity.[7] Who were these people? What were their self-perceptions? Did they constitute a middle class? One scholar has concluded: "But if we look beyond conscious political choices toward more nuanced and complex phenomenons—new ideas of space and time, new attitudes toward the role of law and the possibilities of purposeful individual action, the acceptance of new ways of conceptualizing the place of the individual and society—then we can see that a new public culture was indeed developing in Late Imperial Russia."[8] According to this view, all of the middling groups that were a part of the civil society created by the Great Reforms participated in the development in Russia of a "public sphere," a space between state and society to mediate issues of concern to both.[9]

The idea of a public sphere was so new in nineteenth-century Russia that it was very fluid. With so many groups trying to define and shape it, it was never the same public sphere for very long. Teachers were a key group in its development. Their attempts to redefine state service as public service helped to expand the boundaries of civic activity in Russia. Education was no longer the preserve of government bureaucrats and the nobility, but belonged to local governmental bodies, parents, and teachers. But teachers' involvement in the public sphere extended beyond their own involvement in public education: teachers attempted to transmit the values and skills necessary to participate in this new public culture through their work. By teaching literacy to lower-class children and attempting to make them independent thinkers, teachers were helping to expand the public sphere to previously excluded groups. Thus, teachers' public service contributed greatly to the expansion and persistence of a public culture in postreform Russia.

The creation of a public sphere did not mean that these middling groups were developing a middle-class identity—pursuing their own economic and political self-interest. They may have been in the middle, between the tsar and the people, but they were not middle class because they did not act as a class, for themselves. Teachers' reluctance to articulate their own political agenda and their reliance on the political slogans of the lower classes suggest that their professional consciousness did not lead to the development of a middle-class consciousness or class identity. The evolution of teachers' professional values—autonomy, initiative, and self-worth—took place within the context of the older tradition of the intelligentsia's service ethic from which they were unable or unwilling to separate themselves. Most people find it difficult to reject old values and attitudes completely but continually redefine them according to new circumstances. The expansion of educational opportunity in the second half of the nineteenth century encouraged teachers to create a new kind of intelligentsia, a professional intelligentsia that pursued public service with greater freedom and autonomy for the individual in the workplace, but eschewed self-interested political activity. In doing this, teachers resembled Russian physicians, who also developed a strong public service ethic while at the same time demanding greater freedom for the individual within the context of that service.[10] Kendall Bailes makes the same argument about engineers in the Soviet period.[11] This strongly suggests that the public service ethic survived the 1917 Revolution, despite the enormous political, economic, and social changes that had occurred.

The development of a professional intelligentsia rather than a professional middle class has serious implications for Russian history. The revolutionary intelligentsia's desire for self-abnegation casts a long shadow over the professions. In the political sphere, teachers as well as other professionals who shared their service ethic were unwilling to pursue rational self-interest to become members of those moderate, liberal parties essential for the development of liberal democracies. They remained first and foremost public *servants*. And while certainly not all teachers believed in such a complete abnegation of the self, many did. This lack of unity prevented teachers from organizing any meaningful collective action in support of their own political interests.

Teachers' devotion to "the people" was so strong that it became the most fundamental part of their professional identity. They believed that greater freedom and autonomy were necessary for professionals, not to further their own interests but to serve the interests of others. As we have seen, both men and women teachers developed self-images that emphasized the service ethic. As Seregny has pointed out, rural teachers saw themselves as representatives of the peasantry, particularly to other authorities.[12] Women teachers combined populist and religious ideals with the traditional female notion of self-sacrifice to create an image of themselves as public servants. Those teachers, such as the Petersburg women teachers, who tried to develop a more self-interested approach to their profession did not succeed in universalizing their professional ideal.

The development of a Russian professional intelligentsia should serve as an important corrective to the Anglo-American model of professionalization. As the case of Russian city teachers demonstrates, professional development is not necessarily synonymous with middle-class development. Professional values are shaped primarily by the social groups that form the bulk of the members of a particular profession. In imperial Russia, men and women from the nobility, clergy, and bureaucracy became city teachers. Their desire to perform meaningful public service grew out of a long tradition of government service, which those classes had provided for centuries. In the nineteenth century the radical intelligentsia argued that such government service was morally corrupt, for it enslaved the masses, who in turn worked for the elites. According to the intelligentsia, those who wished to serve were no longer to serve the government but rather "the people." Many of those who entered the professions in the second half of the nineteenth century redefined the intelligentsia call for service to the people. Although few had the desire to become revolutionaries, their valuable public services should not be discredited or seen as morally corrupt because they worked as public servants. These new professionals argued that one could serve the people and still have a rich professional and private life. But because they still saw themselves as part of the intelligentsia, many professionals did not develop an independent class-based political outlook—they identified their political interests with those of the lower classes. In the end, this professional intelligentsia proved to be neither a profession in the Western sense of the word, nor an intelligentsia according to the older Russian tradition, but rather a new social group based on meaningful professional and private lives dedicated to public service.

Appendix
Notes
Bibliography
Index

Appendix

TABLE 1 Number of City Education Professionals by Gender, Level, and Subject

	Petersburg				Moscow			
	1891		1907		1895		1905	
Type of Professional	N	%	N	%	N	%	N	%
Primary teachers								
Male religion	94	23.9	177	19.3	70	14.1	169	13.4
Arts and trades (male and female)	33	8.4	98	10.7	106	21.4	245	19.4
Male classroom	25	6.3	11	1.2	320	64.5	106	8.4
Female classroom	242	61.4	629	68.7			741	58.8
Total	394		915		496		1,261	

	Boys' Gymnasium 1905		Girls' Gymnasium 1905		Boys' Gymnasium 1905		Girls' Gymnasium 1905	
	N	%	N	%	N	%	N	%
Secondary								
Administrators	43	6.4	34	5.2	26	5.2	73	8.6
Teachers								
Religion	87	12.9	51	7.7	29	5.8	74	8.7
Science and language	510	75.9	368	55.8	338	67.9	488	57.5
Art	16	2.4	100	15.2	17	3.4	130	15.3
Other	16	2.4	107	16.2	88	17.7	83	9.8
Total	672		660		498		848	

SOURCES: For primary teachers in Petersburg: Komissiia po narodnomu obrazovaniiu, S-Peterburgskie gorodskie nachal'nye uchilishcha [hereafter SGNU] v 1891 godu (St. Petersburg, 1892), 10; SGNU v 1906 godu, 93. For primary teachers in Moscow: N. M. Bychkov, Deiatel'nost' Moskovskogo gorodskogo obshchestvennogo upravleniia po narodnomu obrazovaniiu (Moscow, 1896), 18; Otchet za 1905/06 uchebnyi god, 96. For secondary education professionals in Petersburg and Moscow: TsGIA, f. 733, op. 204, d. 305, ll. 43–48, d. 451, ll. 8–9, d. 455, ll. 37–40, and d. 306, l. 42.

APPENDIX

TABLE 2 Social Order of City Teachers

	Primary School, 1895							
	Petersburg				Moscow			
	Male		Female		Male		Female	
Child of	N	%	N	%	N	%	N	%
Nobles	23	24.5	89	56.0	8	16.3	159	55.4
Clergy	38	40.4	24	15.1	22	44.9	42	14.6
Merchants and honored citizens	7	7.4	20	12.6	16	32.7	82	28.6
Meshchane and artisans	7	7.4	22	13.8				
Peasants	15	16.0	1	0.6	3	6.1	4	1.4
Other	4	4.3	3	1.9	—	—	—	—

| | Secondary School, Petersburg and Moscow ||||
| | 1840–89 || 1890–1918 ||
Son of	N	%	N	%
Nobles	11	14.7	15	18.3
Bureaucrats	4	5.3	10	12.2
Clergy	12	16.0	13	15.9
Honored citizens	3	4.0	1	1.2
Merchants	6	8.0	4	4.9
Meshchane	12	16.0	10	12.2
Artisans	—	—	2	2.4
Peasants	—	—	5	6.1
Foreigners	11	14.7	10	12.2
Soldiers	11	14.7	7	8.5
Other	5	6.7	5	6.1

SOURCES: For primary schoolteachers in Petersburg: TsGIA f. 91, op. 3, d. 792; in Moscow, Bychkov, *Deiatel'nost'*, 21. For secondary schoolteachers: TsGIA, f. 733, op. 225, d. 1–340.

TABLE 3 Age of City Primary Schoolteachers

	1895				1911			
	Male		Female		Male		Female	
	N	%	N	%	N	%	N	%
Petersburg								
Under 20 years	—	—	11	5.8	—	—	1	0.1
21–25	14	15.9	47	24.6	—	—	159	19.2
26–30	16	18.2	51	26.7	2	18.2	239	28.8
31–40	31	35.2	54	28.3	—	—	173	20.8
41 and over	27	30.7	28	14.7	9	81.8	258	31.1
Moscow								
Under 20 years	—	—	10	3.5	3	1.0	87	5.1
21–25	4	8.2	59	20.6	44	14.3	389	22.6
26–30	3	6.1	63	22.0	62	20.1	363	21.1
31–40	25	51.0	108	37.6	111	36.0	504	29.3
41 and over	17	34.7	47	16.4	88	28.6	379	22.0

SOURCES: Petersburg figures, TsGIA, f. 91, op. 3, d. 792; *Odnodnevnaia perepis' nachal'nykh shkol v imperii proizvedennaia 18 ianvaria 1911 g.* (St. Petersburg, 1913), 52–53. Moscow figures, Bychov, *Deiatel'nost'*, 21; *Odnodnevnaia perepis'*, 98.

APPENDIX

TABLE 4 Length of Service of Primary Schoolteachers

| | 1892 |||| 1906 ||||
| | Male || Female || Male || Female ||
Petersburg	N	%	N	%	N	%	N	%
25 or more years	—	—	—	—	9	81.8	38	6.0
21–24	—	—	—	—	2	18.2	75	11.9
16–20	—	—	—	—	—	—	64	10.1
11–15	19	73.1	3	1.5	—	—	72	11.4
6–10	6	23.1	129	64.2	—	—	112	17.7
1–5	1	3.8	69	34.3	—	—	271	42.9

| | Male || Female ||
Moscow	N	%	N	%
25 or more years	10	10.3	23	3.1
21–24	9	9.3	52	7.0
16–20	12	12.4	58	7.8
11–15	5	5.2	51	6.9
6–10	16	16.5	185	25.0
1–5	45	46.4	372	50.2

SOURCES: Petersburg figures: *SGNU v 1892 godu*, 98; *SGNU v 1906 godu*, 96, 102. Moscow figures: *Otchet za 1905/06 uchebnyi god*, 97–98.

TABLE 5 Marital Status of Primary Schoolteachers

	Petersburg								Moscow			
	1892				1911				1911			
	Male		Female		Male		Female		Male		Female	
	N	%	N	%	N	%	N	%	N	%	N	%
Unmarried	9	34.6	185	72.5	1	9.1	738	88.9	29	22.0	894	73.4
Married	16	61.5	60	23.5	10	90.9	55	6.6	99	75.0	267	21.9
Widowed	1	3.8	10	3.9	—	—	37	4.5	4	3.0	56	4.6

SOURCES: Petersburg figures, *SGNU v 1892 godu*, 97; *Odnodnevnaia perepis'*, 52–53. Moscow figures, Bychkov, *Deiatel'nost'*, 21; *Odnodnevnaia perepis'*, 98.

APPENDIX

TABLE 6 Marital Status and Number of Children of Secondary Schoolteachers in Petersburg and Moscow

	1840–1889 N	1840–1889 %	1890–1918 N	1890–1918 %
Married	56	76.7	57	67.9
Unmarried	10	13.7	20	23.8
Widowed	7	9.6	7	8.3
Number of children				
1	7	14.3	7	14.6
2	9	18.4	22	45.8
3	15	30.6	2	4.2
4	5	10.2	6	12.5
5	2	4.1	5	10.4
6 or more	11	22.4	6	12.5

SOURCE: TsGIA, f. 733, op. 225, d. 1–340.

TABLE 7 Education of City Teachers

	Petersburg 1891 N	Petersburg 1891 %	Petersburg 1907 N	Petersburg 1907 %	Moscow 1895 N	Moscow 1895 %	Moscow 1905 N	Moscow 1905 %
Male primary teachers								
Pedagogical courses and teachers' seminaries	23	92.0	10	90.9	15	30.6	67	66.3
Clerical seminaries	—	—	—	—	21	42.9	23	22.8
Secondary education	1	4.0	—	—	—	—	2	2.0
Universities	—	—	—	—	—	—	2	2.0
Other	1	4.0	1	9.1	13	26.5	7	6.9
Female teachers								
Pedagogical courses	133	54.5	380	60.1	201	70.0	425	56.9
Teachers' seminaries	71	29.1	144	22.8	20	7.0	52	6.9
Women's higher courses	34	13.9	101	16.0	—	—	7	0.9
Secondary education	6	2.5	7	1.1	—	—	10	1.3
Other	—	—	—	—	66	23.0	258	34.3

SOURCES: Petersburg figures: *SGNU v 1891 godu*, 10 and 81; *SGNU v 1906 godu*, 96, 102. Moscow figures: Bychkov, *Deiatel'nost'*, 21–22; *Otchet za 1905/06 uchebnyi god*, 97.

APPENDIX

TABLE 8 Social Order of Students by *Soslovie*

	St. Petersburg Teachers' Institute				Moscow Teachers' Institute			
	1895		1905		1898		1905	
Son of	N	%	N	%	N	%	N	%
Nobles and bureaucrats	6	9.2	7	8.9	10	15.6	6	7.2
Clergy	2	3.1	2	2.5	1	1.6	3	3.6
City orders	27	41.5	16	20.3	24	37.5	30	36.2
Rural orders	30	46.2	54	68.3	27	42.2	41	49.4
Other	—		—		2	3.1	3	3.6
Total	65		79		64		83	

SOURCES: Petersburg figures, TsGIA, f. 733, op. 203, d. 462, l. 1 and op. 204, d. 501, ll. 21–22. Moscow figures, TsGIA, f. 733, op. 203, d. 867, l. 3 and op. 204, d. 503, ll. 27–28.

TABLE 9 Class Hours of Instruction per Week at the Teachers' Institutes

Subject	Grade 1	Grade 2	Grade 3
Religion	2	2	2
Russian and Old Church Slavonic	6	6	3
Arithmetic	5	5	2
Geometry	2	2	2
History	3	3	1
Geography	2	2	1
Natural sciences	4	3	1
Drawing and penmanship	6	2	2
Pedagogy and didactics	2	2	1
Singing	2*	2*	2*
Gymnastics	1*	1*	1*

SOURCE: TsGIA, f. 733, op. 174, d. 28, l. 34.
*After class.

APPENDIX

TABLE 10 Students' Schedule at the Moscow Teachers' Institute

7:45 A.M.	Reveille
8:00 A.M.	Prayers and morning tea
8:45–11:50 A.M.	Three classes
11:50 A.M.	Lunch
12:30–2:30 P.M.	Two classes
2:30–4:30 P.M.	Manual trades, gymnastics, singing
4:30 P.M.	Dinner
8:00 P.M.	Evening tea and study
10:00 P.M.	Evening prayers*

SOURCE: TsGIA, f. 733, op. 204, d. 65, ll. 31–36.
*After evening prayers, a student could go to bed or study until 11:00 P.M.

Notes

Introduction

1. W. Bruce Lincoln, *The Great Reforms: Autocracy, Bureaucracy, and the Politics of Change in Imperial Russia* (DeKalb: Northern Illinois University Press, 1990).

2. For the most recent statement concerning the complexity of Russian workers' identities, see Reginald E. Zelnik, "Introduction: Kanatchikov's *Story of My Life* as Document and Literature," in *A Radical Worker in Tsarist Russia: The Autobiography of Semen Ivanovich Kanatchikov*, ed. and trans. Reginald E. Zelnik (Stanford: Stanford University Press, 1986), xv–xxx.

3. The literature on the Russian professions is small but growing: Nancy Mandelker Frieden, *Russian Physicians in an Era of Reform and Revolution, 1856–1905* (Princeton: Princeton University Press, 1981); Samuel D. Kassow, *Students, Professors and the State in Tsarist Russia* (Berkeley and Los Angeles: University of California Press, 1989); Scott J. Seregny, *Russian Teachers and Peasant Revolution: The Politics of Education in 1905* (Bloomington: Indiana University Press, 1989); Richard Wortman, *The Development of a Russian Legal Consciousness* (Chicago: University of Chicago Press, 1976); William C. Fuller, Jr., *Civil-Military Conflict in Imperial Russia* (Princeton: Princeton University Press, 1985); Robert Johnson, "Liberal Professionals and Professional Liberals: The Zemstvo Statisticians and Their Work," in *The Zemstvo in Russia: An Experiment in Local Self-Government* (Cambridge: Cambridge University Press, 1982), 343–64; Harley Balzer, "Educating Engineers: Economic Politics and Technical Training in Tsarist Russia" Ph.D. diss., University of Pennsylvania, 1980; idem., *Professions in Russia at the End of the Old Regime* (Ithaca: Cornell University Press, forthcoming); Julie V. Brown, "Revolution and Psychosis: The Mixing of Science and Politics in Russian Psychiatric Medicine, 1905–1913," *Russian Review* 46 (July 1987): 283–302; Jonathan Sanders, "Drugs and Revolution: Moscow Pharmacists in the First Russian Revolution," *Russian Review* 44 (1985): 351–77; and idem., "The Union of Unions: Political, Economic, Civil and Human Rights Organizations in the 1905 Russian Revolution," Ph.D. diss., Columbia University, 1985.

4. Frieden, *Russian Physicians;* Wortman, *The Development of a Russian Legal Consciousness.*

5. Talcott Parsons, "Professions," in *International Encyclopedia of the Social Sciences*, ed. David L. Sills (New York, 1968), 12: 545.

6. Ibid., 536–47.

7. Magali Sarfatti Larson, *The Rise of Professionalism: A Sociological Analysis* (Berkeley and Los Angeles: University of California Press, 1977), 14–15.

8. Ibid., xvii–xviii; Parsons, "Professions," 542.

9. Gerald L. Geison, Introduction to *Professions and the French State, 1700–1900* (Philadelphia: University of Pennsylvania Press, 1984), 4.

10. Harold Perkin, *The Rise of Professional Society: England Since 1880* (London: Routledge, 1989), 2.

11. Ibid., 10.

12. Joan Jacobs Brumberg and Nancy Tomes, "Women in the Professions: A Research Agenda for American Historians," *Reviews in American History* (June 1982): 275.

13. The classic statement of women's professions as underdeveloped professions can be found in *The Semi-Professions and their Organization: Teachers, Nurses and Social Workers*, ed. Amitai Etzioni (New York: Free Press, 1969).

14. Brumberg and Tomes, "Women in the Professions," 275.

15. For a discussion of the problems inherent in Russian social development, see Gregory L. Freeze, "The *Soslovie* (Estate) Paradigm and Russian Social History," *American Historical Review* 96 (1986): 11–36.

16. For a discussion of the Russian merchantry, see Thomas C. Owen, *Capitalism and Politics in Russia: A Social History of the Moscow Merchants, 1855–1905* (New York: Cambridge University Press, 1981); Alfred J. Rieber, *Merchants and Entrepreneurs in Imperial Russia* (Chapel Hill: University of North Carolina Press, 1982); and JoAnn Ruckman, *The Moscow Business Elite: A Social and Cultural Portrait of Two Generations, 1840–1905* (DeKalb: Northern Illinois University Press, 1984).

17. Samuel D. Kassow, "Russia's Unrealized Civil Society," in *Between Tsar and People: Educated Society and the Quest for Public Identity in Late Imperial Russia*, ed. Edith W. Clowes, Samuel D. Kassow, and James L. West (Princeton: Princeton University Press, 1991), 367.

18. See esp. Frieden, *Russian Physicians*; Seregny, *Russian Teachers*; and Harley Balzer, "The Problem of Professions in Imperial Russia," in Clowes, Kassow, and West, eds., *Between Tsar and People*, 183–98.

19. For a fuller discussion of the problem of the bourgeoisie in Russia, see the essays in Clowes, Kassow, and West, eds., *Between Tsar and People*.

20. My effort to reinterpret Russian professionalization is indebted to the work of Stuart M. Blumin and David Blackbourn and Geoff Eley. These historians have attempted to reexamine middle-class development in the United States and Germany by emphasizing features of middle-class life that

historians have previously overlooked. Blumin argues that the "convergence of relevant experience" is the best way of analyzing the emergence of a middle class in the United States. And while I am not suggesting that Russian professionals were part of a new middle class, the idea of a "shared social and cultural experience" goes to the heart of their professional development. See David Blackbourn and Geoff Eley, *The Peculiarities of German History: Bourgeois Society and Politics in Nineteenth-Century Germany* (New York: Oxford University Press, 1984); and Stuart M. Blumin, *The Emergence of the Middle Class: Social Experience in the American City, 1760–1900* (Cambridge: Cambridge University Press, 1989), esp. 10–11.

21. For a fuller discussion, see Philip Pomper, *The Russian Revolutionary Intelligentsia* (Arlington Heights: AHM Publishing Co., 1970).

22. Frieden, *Russian Physicians*, 14.

23. Ben Eklof, *Russian Peasant Schools: Officialdom, Village Culture, and Popular Pedagogy, 1861–1914* (Berkeley and Los Angeles: University of California Press, 1986); Jeffrey Brooks, *When Russsia Learned to Read* (Princeton: Princeton University Press, 1985).

24. The literature on Russian education is enormous. For an introduction to the debates, see Patrick L. Alston, *Education and the State in Tsarist Russia* (Stanford: Stanford University Press, 1969); Kassow, *Students, Professors and the State;* James C. McClelland, *Autocrats and Academics: Education, Culture and Society in Tsarist Russia* (Chicago: University of Chicago Press, 1979); Charles Timberlake, "Higher Learning, the State and the Professions in Russia," in *The Transformation of Higher Learning, 1860–1930,* ed. Konrad H. Jarausch (Chicago: University of Chicago Press, 1983), 321–44; Allen Sinel, *The Classroom and the Chancellery: State Educational Reform in Russia under Count Dmitrii Tolstoi* (Cambridge: Harvard University Press, 1973); and S. V. Rozhdestvenskii, *Istoricheskii obzor deiatel'nosti Ministerstva narodnogo prosveshcheniia 1802–1902* (St. Petersburg, 1902).

25. Balzer, "Educating Engineers," 115–202; Alston, *Education and the State.*

26. For the social profile of Moscow and Petersburg teachers, see Appendix, table 2.

27. Eklof, *Russian Peasant Schools*, 186–94; Seregny, *Russian Teachers*, 12–18.

28. The 1897 figures can be found in L. K. Erman, "Sostav intelligentsii v Rossii v kontse XIX i nachale XX v.," *Istoriia SSSR* 1 (1963): 168. The Moscow figures are found in Joseph Bradley, *Muzhik and Muscovite: Urbanization in Late Imperial Russia* (Berkeley and Los Angeles: University of California Press, 1985), appendix A. The statistics comparing teachers in Russia's major cities can be found in N. K., "Nachal'noe obrazovanie v bol'shikh russkikh gorodakh," *Vestnik vospitaniia* 6 (1899): 165. For further information on Moscow and Petersburg teachers, see Appendix, table 1.

29. N. K., "Nachal'noe obrazovanie," 144–82.

30. For the sake of greater readability, I will use the terms "city teachers" and "teachers in Moscow and Petersburg" interchangeably. At all times, however, my discussion will concern itself with Moscow and Petersburg teachers alone.

31. For a fuller discussion, see Christine Ruane Hinshaw, "The Soul of the School: The Professionalization of Urban Schoolteachers in St. Petersburg and Moscow, 1890–1907," Ph.D. diss., University of California, Berkeley, 1986, chaps. 1 and 3.

32. N. K., "Nachal'noe obrazovanie," 146.

33. For a fuller discussion of the organization of Moscow and Petersburg schools, see *Dvadtsatipiatiletie nachal'nykh uchilishch goroda S.-Peterburga, 1877–1902* (St. Petersburg, 1902); N. Malinovskii, "Chto sdelano za sorok let moskovskim gorodskim upravleniem po narodnomu obrazovaniiu," *Russkaia mysl'* 4 (April 1904): 40–67 and 12 (December 1904): 1–38; M. Shchepkin, "Upravlenie gorodskimi uchilishchami v Moskve: Istoricheskii ocherk," *Russkaia mysl'* 26 (March 1905): 231–56.

34. For a brief history of what happened to teachers after the 1917 Revolution, see Sheila Fitzpatrick, *The Commissariat of Enlightenment: Soviet Organization of Education and the Arts under Lunacharsky, October 1917–1921* (Cambridge: Cambridge University Press, 1970), 34–43. For examples of Soviet writing on teachers, see V. R. Leikina-Svirskaia, *Intelligentsia v Rossii vo vtoroi polovine XIX veka* (Moscow: Mysl', 1971); idem., *Russkaia intelligentsiia v 1900–1917 godakh* (Moscow: Mysl', 1981); F. G. Panachin, *Uchitel'stvo i revoliutsionnoe dvizhenie v Rossii (XIX–nachalo XX v.) Istoriko-pedagogicheskie ocherki* (Moscow: Pedagogika, 1986); A. V. Ososkov, *Nachal'noe obrazovanie v dorevoliutsionnoi Rossii, 1861–1917* (Moscow: Prosveshchenie, 1982); N. M. Pirumova, *Zemskaia intelligentsiia i ee rol' v obshchestvennoi bor'be* (Moscow: Nauka, 1986); and A. V. Ushakov, *Revoliutsionnoe dvizhenie demokraticheskoi intelligentsii v Rossii, 1895–1904* (Moscow: Mysl', 1976).

35. A. N. Stepanov, "Uchastie uchitel'stva Peterburga v pervoi russkoi revoliutsii," *Sovetskaia pedagogika* 1 (1941): 86–93.

36. Eklof, *Russian Peasant Schools*, 179–214; Seregny, *Russian Teachers*, 12–18.

37. For the literature on other European countries, see Dina Mira Copelman, "Women in the Classroom Struggle: Elementary Schoolteachers in London, 1870–1914," Ph.D. diss., Princeton University, 1985; Jo Burr Margadant, *Madame le Professeur: Women Educators in the Third Republic* (Princeton: Princeton University Press, 1990); Frances Kelleher, "Gender, State Policy and Professional Politics: Primary Schoolteachers in France, 1880–1920," Ph.D. diss., New York University, 1988; and Joanne Schneider, "*Volksschullehrerinnen:* Bavarian Women Defining Themselves

Through Their Profession," in *German Professions*, ed. Geoffrey Cocks and Konrad H. Jaraush (New York: Oxford University Press, 1990), 85–103.

38. For a discussion of the women's liberation movement and the role of women in the revolutionary movement, see Linda Harriet Edmondson, *Feminism in Russia, 1900–1917* (Stanford: Stanford University Press, 1984); Barbara Alpern Engel, *Mothers and Daughters: Women of the Intelligentsia in Nineteenth-Century Russia* (Cambridge: Cambridge University Press, 1983); and Richard Stites, *The Women's Liberation Movement in Russia: Feminism, Nihilism, and Bolshevism, 1860–1930* (Princeton: Princeton University Press, 1983). On women's education, see Ruth Dudgeon, "The Forgotten Minority: Women Students in Imperial Russia, 1872–1917," *Russian History* 9 (1982): 1–26; Christine Johanson, *Women's Struggle for Higher Education in Russia, 1855–1900* (Kingston and Montreal: McGill-Queen's University Press, 1987); and E. O. Likhacheva, *Materialy dlia istorii zhenskogo obrazovaniia v Rossii, 1856–1880* (St. Petersburg, 1901).

1. Pedagogy and Professionalism

1. For a discussion of prereform teachers, see N. V. Chekhov, *Narodnoe obrazovanie v Rossii s 60-kh godov* (Moscow, 1912), 107–110; Eklof, *Russian Peasant Schools*, chap. 1.

2. For a discussion of secondary schoolteachers, see Sinel, *The Classroom and the Chancellery*.

3. For a discussion of teacher training and its effect on professionalization, see Jurgen Herbst, *And Sadly Teach: Teacher Education and Professionalization in American Culture* (Madison: University of Wisconsin Press, 1989).

4. Graduates from the historical-philological institutes in St. Petersburg and Nezhin and graduates of the higher technical schools could teach in the boys' secondary schools. See F. G. Panachin, *Pedagogicheskoe obrazovanie v Rossii: Istoriko-pedagogicheskie ocherki* (Moscow, 1979), 78.

.5. For a discussion of the problem confronting the Russian universities, see Kassow, *Students, Professors and the State;* McClelland, *Autocrats and Academics*.

6. For a discussion of child-centered pedagogy, see Michael Heafford, *Pestalozzi: His Thought and Its Relevance Today* (London: Metheuen and Co., 1967); Lewis Flint Anderson, *Pestalozzi* (New York: McGraw-Hill Book Company, 1931); Robert B. Downs, *Friedrich Froebel* (Boston: Twayne Publishers, 1978); and Johann Friedrich Herbart, *The Science of Education* trans. Henry and Emmie Felkin (Boston: D. C. Heath, n.d.).

7. Cynthia H. Whittaker, *The Origins of Modern Russian Education: An Intellectual Biography of Count Sergei Uvarov, 1786–1855* (DeKalb: North-

ern Illinois University Press, 1984), 70; and N. A. Konstantinov, E. N. Medynskii, and M. F. Shabaeva, *Istoriia pedagogiki*, 5th ed. (Moscow: Prosveshchenie, 1982), 215–33. For a further discussion of the impact of child-centered pedagogy on Russian education, see Ben Eklof, "Worlds in Conflict: Patriarchical Authority, Discipline, and the Russian School, 1861–1914," *Slavic Review* 50 (Winter 1991): 792–806.

8. Panachin, *Pedagogicheskoe obrazovanie v Rossii*, 75–76.
9. Sinel, *The Classroom and the Chancellery*, 219–20.
10. N. S., "Po voprosu o spetsial'noi podgotovke prepodavatelei v srednie shkoly," *Pedagogicheskii sbornik* 8 (August 1899): 131.
11. Kassow, *Students, Professors and the State*, 37–47.
12. P. Vipper, "Spetsial'naia podgotovka prepodavatelia srednei shkoly ili podniatie ego polozheniia?" *Vestnik vospitaniia* 6 (June 1898): 52–74.
13. V. Ivanovskii, "O prepodavanii pedagogiki v universitetakh," *Vestnik vospitaniia* 7 (July 1906): 134.
14. See ibid., 109–35; S. Zenchenko, "O podgotovke prepodavatelei srednikh uchebnykh zavedenii k pedagogicheskoi deiatel'nosti," *Vestnik vospitaniia* 4 (April 1898): 60–96; and N. S., "Po voprosu o spetsial'noi podgotvke prepodavatelei v srednie shkoly," 128–36.
15. N. S., "Po voprosu," 134.
16. Zenchenko, "O podgotovke," 83–86.
17. Panachin, *Pedagogicheskoe obrazovanie v Rossii*, 80.
18. Wortman, *The Development of a Russian Legal Consciousness;* Daniel Brower, *Training the Nihilists: Education and Radicalism in Tsarist Russia* (Ithaca: Cornell University Press, 1975); Engel, *Mothers and Daughters*.
19. Kassow, *Students, Professors and the State*, chaps. 2–4.
20. Barbara Corrado Pope, "The Influence of Rousseau's Ideology of Domesticity," in *Connecting Spheres: Women in the Western World, 1500 to the Present*, ed. Marilyn J. Boxer and Jean H. Quataert (New York: Oxford University Press, 1987), 136–45.
21. Carol S. Nash, "Educating New Mothers: Women and the Enlightenment in Russia," *History of Education Quarterly* (Fall 1981): 301–16.
22. N. I. Pirogov, "Voprosy zhizni," in *Izbrannye pedagogicheskie sochineniia* (Moscow, 1985), 29–51. For more on the impact of Pirogov's article on the women's movement, see Stites, *The Women's Liberation Movement in Russia*, 30–33; Engel, *Mothers and Daughters*, 52–53.
23. Quoted in Likhacheva, *Materialy*, 17.
24. Eduard Dneprov, "Zhenskoe obrazovanie v poreformennoi Rossii," in *Bestuzhevskie kursy—pervyi zhenskii universitet v Rossii*, ed. E. D. Fedosova (Moscow: Pedagogika, 1980), 13–16.
25. For a discussion of the controversy surrounding higher education for women, see Johanson, *Women's Struggle;* Likhacheva, *Materialy;* Stites, *The Women's Liberation Movement in Russia;* Engel, *Mothers and Daughters;*

NOTES TO PAGES 30–35

Dudgeon, "The Forgotten Minority," 1–26; G. A. Tishkin, *Zhenskii vopros v Rossii v 50–60gg. XIX v.* (Leningrad, 1984), 212–18.

26. Quoted in Stites, *The Women's Liberation Movement in Russia*, 33.

27. K. El'nitskii, "Prepodavanie obshchei pedagogiki v zhenskoi gimnazii," *Russkaia shkola* 3 (March 1905): 87.

28. Eklof, *Russian Peasant Schools*, 186–90.

29. I. Solov'ev, "Pedagogika kak uchebnyi predmet v zhenskikh gimnaziiakh," *Vestnik vospitaniia* 4 (April 1913): 184.

30. M. I. Demkov, *Istoriia russkoi pedagogii: Novaia russkaia pedagogika* (Moscow, 1909), 497–507.

31. El'nitskii, "Prepodavanie obshchei pedagogiki," 85; P. Brakengeim, "K voprosu o prepodavanii pedagogiki v zhenskikh gimnaziiakh," *Vestnik vospitaniia* 6 (June 1895): 83.

32. P. Golovachev, "K voprosu o prepodavanii pedgogiki v zhenskikh gimnaziiakh," *Vestnik vospitaniia* 8 (August 1893): 69.

33. Brakengeim, "K vosprosu," 87.

34. Ibid., 84; E. D'iakonova, "Zhenskoe obrazovanie," *Zhenskoe delo* 12 (December 1899): 55.

35. In 1903 a four-year women's pedagogical institute was established in St. Petersburg. It served as the Russian equivalent of women's teaching colleges in Western Europe and America and provided its students with the most sophisticated pedagogical training available in Russia. For a brief history of the institute, see Panachin, *Pedagogicheskoe obrazovanie v Rossii*, 101.

36. The Guerrier courses were closed by the government in 1888 and reopened only in 1900. Thus, the Bestuzhev courses were the primary source for women teachers with a higher education.

37. Quoted in Johanson, *Women's Struggle*, 99.

38. *Dopolnenie ko vtoromu izdaniiu pamiatnoi knizhki okonchivshikh kurs na S-Peterburgskikh vysshikh zhenskikh kursakh* (St. Petersburg, 1897), statistical table following p. 28; Dudgeon, "The Forgotten Minority," 11.

39. Eklof, *Russian Peasant Schools*, 205–06.

40. "Pervyi god moei uchitel'skoi deiatel'nosti," *Russkaia shkola* 9–10 (September–October 1893): 38–64.

41. A. N. Stepanov, "Eksperty po uchebnoi chasti Peterburgskoi gorodskoi dumy," *Narodnoe obrazovanie* 5–6 (1946): 69.

42. Kommissiia po narodnomu obrazovaniiu, *S.-Peterburgskie gorodskie nachal'nye uchilishcha v 1892 godu* (St. Petersburg, 1893), 104; idem, *S.Peterburgskie gorodskie nachal'nye uchilishcha v 1895 godu* (St. Petersburg, 1896), 166.

43. S. N. Valk, ed., *Sankt-Peterburgskie vysshie zhenskie (Bestuzhevskie) kursy, 1878–1918: Sbornik statei* (Leningrad: Izdatel'stvo Leningradskogo universiteta, 1973), 239 and 243.

44. Sinel, *The Classroom and the Chancellery*, 220.
45. TsGIA, f. 733, op. 204, d. 463, ll. 70–73.
46. Sinel, *The Classroom and the Chancellery*, 224; TsGIA, f. 733, op. 203, d. 462, l. 12.
47. TsGIA, f. 733, op. 203, d. 65, l. 91.
48. N. N. Kuz'min, *Uchitel'skie instituty v Rossii* (Cheliabinsk, 1975), 10; Sinel, *The Classroom and the Chancellery*, 221; TsGIA, f. 733, op. 204, d. 154, l. 4 and d. 503, l. 12.
49. TsGIA, f. 733, op. 204, d. 65, ll. 31–36 and d. 170, ll. 15–16.
50. Ibid., d. 65, ll. 15–19.
51. Demkov, *Ocherki po istorii russkoi pedagogiki* 82–83.
52. M. D. O., "O nauchnoi i pedagogicheskoi podgotovke v uchitel'skikh institutakh," *Vestnik vospitaniia* 7 (July 1904): 129–39.
53. TsGAOR, f. 6862, op. 1, d. 84, ll. 114–15.
54. A. Razd-kii, "Tri goda v uchitel'skom institute," *Obrazovanie* 12 (December 1900): 91–103.
55. V. A. Samsonov, "Anketnye dannye o prakticheskoi i teoreticheskoi podgotovke uchitelei gorodskikh po Polozheniiu 1872 goda uchilishch," in *Trudy pervogo vserossiiskogo s"ezda uchitelei gorodskikh po polozheniiu 1872g. uchilishch* (St. Petersburg, 1910), 1: 285–90.
56. Ibid., 289.
57. Etzioni, ed., *The Semi-Professions*, v–xvii.

2. City Teachers' Daily Lives

1. Eduard Dneprov, "A Systems Approach to the Study of Public Education in Prerevolutionary Russia," *Soviet Studies in History* 25 (Winter 1986–1987): 11–30. The Ministry of Education eventually had to share its control over male secondary schools with the introduction of commercial schools run by the Ministry of Finance.
2. N. B., "Popechiteli i popechitel'nitsy gorodskikh nachal'nykh shkol v Moskve," *Russkaia shkola* 1 (January 1906): 164. It is interesting to note that this article was published anonymously. I was not able to locate any published accounts of conflicts between Moscow trustees and teachers. Teachers who complained publicly about these problems could be fired. Until the archives of the Moscow city schools are opened to scholars, this information remains elusive. Nevertheless, the continuing complaints by teachers about the problems they had with the trustees suggests this was a serious problem.
3. Ibid., 167.
4. Ibid., 166–67.
5. The *eksperty* were A. Ia. Gerd, I. I. Paul'son, V. P. Volens, and D. D. Semenov. All these men were distinguished educators before assuming their role as *eksperty*. See Stepanov, "Eksperty po uchebnoi chasti Pe-

NOTES TO PAGES 48–57

terburgskoi gorodskoi dumy," 68–72; and *Dvadtsatipiatiletie nachal'nykh uchilishch*, 31–37.

6. N. V. Tulupov, "Petr Mikhailovich Shestakov," *Dlia narodnogo uchitelia* 1 (January 1915): 2–6; N. V. Chekhov, "Moi vospominaniia o P. M. Shestakove," *Dlia narodnogo uchitelia* 1 (January 1915): 6–10; TsGIA, f. 733, op. 174, d. 689, ll. 1–28.

7. A. Petrishchev, "Iz zametok shkol'nogo uchitelia," *Russkoe bogatstvo* 10 (October 1904): 82 and 94–95.

8. Eklof, *Russian Peasant Schools*, 223.

9. A. V. Filatova, *Vospominaniia uchitel'nitsy 1874–1907* (Moscow, 1929), 16.

10. TsGIA, f. 91, op. 3, d. 575, l. 211.

11. Thomas Darlington, *Education in Russia* (London, 1909), 296–99.

12. Kommissiia po narodnomu obrazovaniiu, *S-Petersburgskie gorodskie nachal'nye uchilishcha v 1896 godu*, 196.

13. Kommissiia po narodnomu obrazovaniiu, *S-Petersburgskie gorodskie nachal'nye uchilishcha v 1892 godu*, 9–10; "Iz obshchestvennoi khroniki," *Vestnik Evropy* 4 (April 1895): 857–62.

14. Kommissiia po narodnomu obrazovaniiu, *S-Peterburgskie gorodskie nachal'nye uchilishcha v 1893 godu*, 11–12.

15. L. Antokol'skii, "Leningradskoe uchitel'stvo v ego proshlom i nastoiashchem," *Na fronte kommunisticheskogo prosveshcheniia* 10–11 (October–November 1932): 100.

16. TsGIA, f. 91, op. 3, d. 793, l. 613.

17. Eklof, "Worlds in Conflict," 795.

18. Darlington, *Education in Russia*, 275–91.

19. For a discussion of the classical controversy, see ibid., 375–407; Sinel, *The Classroom and the Chancellery*, 130–213.

20. Sinel, *The Classroom and the Chancellery*, 175.

21. Aleksandr Davydov, *Vospominaniia* (Paris, 1982), 116.

22. Alston, *Education and the State*, 99.

23. Quoted in ibid., 262.

24. Ibid., 260.

25. For a fuller discussion of the ministry's attempts to reform the secondary schools, see ibid., 140–71.

26. Darlington, *Education in Russia*, 359; Alston, *Education and the State*, 222.

27. TsGIA, f. 733, op. 203, d. 431, l. 5. The pay scale in the ministry's girls' schools in 1900 was:

Gymnasiums	Grades 1–4	45 rubles per lesson
	Grades 5–7	60 rubles per lesson
	Grade 8	70 rubles per lesson
Pro-Gymnasiums	All grades	35 rubles per lesson

28. Darlington, *Education in Russia*, 359.
29. "Material'noe polozhenie uchitelei srednei shkoly v Moskve," *Vestnik vospitaniia* 4 (April 1908): 158.
30. TsGIA, f. 733, op. 204, d. 76, ll. 55–72.
31. This table appears in Alston, *Education and the State*, 289–90.
32. "Material'noe polozhenie uchitelei srednei shkoly v Moskve," 156.
33. Ibid., 157–58.
34. Petrishchev, "Iz zametok shkol'nogo uchitelia," 99.
35. "Material'noe polozhenie uchitelei srednei shkoly v Moskve," 154–55.
36. V. Fediavskaia, "Vospominaniia uchitel'nitsy muzhskoi gimnazii," *Vestnik vospitaniia* 2 (February 1907): 160.
37. Frieden, *Russian Physicians*, 212–13.

3. Women Teachers and Professionalization

1. Etzioni, ed., *The Semi-Professions*, vi.
2. For an introduction to the literature on women in the professions, see Nancy F. Cott, *The Grounding of Modern Feminism* (New Haven: Yale University Press, 1987); Penina Migdal Glazer and Miriam Slater, *Unequal Colleagues: The Entrance of Women into the Professions* (New Brunswick: Rutgers University Press, 1987). The problems women teachers faced are discussed in Copelman, "Women in the Classroom Struggle"; Margadant, *Madame le Professeur;* Kelleher, "Gender, State Policy and Professional Politics"; and Schneider, "*Volksschullehrerinnen*," 85–103.
3. Joan Wallach Scott, "Gender: A Useful Category of Historical Analysis," *American Historical Review* 91 (December 1986): 1053–75.
4. F. Povaliev, "Otvety na pis'mo uchitel'nitsy N. Nikiforovoi, pomeshchannoe v zhurnale R.N.U. za 1883 g., No. 3," *Russkii nachal'nyi uchitel'* 12 (December 1885): 538. Hereafter cited as *RNU*.
5. Eklof, *Russian Peasant Schools*, 186–94.
6. K. Zhivilo, "Otvety na pis'mo uchitel'nitsy N. Nikiforovoi pomeshchannoe v zhurnale R.N.U. za 1883 g.," *RNU* 12 (December 1885): 531.
7. Seregny, *Russian Teachers*, 14–15, 206.
8. Eklof does suggest that women teachers may have had a positive influence on peasant girls. See Eklof, *Russian Peasant Schools*, 189.
9. Ibid.
10. Seregny, *Russian Teachers*.
11. There was conflict between men and women teachers in other parts of Europe as well during this period. For the French example, see Peter V. Meyers, "From Conflict to Cooperation: Men and Women Teachers in the Belle Epoque," *Historical Reflections* 7 (1980): 493–505.
12. "Sel'skie uchitelia o sel'skikh uchitel'nitsakh (Tri pis'ma v redaktsiiu)," *RNU* 6–7 (1883): 413–18.

NOTES TO PAGES 69–77

13. P. Sitnikov, "Po povodu pisem sel'skikh uchitelei o sel'skikh uchitel'nitsakh," *RNU* 8–9 (August–September 1883): 532.
14. Zhivilo, "Otvety na pis'mo uchitel'nitsy," 532–33.
15. Ibid., 530–31.
16. For an example, see Filatova, *Vospominaniia uchitel'nitsy*.
17. Natalia Nikiforova, "Pis'mo uchitel'nitsy," *RNU* 12 (December 1883): 688.
18. Kra-kaia, "Pis'mo uchitel'nitsy (Otvet na pis'ma uchitelei)," *RNU* 8–9 (August–September 1883): 530.
19. Ibid.
20. Nikiforova, "Pis'mo uchitel'nitsy," 688.
21. Eklof, *Russian Peasant Schools*, 190.
22. V. B-va, "Otvet na pis'ma uchitelei," *RNU* 3 (March 1884): 155–56.
23. Nikiforova, "Pis'mo uchitel'nitsy," 686–87.
24. For a discussion of the attempts of other women to use their traditional religious and familial role to create a new place for women in their society, see Barbara Weltner, "The Cult of True Womanhood: 1820–1860," in *The American Family in Social-Historical Perspective*, ed. Michael Gordon (New York: St. Martin's Press, 1978), 313–33; Catherine M. Prelinger, "The Nineteenth-Century Deaconessate in Germany: The Efficacy of a Family Model," in *German Women in the Eighteenth and Nineteenth Centuries: A Social and Literary History*, ed. Ruth-Ellen B. Joeres and Mary Jo Maynes (Bloomington: Indiana University Press, 1986), 215–29; and Bonnie G. Smith, *Ladies of the Leisure Class: The Bourgeoises of Northern France in the Nineteenth Century* (Princeton: Princeton University Press, 1981).
25. Engel, *Mothers and Daughters*, esp. 127–55.
26. Brenda Meehan-Waters, "The Authority of Holiness: Women Ascetics and Spiritual Elders in Nineteenth-Century Russia," in *Church, Nation and State in Russia and Ukraine*, ed. Geoffrey A. Hosking (London: Macmillan, 1991), 48.
27. Chekhov, *Narodnoe obrazovanie v Rossii*, 111; Christine Worobec, *Peasant Russia: Family and Community in Post-Emancipation Russia* (Princeton: Princeton University Press, 1991), 124; L. Tul'tseva, "Chernichki," *Nauka i religiia* 11 (1970): 81–82.
28. This development bears a sharp resemblance to the teaching nuns found in Catholic countries. For a brief discussion, see Margadant, *Madame le Professeur*, 37–40.
29. For a fuller discussion of this issue, see Christine Ruane, "The Vestal Virgins of St. Petersburg: Schoolteachers and the 1897 Marriage Ban," *Russian Review* 50 (April 1991): 163–82.
30. Johanson, *Women's Struggle*, 20–21.
31. *Dvadtsatipiatiletie nachal'nykh uchilishch*, 10–16.

32. Stepanov, "Eksperty po uchebnoi chasti," 68–72.
33. Likhacheva, *Materialy*, 3; Stites, *The Women's Liberation Movement in Russia*, 33.
34. For a discussion of similar attitudes toward working-class women, see Rose L. Glickman, *Russian Factory Women: Workplace and Society, 1880–1914* (Berkeley and Los Angeles: University of California Press, 1984), 89–96.
35. N. K., "Nachal'noe obrazovanie v bol'shikh russkikh gorodakh," 166; Eklof, *Russian Peasant Schools*, 186–94.
36. D. D. Semenov, "Pervoe desiatiletie s-peterb. gorodskikh nachal'nykh uchilishch," *Russkaia starina* 10 (October 1887): 186.
37. The top pay for Riga teachers was 1,100 rubles. It is interesting to note that men teachers dominated in the Riga primary schools, which might explain the better wages in that city. See N. K., "Nachal'noe obrazovanie v bol'shikh russkikh gorodakh," 166 and 170.
38. By 1902 the effect of the new hiring policy could be seen in the educational profile of Petersburg teachers. Out of 480 teachers, 68 were graduates of the women's higher courses and 289 graduated from the three-year pedagogical courses. See *Dvadtsatipiatiletie nachal'nykh uchilishch*, 433.
39. "Poriadok opredeleniia na uchitel'skie dolzhnosti v nachal'nykh uchilishchakh goroda S.-Peterburga," *Izvestiia S.-Peterburgskoi gorodskoi dumy* 19 (October 1897): 129–32; A. Strannoliubskii, "Nesostoiatel'nost' S.-Peterburgskoi Gorodskoi Dumy v dele narodnogo obrazovaniia," *Obrazovanie* 10 (October 1897): 151.
40. *Novoe vremia*, 7765 (9 October 1897): 3.
41. Kommissiia po narodnomu obrazovaniiu, *S-Peterburgskie gorodskie nachal'nye uchilishcha v 1892 godu*, 97.
42. "Otmena bezbrachiia uchitel'nits," *Zhenskii vestnik* 12 (December 1913): 290.
43. For a critique of the city's educational policies, see Strannoliubskii, "Nesostoiatel'nost'," 143–70. For a more general discussion of the city's financial problems, see James Bater, *St. Petersburg: Industrialization and Change* (Montreal: McGill-Queen's University Press, 1976), 259–63.
44. Ministerstva narodnogo prosveshcheniia, *Odnodnevnaia perepis' nachal'nykh shkol Rossiiskoi imperii proizvedennaia 18 ianvaria 1911* (Petrograd, 1916), 2: 52–53.
45. "Zametka po povodu novoi organizatsii S.-Peterburgskikh nachal'nykh gorodskikh uchilishch," *Russkaia shkola* 9–10 (September–October 1897): 170–87.
46. Ibid., 174, 186. V. A. Latyshev, the director of the Petersburg schools, made a similar argument against school reform in 1910 without using gender-specific language, but emphasizing the importance of the one-room

schoolhouse for pupils and teachers. See V. A. Latyshev, "S.-Peterburgskie gorodskie nachal'nye uchilishcha," *RNU* 8–9 (August–September 1910): 219–38.

47. For a discussion of this development in Russian schools, see Eklof, *Russian Peasant Schools;* E. D. Dneprov, "A Systems Approach," 11–30. For a discussion of the American experience, see David B. Tyack, *The One Best System: A History of American Education* (Cambridge: Harvard University Press, 1974).

48. Recent studies that examine this phenomenon in Great Britain are Copelman, "Women in the Classroom Struggle," chap. 5; Samuel Cohn, *The Process of Occupational Sex-Typing: The Feminization of Clerical Labor in Great Britain* (Philadelphia: Temple University Press, 1985).

49. International Labor Office, "Discrimination in Employment or Occupations on the Basis of Marital Status," *International Labor Review* 85 (March–April 1962): 262–83, 368–89.

50. Cohn, *The Process of Occupational Sex-Typing*, 109.

51. Petersburg school officials did not publish the numbers of eligible candidates for teaching positions. The only numbers available are from 1893, when the waiting list for teachers was 215. On how a teacher became a candidate for a city teaching position, see *Dvadtsatipiatiletie nachal'nykh uchilishch*, 105–10.

4. Politics and Professionalization

1. For the figures on rural women schoolteachers, see Eklof, *Russian Peasant Schools*, 186–87. For comparable figures on city schoolteachers, see Appendix, table 1.

2. Quoted in Alston, *Education and the State*, 266.

3. For a discussion of the importance of voluntary associations in imperial Russia and particularly the values they helped to foster, see Joseph Bradley, "Voluntary Associations, Civic Culture, and *Obshchestvennost'* in Moscow," in Clowes, Kassow, and West, eds., *Between Tsar and People*, 131–48.

4. Frieden, *Russian Physicians;* Balzer, "The Problem of Professions in Imperial Russia," 183–98.

5. D. D. Semenov, "Ocherki pedagogicheskoi deiatel'nosti Iosifa Ivanovicha Paul'sona," *Vestnik vospitaniia* 6 (June 1898): 94.

6. A. I. Piskunov, ed., *Ocherki shkoly i pedagogicheskoi mysli narodov SSSR: Vtoraia polovina XIX v.* (Moscow, 1976), 350–51.

7. Ibid., 353; Alston, *Education and the State*, 156.

8. A. D. Stepanskii, *Samoderzhavie i obshchestvennye organizatsii Rossii na rubezhe XIX–XX vv.* (Moscow: Moskovskii gosudarstvennyi istoriko-arkhivnyi institut, 1980).

NOTES TO PAGES 93-98

9. Peter A. Zaionchkovsky, *The Russian Autocracy in Crisis, 1878–1882*, trans. Gary Hamburg (Gulfbreeze: Academic International Press, 1979), esp. 70–75.
10. See Seregny, *Russian Teachers*, chap. 3; Eklof, *Russian Peasant Schools*, chaps. 7, 8.
11. Darlington, *Education in Russia*, 217; Stepanov, "Eksperty po uchebnoi chasti," 69; *Dvadtsatipiatiletie nachal'nykh uchilishch*, 123–29.
12. Piskunov, *Ocherki shkoly i pedagogicheskoi mysli narodov SSSR*, 358.
13. Ibid., 357–58; E. Zviagintsev, "Iz zhizni moskovskikh prosvetitel'nykh obshchestv," *Vestnik vospitaniia* 3 (March 1911): 22–34.
14. Piskunov, *Ocherki shkoly i pedagogicheskoi mysli narodov SSSR*, 353–55. For a history of the St. Petersburg Literacy Committee, see D. D. Protopopov, *Istoriia S.-Peterburgskogo komiteta gramotnosti* (St. Petersburg, 1898).
15. Chekhov, *Narodnoe obrazovanie v Rossii*, 116.
16. See Bradley, "Voluntary Associations, Civic Culture, and *Obshchestvennost'* in Moscow," 131–33.
17. "Pervoe godovoe sobranie S.-Peterburgskogo pedagogicheskogo obshchestva vzaimnoi pomoshchi," *Russkaia skhola* 3 (March 1984): 212; "Spisok chlenov S.-Peterburgskogo Pedagogicheskogo Obshchestva Vzaimnoi pomoshchi," *Spravochnyi listok S.-Peterburgskogo pedagogicheskogo obshchestva vzaimnoi pomoshchi* 27 (January–April 1904): 97–120. Hereafter *Spravochnyi listok*.
18. For a discussion of the famine, see Richard G. Robbins, Jr., *Famine in Russia, 1891–1892: The Imperial Government Responds to a Crisis* (New York: Columbia University Press, 1975); Frieden, *Russian Physicians*, 135–60.
19. Frieden, *Russian Physicians*, 135–60; Shmuel Galai, *The Liberation Movement in Russia, 1900–1905* (Cambridge: Cambridge University Press, 1973), 62–63.
20. Piskunov, *Ocherki shkoly i pedagogicheskoi mysli narodov SSSR*, 355.
21. Members listed on both organizations' governing boards include N. N. Skalon, A. N. Strannoliubskii, and Ia. Gurevich. The names of some of the members of both societies are in Protopopov, *Istoriia S.-Peterburgskogo komiteta gramotnosti, 1861–1895*, xviii; "Pervoe godovoe sobranie S.-Petersburgskogo pedagogicheskogo obshchestva vzaimnoi pomoshchi," 212–14.
22. Alston, *Education and the State*, 226. According to one report, very few professors were members of the society. Most members taught in the secondary schools of the Ministries of Education and War or in the Petersburg municipal schools. See " 'S.-Peterburgskoe pedagogicheskoe obshchestvo vzaimnoi pomoshchi' ili 'Pedagogicheskii fond,' " *Russkaia shkola* 5–6 (May–June 1894): 283.

23. See Frieden, *Russian Phyisicians,* 161–200; Galai, *The Liberation Movement,* 5–108.
24. Seregny, *Russian Teachers,* 56; V. I. Charnolusskii, *Uchitel'skie obshchestva, kassy, kursy, i s˝ezdy* (St. Petersburg, 1901), 7–11.
25. *Doklad Obshchemu Sobraniiu Komissii po uvekovecheniiu pamiati K.D. Ushinskogo pri Spb. Pedagogicheskom Obshchestve Vzaimopomoshchi* (St. Petersburg, 1896), 3.
26. Ibid., 3–4.
27. *Spravochnyi listok* 29 (October–December 1904): 40–49.
28. For a discussion of the women's perceived immaturity, see Laura Engelstein, "Gender and the Juridical Subject: Prostitution and Rape in Nineteenth-Century Russian Criminal Codes," *Journal of Modern History* 60 (September 1988): 458–95.
29. The one interesting exception to this rule was N. V. and Mariia Chekhov. He was one of the prominent leaders of the teachers' movement, while she was one of the leading feminist organizers. While Mariia was herself a schoolteacher, she never participated actively in the teachers' movement. Her husband, however, was a staunch supporter of women's rights and spoke frequently on that subject.
30. "Khronika," *Vestnik vospitaniia* 6 (June 1895): 168–69.
31. "Khronika," *Vestnik vospitaniia* 1 (January 1898): 128–32.
32. "Obshchestvo popecheniia ob uluchshenii byta uchashchikh v nachal'nykh uchilishchakh g. Moskvy," *Vestnik vospitaniia* 3 (March 1903): 91–96.
33. Alston, *Education and the State,* 156.
34. Ibid.
35. TsGIA, f. 733, op. 204, d. 167, l. 1.
36. "Moskovskoe Pedagogicheskoe Obshchestvo," *Spravochnyi listok* 29 (October–December 1904): 82–85.
37. Seregny, *Russian Teachers,* 39–41.
38. Dneprov, "A Systems Approach," 24–25.
39. "Pervyi s˝ezd russkikh deiatelei po tekhnicheskomu i professional'nomu obrazovaniiu v 1889–1890 gg.," *Zhurnal Ministerstva narodnogo prosveshcheniia* 278 (November–December 1891): 19–22.
40. Ibid., 23–39.
41. "S˝ezd deiatelei po tekhnicheskomu i professional'nomu obrazovaniiu," *Russkaia mysl'* 2 (February 1896): 225. For the reports delivered at the congress, see "S˝ezd russkikh deiatelei po tekhnicheskomy i professional'nomy obrazovaniiu," in *Trudy* 2 vols. (St. Petersburg, 1899); and I. I. Ianzhul, *Ekonomicheskaia otsenka narodnogo obrazovaniia* (St. Petersburg, 1896).
42. K., "Voprosy narodnoi shkoly na II s˝ezde deiatelei po tekhnicheskomu i professional'nomu obrazovaniiu," *Russkaia mysl'* 4 (April 1896): 81; Darlington, *Education in Russia,* 330.

43. K., "Voprosy narodnoi shkoly na II s˝ezde deiatelei po tekhnicheskomu i professional'nomu obrazovaniiu," 89; Alston, *Education and the State*, 144.

44. TsGAOR, f. 6862, op. 1, d. 20, l. 5; E. O. Vakhterova, *V. P. Vakhterov, ego zhizn' i rabota* (Moscow, 1961), 128–29; and Seregny, *Russian Teachers*, 63–64.

45. For a discussion of this "thaw" in ministry attitudes, see Alston, *Education and the State*, 140–71.

46. S. Volkov, "Pervyi s˝ezd narodnykh uchitelei i uchitel'nits," *Russkaia mysl'* 10 (October 1901): 209.

47. Quoted in ibid., 217.

48. N. V. Tulupov, "Pervyi vserossiiskii s˝ezd predstavitelei Obshchestv vspomoshchestvovaniia litsam uchitel'skogo zvaniia," *Russkaia mysl'* 3 (March 1903): 112.

49. Seregny, *Russian Teachers*, 64.

50. TsGIA, f. 733, op. 195, d. 623, ll. 88, 91, and 97–98.

51. Ibid., ll. 97–98; L. Kleinbort, "Chego khotiat narodnye uchitelia?" *Obrazovanie* 3 (March 1903): 97.

52. Kleinbort, "Chego khotiat narodnye uchitelia?"

53. Ibid., 98.

54. Tulupov, "Pervyi vserossiiskii s˝ezd," 129.

55. *Ibid.*; Kleinbort, "Chego khotiat narodnye uchitelia?" 115–16.

56. See Frieden, *Russian Physicians*, 179–200.

57. K. K., "Sudy obshchestva ofitserov," in *Entsiklopedicheskii slovar'* (St. Petersburg: Brokgauz and Efron), 32: 16–18.

58. Kleinbort, "Chego khotiat narodnye uchitelia?" 101.

59. Seregny, *Russian Teachers*, 78–80.

60. Quoted in Scott J. Seregny, "Professional and Political Activism: The Russian Teachers' Movement 1864–1908," Ph.D. diss., University of Michigan, 1982, 311; see also 303–16.

61. Chlen s˝ezda, "Lishennye dara slova," *Obrazovanie* 3 (March 1903): 31–33.

62. Ibid., 34–66; Alston, *Education and the State*, 215–16.

63. Chlen s˝ezda, "Lishennye dara slova," 37–38.

64. Ibid., 38.

65. Ushakov, *Revoliutsionnoe dvizhenie*, 34.

66. Seregny, "Professional and Political Activism," 374–77.

67. For a history of the Union of Liberation, see Galai, *The Liberation Movement;* and Terence Emmons, *The Formation of Political Parties and the First National Elections in Russia* (Cambridge: Harvard University Press, 1983), 21–36.

68. Seregny, "Professional and Political Activism," 378 and 380–81.

69. Ibid., 379. In addition to the nonparty Union of Teachers, the SRs also claimed a party teachers' union. The evidence suggests, however, that this union was probably the same as the Union of Teachers, with the main

activist of both unions being S. I. Akramovskii. For a discussion of this confusing issue, see ibid., 379–85.

70. *Dnevnik pervogo Vserossiiskogo s"ezda predstavitelei obshchestv vspomoshchestvovaniia litsam uchitel'skogo zvaniia* 10 (5 January 1903): 8.

71. Ibid., 18–19.

72. Petrishchev, "Iz zametok shkol'nogo uchitelia," 82.

73. Govorov, *Brachnyi vopros*, 16.

74. Ibid. These same objections were raised against married women teachers in Germany. See Schneider, "*Volksschullehrerinnen,*" 93.

75. Govorov sent a questionnaire to teachers in the Moscow area and received seventy replies, including some from men teachers, but the vast majority of respondents were women teachers from the city of Moscow—fifty in all. And, although this evidence does not come from Petersburg itself, it reflects the views of the teachers and the society as a whole toward this issue. Govorov, *Brachnyi vopros*, 7.

76. Ibid., 10.

77. Ibid., 47–49.

78. Ibid., 51, emphasis in the original.

79. Of those who replied to the questionnaire, 80 percent thought married women teachers should be permitted to continue to teach, while 20 percent disapproved. See ibid., 7.

80. Ibid., 26.

81. Ibid., 24.

82. Carroll Smith-Rosenberg, *Disorderly Conduct: Visions of Gender in Victorian America* (New York: Alfred A. Knopf, 1985), 197–218; Elaine Showalter, *The Female Malady: Women, Madness and English Culture, 1830–1980* (New York: Penguin, 1985), 121–66.

83. Vasilii V. Rozanov, *Semeinyi vopros v Rossii* (St. Petersburg, 1903), 1: 405–08.

84. *Izvestiia S-Peterburgskoi gorodskoi dumy* 35 (December 1905): 2101.

85. Ibid., 2092–2102.

86. "Organizatsiia II s"ezda predstavitelei obshchestva vspomoshchestvovaniia litsam uchitel'skogo zvaniia," *Spravochnyi listok* 26 (October–December 1903): 9–11.

87. Ibid., 11.

88. Ushakov, *Revoliutsionnoe dvizhenie*, 36–37.

89. TsGIA, f. 733, op. 195, d. 623, l. 125.

90. "Zasedanie Komissii imeni K.D. Ushinskogo," *Spravochnyi listok* 26 (October–December 1903): 17; TsGAOR, f. 6862, op. 1, d. 87, l. 76.

91. "Otchet Komissii po uchastiiu S.-Peterburgskogo Pedagogicheskogo Obshchestva Vzaimnoi Pomoshchi v 3-m S"ezde russkikh deiatelei po tekhnicheskomu i professional'nomu obrazovaniiu v Rossii," *Spravochnyi listok* 26 (October–December 1903): 32–34.

92. Frieden, *Russian Physicians*, 242–59; Emmons, *The Formation of Political Parties*, 31.
93. TsGIA, f. 733, op. 195, d. 623, l. 127. This tactic of drowning out speeches with music was common during those years. At the Ninth Congress of the Pirogov Society, which was occurring at the same time as the Third Technical Congress, the last speaker announced the end of the congress without reading the resolutions adopted by the delegates. A military band immediately began to play while the audience jeered. See Frieden, *Russian Physicians*, 260–61.
94. Darlington, *Education in Russia*, 344–45.
95. Ushakov, *Revoliutsionnoe dvizhenie, 1895–1904*, 37; Alston, *Education and the State*, 170; and Frieden, *Russian Physicians*, 260.
96. On the importance of the Third Technical Congress for the Liberation movement, see Sanders, "The Union of Unions," 110–12.
97. Abraham Ascher, *The Revolution of 1905: Russia in Disarray* (Stanford: Stanford University Press, 1988), 46–47.
98. *Spravochnyi listok* 27 (January–March 1904): 90–95 and 28 (April–May 1904): 14–16.
99. Emmons, *The Formation of Political Parties*, 8; Harcave, *The Russian Revolution of 1905* (London, 1964), 44–45.
100. Emmons, *The Formation of Political Parties*, 8–9.
101. Ascher, *The Revolution of 1905*, 53–70.
102. *Spravochnyi listok* 27, 28, and 29 (1904): passim.
103. Terence Emmons, "Russia's Banquet Campaign," *California Slavic Studies* 10 (1977): 45–86.
104. Emmons, *The Formation of Political Parties*, 30–36.
105. According to Dal', "*korporatsiia*" was sometimes used to refer to a union of individuals from a particular occupation. See Vladimir Dal', *Tolkovyi slovar' zhivogo velikorusskogo iazyka* (Moscow, 1981), 2: 170. I have chosen to translate this term as "association," which comes closest to the actual structure of the Moscow organization. The American Teachers' Association is an equivalent organization.
106. P., "Iz zhizni korporatsii Moskovskikh gorodskikh uchitelei," *Uchitel'* 5 (31 March 1907): 26; TsGAOR, f. 6862, op. 1, d. 20, l. 45.

5. The Revolution of 1905

1. An excellent account of the 1905 Revolution can be found in Ascher, *The Revolution of 1905*.
2. L. Mezhinskaia, "Peterburgskoe uchitel'stvo v 1905 godu," *Narodnyi uchitel'* 11 (November 1925): 39; E. Medynskii, *Istoriia russkoi pedagogiki* (Moscow, 1941), 379.
3. Medynskii, *Istoriia russkoi pedagogiki*, 387; G. Rokov, "Shkol'nye volneniia 1905 goda," *Vestnik vospitaniia* 9 (September 1905): 110–17.

NOTES TO PAGES 132–143

4. Rokov, "Shkol'nye volneniia," 121–24; Alston, *Education and the State*, 175–76.
5. Alston, *Education and the State*, 176–78.
6. "Zapiski prepodavatelei moskovskikh srednikh uchebnykh zavedenii," *Pravo* 6 (13 February 1905): 424–25.
7. TsGAOR, f. 6862, op. 1, d. 69, ll. 8–9 and d. 20, ll. 69–70.
8. P., "Iz zhizni korporatsii moskovskikh gorodskikh uchitelei," 26.
9. TsGAOR, f. 6862, op. 1, d. 84, l. 5 and d. 75, l. 47.
10. Ibid., d. 61, l. 29 and d. 35, l. 5.
11. Ibid., ll. 5–6 and d. 84, l. 6.
12. Ibid., d. 61, l. 29.
13. Laura Engelstein, *Moscow, 1905* (Stanford: Stanford University Press, 1982), 54.
14. TsGAOR, f. 6862, op. 1, d. 84, l. 5.
15. *Spravochnyi listok* 30 (March 1905–April 1906): 40–42.
16. Ibid.
17. Mezhinskaia, "Peterburgskoe uchitel'stvo v 1905 godu," 39.
18. TsGAOR, f. 6862, op. 1, d. 69, l. 6; Sanders, "The Union of Unions," 124–25 and 137–38.
19. TsGAOR, f. 6862, op. 1, d. 84. l. 32.
20. Ibid., d. 69, l. 35; *Pravo* 12 (27 March 1905): 924.
21. Mezhinskaia, "Peterburgskoe uchitel'stvo v 1905 godu," 39–40.
22. Alston, *Education and the State*, 181.
23. Mezhinskaia, "Peterburgskoe uchitel'stvo v 1905 godu," 39–40.
24. P. Sakulin, "Moskovskoe pedagogicheskoe obshchestvo v 1905 godu," *Vestnik vospitaniia* 3 (March 1906): 57.
25. *Pravo* 16 (24 April 1905): 1324–29. It is interesting to note that Aleksandra Kollontai attended this meeting of the Ushinskii Commission. This demonstrates how fluid attendance was at the various meetings held during 1905.
26. TsGAOR, f. 6862, op. 1, d. 85, ll. 35–37 and d. 46, ll. 18–19; E. Vakhterova, "O vserossiiskom uchitel'skom soiuze," *Vestnik vospitaniia* 1 (January 1906): 121; Ronald Hideo Hayashida, "The Unionization of Russian Teachers, 1905–1908: An Interest Group Under the Autocracy," *Slavic and European Education Review* 2 (1981): 6; Alston, *Education and the State*, 181; and Seregny, *Russian Teachers*, 118–25.
27. Alston, *Education and the State*, 260–66.
28. TsGAOR, f. 6862, op. 1, d. 46, ll. 17–18.
29. For a discussion of the *soslovie* mentality among Russian businessmen, see Jo Ann Ruckman, *The Moscow Business Elite*. Ruckman also points toward a generational difference among Moscow merchants, with the older merchants maintaining a *soslovie* attitude toward politics, and the younger generation exhibiting a greater willingness to participate in political life.

30. Engelstein, *Moscow, 1905*, 6.
31. Seregny, *Russian Teachers*, 115–25.
32. P. Miliukov, " 'Politicheskii ili 'professional'nyi' soiuzy?" in *God bor'by: Publitsisticheskaia khronika, 1905–1906* (St. Petersburg, 1907), 41–47.
33. TsGAOR, f. 6862, op. 1, d. 46, ll. 18–24 and d. 57, ll. 20–1.
34. Vakhterova, "O vserossiiskom uchitel'skom soiuze," 122.
35. On the participation of the VSU in the Union of Unions, see Sanders, "The Union of Unions." Sanders identifies the various political affiliations of the union's leadership.
36. Seregny, "Professional and Political Activism," 614.
37. For an introduction to this issue in 1905, see Seregny, *Russian Teachers*, 115–25; Gerald Surh, *1905 in St. Petersburg: Labor, Society, and Revolution* (Stanford: Stanford University Press, 1989), 304–10; Kassow, *Students, Professors and the State*, 219–28; and Sanders, "The Union of Unions," 888–901.
38. TsGAOR, f. 6862, op. 1, d. 69, l. 34, emphasis added.
39. Vakhterova, "O vserossiiskom uchitel'skom soiuze," 129.
40. I. L. Tsvetkov, "Uchitel'skoe dvizhenie 1905 goda," *Narodnyi uchitel'* 11 (November 1925): 21.
41. N. Popova, "K istorii vserossiiskogo uchitel'skogo soiuza (Moskovskaia oblastnaia organizatsiia Vserossiiskogo Uchitel'skogo Soiuza)," *Vestnik vospitaniia* 4–5 (April–May 1917): 47.
42. Engelstein, *Moscow, 1905*, 73 and 94.
43. Kassow, *Students, Professors and the State*, chap. 6.
44. Engelstein, *Moscow, 1905*, 139–48; Ascher, *The Revolution of 1905*, 233.
45. TsGAOR, f. 6862, op. 1, d. 84, ll. 224–25.
46. Ibid., d. 62, ll. 20–21.
47. Ibid., d. 56, l. 19.
48. Ibid., d. 62, l. 25.
49. Ibid., d. 56, l. 13 and ll. 22–23.
50. Ibid., d. 62, l. 25; P., "Iz zhizni korporatsii moskovskikh gorodskikh uchitelei," 29.
51. For a detailed discussion of the rail strike, see Henry Reichman, *Railwaymen and Revolution: Russia, 1905* (Berkeley and Los Angeles: University of California Press, 1987).
52. P., "Iz zhizni korporatsii moskovskikh gorodskikh uchitelei," 27; Engelstein, *Moscow, 1905*, 116–20.
53. TsGAOR, f. 6862, op. 1, d. 84, l. 7.
54. Ibid.
55. "Uchitel'skaia zabastovka v S-Peterburge v dni 14–21 oktiabria 1905 g.," *Vestnik VSU* (November 1905): 1–8; A. N. Stepanov, "Uchastie uchitel'stva Peterburga v pervoi russkoi revoliutsii," 90.

56. Stepanov, "Uchastie ucheitel'stva Peterburga v pervoi russkoi revoliutsii"; Mezhinskaia, "Peterburgskoe uchitel'stvo v 1905 godu," 43.
57. TsGAOR, f. 6862, op. 1, d. 87, l. 79.
58. Alston, *Education and the State*, 186–87.
59. Ibid., 185; TsGAOR, f. 6862, op. 1, d. 61, ll. 46–47.
60. TsGAOR, f. 6862, op. 1, d. 67, l. 17. The union's platform can be found in "Po voprosu, vozbuzhdennomu biuro vserossiiskogo soiuza uchitelei, o merakh k uluchsheniiu narodnogo obrazovaniia," *Izvestiia S-Peterburgskogo gorodskoi dumy* 37 (December 1906): 1216–21.
61. Stepanov, "Uchastie uchitel'stva Peterburga v pervoi russkoi revoliutsii," 91.
62. TsGAOR, f. 6862, op. 1, d. 59, l. 165.
63. O. Vitten, "Nekotorye etapy, proidennye uchitel'stvom v minuvshem godu," *Vestnik soiuza uchitelei* 1 (April 1906): 11–15; Popova, "K istorii vserossiiskogo uchitel'skogo soiuza," 106.
64. Stepanov, "Uchastie uchitel'stva Peterburga v pervoi russkoi revoliutsii," 91.
65. P., "Iz zhizni korporatsii moskovskikh gorodskikh uchitelei," 28.
66. TsGAOR, f. 6862, op. 1, d. 61, l. 42 and d. 60, l. 1.
67. Kassow sees a similar pattern among university students. He argues that students developed a corporate identity in tsarist Russia. They were united when they felt the government violated what they believed to be their rights as students, but contrary to what others have argued, Kassow believes students remained divided in their political attitudes. See Kassow, *Students, Professors and the State*.
68. For a more detailed discussion of the December Uprising in Moscow, see Engelstein, *Moscow, 1905*, 162–225.
69. Ibid., 181–86.
70. Ibid., 196.
71. TsGAOR, f. 6862, op. 1, d. 84, ll. 225–26.
72. Ibid, l. 3 and l. 225.
73. Ibid, l. 8.
74. P., "Iz zhizni korporatsii moskovskikh gorodskikh uchitelei," 28–29; TsGAOR, f. 6862, op. 1, d. 84, ll. 131–32.
75. Quoted in Stepanov, "Uchastie uchitel'stva Peterburga v pervoi russkoi revoliutsii," 87.
76. E. A. Chebysheva-Dmitrieva, "Uchashchiesia i uchashchie gorodskikh nachal'nykh uchilishch Peterburga," in *Trudy pervogo Vserossiiskogo s"ezda po obrazovaniiu zhenshchin* (St. Petersburg, 1915), 2: 313.
77. *Izvestiia S-Peterburgskoi gorodskoi dumy* 35 (December 1905): 2105–07.
78. Ibid., 2092–2102.

79. Ibid., 10 (March 1906): 2084.
80. Alston, *Education and the State*, 183 and 190.
81. Rokov, "Shkol'nye volneniia 1905 goda," 144.
82. TsGIA, f. 733, op. 166, d. 810, passim.
83. Alston, *Education and the State*, 190.
84. Ibid., 188–89.
85. TsGAOR, f. 6862, op. 1, d. 34, l. 20.
86. Alston, *Education and the State*, 189–90.
87. Ibid., 192–93.
88. Ibid., 195.
89. Ibid., 193.
90. Seregny, *Russian Teachers*, 201.

6. City Teachers After the 1905 Revolution

1. P., "Iz zhizni korporatsii moskovskikh gorodskikh uchitelei," 29.
2. Roberta Thompson Manning, *The Crisis of the Old Order in Russia: Gentry and Government* (Princeton: Princeton University Press, 1982), 187–95.
3. Seregny, *Russian Teachers*, 199.
4. "Svedeniia o postradavshikh chlenakh VSU," *Vestnik uchitelei* 2 (7 May 1906): 95.
5. Popova, "K istorii vserossiiskogo uchitel'skogo soiuza," 105.
6. Eklof, *Russian Peasant Schools*, 115–19; Alston, *Education and the State*, chap. 7; Eduard Dneprov, "The Autocracy and Public Education in Postreform Russia," *Soviet Studies in History* 25 (Winter 1986–1987):64; and Konstantinov, Medynskii, and Shabaeva, *Istoriia pedagogiki* 299–302.
7. Robert W. Thurston, *Liberal City, Conservative State: Moscow and Russia's Urban Crisis, 1906–1914* (New York: Oxford University Press, 1987), chap. 7; "Moskovskaia gorodskaia uprava," in *Sovremennoe khoziaistvo goroda Moskvy*, ed. I. A. Verner (Moscow, 1913), 26–104.
8. Quoted in Sanders, "The Union of Unions," 655. The activities and membership of the feminist organizations in Petersburg have not been well researched. It is difficult to say precisely how many teachers participated and in what kinds of events. For a general discussion, see Edmondson, *Feminism in Russia, 1900–1917*, 87.
9. Chebysheva-Dmitrieva, "Uchashchiesia i uchashchie gorodskikh nachal'nykh uchilishch Peterburga," 2:313.
10. Ibid., 307–14.
11. "Otmena bezbrachiia uchitel'nits," *Zhenskii vestnik* 12 (December 1913): 290.
12. Ibid.
13. Bater, *St. Petersburg*, 359.

14. For a fuller discussion of this important issue, see Olga Crisp and Linda Edmondson, eds., *Civil Rights in Imperial Russia* (Oxford: Clarendon Press, 1989).
15. Thurston, *Liberal City, Conservative State*, chap. 7. Thurston describes Moscow's teachers as demoralized during this period and attributes their poor morale to low wages. While it is true that teachers believed themselves poorly paid, this was not the main issue between teachers and city officials after 1905. See ibid., 159–60.
16. "Moskovskaia gorodskaia uprava," 37–38.
17. Ibid., 31.
18. Ibid., 46.
19. Ibid., 31.
20. For a discussion of the pedagogical issues at the 1912 Congress, see V-ch, "Voprosy vospitaniia i obucheniia na S˝ezde deiatelei po narodnomu obrazovaniiu v moskovskom gorodskom obshchestvennom upravlenii," *Russkii uchitel'* 4 (April 1912): 337–48. The earlier reforms passed by the Moscow city duma were discussed at length.
21. TsGAOR, f. 102, op. 13, d. 104, ll. 19–21; V-ch, "Professional'nye nuzhdy Moskovskogo uchitel'stva," *Russkii uchitel'* 3 (1912): 282.
22. "K s˝ezdu uchitelei," *Russkie vedomosti* (29 January 1912): 5.
23. TsGAOR, f. 102, op. 13, d. 104, l. 42; V-ch, "Professional'nye nuzhdy Moskovskogo uchitel'stva," 284.
24. *Statisticheskii ezhegodnik Moskovskoi gubernii za 1915 god* (Moscow, 1916), 211–12.
25. TsGAOR, f. 102, op. 13, d. 104, l. 19. Two police agents attended the 1912 teachers' meeting. One was Ivan Iakovich Drillikh, whose code name was "Blondinka." Drillikh was a frequent contributor to *Russkoe slovo* and *Kievskaia mysl'*. The second agent was Vasilii Aleksandrovich Kozlov, code name "*Liza*". Kozlov was a journalist by profession. See S. V. Chlenov, *Moskovskaia okhranka i ee sekretnye sotrudniki* (Moscow, 1919), 65–66. I am grateful to Jonathan Daly for bringing this information to my attention.
26. E. Matern, "O s˝ezde uchashchikh v nachal'nykh uchilishchakh g. Moskvy," *Dlia narodnogo uchitelia* 7 (1910): 1–4; I. L. Tsvetkov, "Pervyi s˝ezd deiatelei po narodnomu obrazovaniiu v Moskovskom gorodskom obshchestvennom upravlenii," *Russkaia shkola* 9–10 (September–October 1912): 74.
27. Tsvetkov, "Pervyi s˝ezd deiatelei"; V-ch, "Professional'nye nuzhdy Moskovskogo uchitel'stva," 282–83; TsGAOR, f. 102, op. 13, d. 104, l. 19.
28. TsGAOR, f. 102, op. 13, d. 104, ll. 51–53; Tsvetkov, "Pervyi s˝ezd," 80–82.
29. V-ch, "Professional'nye nuzhdy moskovskogo uchitel'stva," 288.
30. TsGAOR, f. 102, op. 13, d. 104, l. 52.
31. "Zakrytie uchitel'skogo s˝ezda," *Dlia narodnogo uchitelia* 4 (1912): 27–28.

32. TsGAOR, f. 102, op. 13, d. 104, ll. 53–54.
33. D-ch, "Rezul'taty moskovskogo s"ezda," *Russkii uchitel'* 6–9 (September 1913): 623–39.
34. *Spravochnyi listok (1907–1909)*, 7 and 9–11; "Khronika uchitel'skikh obshchestv," *Dlia narodnogo uchitelia* 2 (1909): 20–23.
35. *Spravochnyi listok, 1907–1909*, 13.
36. P. Zhulev, "Uchitel'skie obshchestva vzaimopomoshchi," *Russkaia shkola* 1 (January 1912): 1–20.
37. Ibid., 11.
38. In addition to Zhulev's article, see N. Iordanskii, " 'Soveshchanie' uchashchikh narodnoi shkoly i uchitel'skie kluby," *Dlia narodnogo uchitelia* 21 (1908): 5–9; N. V. Chekhov, "Uchitel'skie Obshchestva, ikh zadachi i organizatsiia," *Dlia narodnogo uchitelia* 5 (1913): 38–41, 6 (1915): 35–39, 7 (1915): 36–39, 8 (1915): 39–43, 9 (1915): 39–45, and 10 (1915): 40–47.
39. N. V. Tulupov, "Uchitel'skii dom Obshchestva Vzaimnoi Pomoshchi pri Moskovskom Uchitel'skom Institute," *Dlia narodnogo uchitelia* 10 (1909): 3; M. Shorin, "Ob 'uchitel'skikh domakh' pri uchitel'skikh obshchestvakh vzaimopomoshchi," *Voprosy i nuzhdy uchitel'stva* 3 (1909): 30–31.
40. Tulupov, "Uchitel'skii dom," 3–7; M. S-ov, "Pervyi v Rossii Uchitel'skii Dom," *Dlia narodnogo uchitelia* 1 (1912): 9–14.
41. S-ov, "Pervyi v Rossii Uchitel'skii Dom," 7–13; Tulupov, "Uchitel'skii dom," 4.
42. N. Kanatchikov, "Pedagogicheskie kursy pri Uchitel'skom Dome v Moskve 1912 g.," *Dlia narodnogo uchitelia* 12 (1912): 21.
43. TsGAOR, f. 102, op. 13, d. 104, l. 2.
44. P. Zhulev, "Vtoroi Vserossiiskii s"ezd predstavitelie uchitel'skikh obshchestv vzaimopomoshchi," *Russkii uchitel'* 3 (1912): 253–58.
45. Joseph Bradley, "Russia's Parliament of Public Opinion: Association, Assembly, and the Autocracy, 1906–1914," unpublished paper presented at a conference on "Reform in Russia and Soviet History: Its Meaning and Function," Kennan Institute, 1990.
46. Zhulev, "Vtoroi Vserossiiskii s"ezd predstavitelei uchitel'skikh obshchestv vzaimopomoshchi," 257–63; *Spravochnyi listok (1907–1909)*, 12; "Kratkii ocherk organizatsii II Vserossiiskogo, imeni K. D. Ushinskogo, s"ezda predstavitelei uchitel'skikh obshchestv," in *Dnevnik II Vserossiiskogo, imeni K. D. Ushinskogo, S"ezda predstavitelei obshchestv vspomoshchestvovaniia litsam uchitel'skogo zvaniia* 1 (29 December 1913): 1–2.
47. "Kratkii ocherk organizatsii II Vserossiiskogo," 2.
48. S. Zolotarev, "Vtoroi s"ezd predstavitelei uchitel'skikh obshchestv," in *Professional'nye uchitel'skie organizatsii na Zapade i v Rossii: sbornik statei* (Petrograd, 1915), 283–84.
49. Ibid., 284–85. For a list of the delegates, see *Dnevnik II S"ezda* 1–4 (29 December 1913–3 January 1914): passim.

50. Zolotarev, "Vtoroi s″ezd," 286.
51. *Dnevnik II S″ezda* 1 (29 December 1913): 13–16.
52. Zolotarev, "Vtoroi s″ezd," 287.
53. *Dnevnik II S″ezda* 6 (16 January 1914): 2–22.
54. *Dnevnik II S″ezda* 1–4 (29 December 1913–3 January 1914): passim.
55. *Dnevnik II S″ezda* 6 (16 January 1914): 10.
56. Zolotarev, "Vtoroi s″ezd," 288.
57. *Dnevnik II S″ezda* 6 (16 January 1914): 22.

Conclusion

1. W. Bruce Lincoln, *In the Vanguard of Reform: Russia's Enlightened Bureaucrats 1825–1861* (DeKalb: Northern Illinois University Press, 1982); Andrzej Walicki, *The Slavophile Controversy: History of a Conservative Utopia in Nineteenth Century Russian Thought*, trans. H. Andrews-Rusiecka (Oxford: Clarendon Press, 1975).

2. Pomper, *The Russian Revolutionary Intelligentsia*; Franco Venturi, *Roots of Rebellion: A History of the Populist and Socialist Movement in 19th Century Russia* (London: Weidenfeld and Nicholson, 1960); and Abbott Gleason, *Young Russia: The Genesis of Russian Radicalism in the 1860s* (Chicago: University of Chicago Press, 1980).

3. Rieber, *Merchants and Entrepreneurs*; Owen, *Capitalism and Politics*; Ruckman, *The Moscow Business Elite*; and essays by Owen, Rosenthal, and West in Clowes, Kassow, and West, eds., *Between Tsar and People*.

4. Sidney Monas, "The Twilit Middle Class of Nineteenth-Century Russia," in Clowes, Kassow, and West, eds., *Between Tsar and People*, 31.

5. Seregny, *Russian Teachers*, 108–45; Panachin, *Uchitel'stvo i revoliutsionnoe dvizhenie v Rossii*, 117–27.

6. TsGAOR, f. 6862, op. 1, d. 69, l. 34.

7. Clowes, Kassow, and West, eds., *Between Tsar and People*; Rieber, *Merchants and Entrepreneurs*; Owen, *Capitalism and Politics*; Ruckman, *The Moscow Business Elite*; Kassow, *Students, Professors and the State*; and Frieden, *Russian Physicians*.

8. Kassow, "Russia's Unrealized Civil Society," 367.

9. For a further discussion of the concept of the "public sphere," see Jurgen Habermas, "The Public Sphere," in *Rethinking Popular Culture: Contemporary Perspectives in Cultural Studies*, ed. Chandra Mukerji and Michael Schudson (Berkeley and Los Angeles: University of California Press, 1991), 398–404.

10. Frieden, *Russian Physicians*.

11. Kendall Bailes, *Technology and Society under Lenin and Stalin: Origins of the Soviet Technical Intelligentsia, 1917–1941* (Princeton: Princeton University Press, 1978).

12. Seregny, *Russian Teachers*.

Bibliography

Archival Sources

Tsentral'nyi Gosudarstvennyi Istoricheskii Arkhiv SSSR (TsGIA)
  Fond 91 Vol'noe Ekonomicheskoe Obshchestvo.
  Fond 733 Ministerstvo narodnogo prosveshcheniia, Departament narodnogo prosveshcheniia.
  Fond 1284 Ministerstvo vnutrennikh del, Departament obshchikh del.
Tsentral'nyi Gosudarstvennyi Arkhiv Oktiabr'skoi Revoliutsii SSSR (TsGAOR)
  Fond 102 Departament politsii, Osobyi otdel.
  Fond 6862 Komissiia po izucheniiu istorii professional'nogo dvizheniia pri Ts. K. profsoiuza rabotnikov prosveshcheniia.
Leningradskii Gosudarstvennyi Istoricheskii Arkhiv (LGIA)
  Fond 412 S-Peterburgskii Uchitel'skii Institut.
  Fond 918 Zhenskii Pedagogicheskii Institut.

Published Sources

Aleksandrov, P. P. *Za Narvskoi zastavoi: vospominaniia starogo ragochego.* Leningrad, 1963.
Allen, Ann Taylor. "Spiritual Motherhood: German Feminists and the Kindergarten Movement, 1848–1911." *History of Education Quarterly* 22 (Fall 1982): 319–39.
Alston, Patrick L. *Education and the State in Tsarist Russia.* Stanford: Stanford University Press, 1969.
Anderson, Lewis Flint. *Pestalozzi.* New York: McGraw-Hill, 1931.
Anikina, A. "Opyt 'kharakteristik' uchennikov narodnoi shkoly." *Voprosy i nuzhdy uchitel'stva* 5 (1910): 3–15.
Antokol'skii, L. "Leningradskoe uchitel'stvo v ego proshlom i nastoiashchem." *Na fronte kommunisticheskogo prosveshcheniia* 10–11 (October–November 1932): 99–106.
Ascher, Abraham. *The Revolution of 1905: Russia in Disarray.* Stanford: Stanford University Press, 1988.
B., N. "Popechiteli i popechitel'nitsy gorodskikh nachal'nykh shkol v Moskve." *Russkaia shkola* 1 (January 1906): 164–69.

BIBLIOGRAPHY

Balzer, Harley. "Educating Engineers: Economic Politics and Technical Training in Tsarist Russia," Ph.D. diss., University of Pennsylvania, 1980.
Bater, James. *St. Petersburg: Industrialization and Change.* Montreal: McGill-Queen's University Press, 1976.
Bradley, Joseph. *Muzhik and Muscovite: Urbanization in Late Imperial Russia.* Berkeley and Los Angeles: University of California Press, 1985.
―――. "Russia's Parliament of Public Opinion: Association, Assembly, and the Autocracy, 1906–1914." Presented at a conference on "Reform in Russian and Soviet History: Its Meaning and Function," 1990.
Brakengeim, P. "K voprosu o prepodavanii pedagogiki v zhenskikh gimnaziiakh." *Vestnik vospitaniia* 6 (June 1895): 82–88.
Brooks, Jeffrey. *When Russia Learned to Read.* Princeton: Princeton University Press, 1985.
Brower, Daniel. *Training the Nihilists: Education and Radicalism in Tsarist Russia.* Ithaca: Cornell University Press, 1975.
Brown, Julie V. "Revolution and Psychosis: The Mixing of Science and Politics in Russian Psychiatric Medicine, 1905–1913." *Russian Review* 46 (July 1987): 283–377.
Bychkov, N. M. *Deiatel'nost' Moskovskogo gorodskogo obshchestvennogo upravleniia po narodnomu obrazovaniiu.* Moscow, 1896.
―――. "K voprosu o vseobshchem obuchenii v gorodakh." *Vestnik vospitaniia* 4 (April 1896): 1–39.
Charnolusskii, V. I. "Spisok uchitel'skikh obshchestv, sobranii i klubov, uchrezhdennykh do 1907 g." *Russkii uchitel'* 4 (1912): 411–16, 5 (1912): 503–06, 6–9 (1912): 599–606, 10 (1912): 702–25.
―――. *Uchitel'skie obshchestva, kassy, kursy, i s″ezdy.* St. Petersburg, 1901.
Chebysheva-Dmitrieva, E. A. "Uchashchiesia i uchashchie gorodskikh nachal'nykh uchilishch Peterburga." In *Trudy pervogo Vserossiiskogo s″ezda po obrazovaniiu zhenshchin.* 2 vols. St. Petersburg, 1915.
Chekhov, N. V. "Moi vospominaniia o P. M. Shestakove." *Dlia narodnogo uchitelia* 1 (January 1915): 6–10.
―――. *Narodnoe obrazovanie v Rossii s 60-kh godov.* Moscow, 1912.
―――. "Zatrudneniia, vstrechaiushchiiasia pri obuchenii russkomu iazyku v nachal'noi shkole," *Voprosy i nuzhdy uchitel'stva* 3 (Moscow, 1908).
Chermenskii, E. D. *Burzhuaziia i tsarizm v pervoi russkoi revoliutsii.* Moscow, 1970.
Chlen s″ezda. "Lishennye dara slova." *Obrazovanie* 3 (March 1903): 31–38.
Chlenov, S. V. *Moskovskaia okhranka i ee sekretnye sotrudniki.* Moscow, 1919.
Clowes, Edith W., Samuel D. Kassow, and James L. West, eds. *Between Tsar and People: Educated Society and the Quest for Public Identity in Late Imperial Russia.* Princeton: Princeton University Press, 1991.

Cogan, Morris. "Toward a Definition of Profession." *The Harvard Educational Review* 23 (Winter 1953): 33–50.

Cohn, Samuel. *The Process of Occupational Sex-Typing: The Feminization of Clerical Labor in Great Britain.* Philadelphia: Temple University Press, 1985.

Conroy, Mary Schaeffer. "School Hygiene in Late Tsarist Russia." *Slavic and European Education Review* 2 (1981): 17–26.

Copelman, Dina. "Women in the Classroom Struggle: Elementary Schoolteachers in London, 1870–1914." Ph.D. diss., Princeton University, 1985.

Cott, Nancy. *The Grounding of Modern Feminism.* New Haven: Yale University Press, 1987.

Crisp, Olga, and Linda Edmondson, eds. *Civil Rights in Imperial Russia.* Oxford: Clarendon Press, 1989.

Darlington, Thomas. *Education in Russia.* London, 1909.

Davydov, Aleksandr. *Vospominaniia.* Paris, 1982.

D-ch. "Rezul'taty moskovskogo s˝ezda." *Russkii uchitel'* 6–9 (September 1913): 623–39.

Demkov, M. I. *Istoria russkoi pedagogii: Novaia russkaia pedagogika.* Moscow, 1909.

———. *Ocherki po istorii russkoi pedagogiki.* Moscow, 1909.

D'iakonova, E. "Zhenskoe obrazovanie." *Zhenskoe delo* 12 (December 1899): 47–58.

Dneprov, Eduard. "The Autocracy and Public Education in Postreform Russia," ed. Ben Eklof. *Soviet Studies in History* 25 (Winter 1986–1987): 31–77.

———. " 'Relentlessly Running in Place:' The Historiography of Schools and Pedagogical Thought in Medieval Russia (Some Conclusions, Problems and Perspectives)," *History of Education Quarterly* 24, 4 (Winter 1986): 537–51.

———. "A Systems Approach to the Study of Public Education in Prerevolutionary Russia," ed. Ben Eklof. *Soviet Studies in History* 25 (Winter 1986–1987): 11–30.

———"Zhenskoe obrazovanie v poreformennoi Rossii." Introduction to *Bestuzhevskie kursy—pervyi zhenskii universitet v Rossii*, ed. E. D. Fedosova. Moscow: Pedagogika, 1980.

Dnevnik pervogo Vserossiiskogo s'ezda predstavitelei obshchestv vspomoshchestvovaniia litsam uchitel'skogo zvaniia. Moscow, 1903.

Dnevnik II Vserossiiskogo, imeni K.D. Ushinskogo, S˝ezda predstavitelei obshchestv vspomoshchestvovaniia litsam uchitel'skogo zvaniia. St. Petersburg, 1914.

Doklad Obshchemu Sobraniiu Komissii po uvekovecheniiu pamiati K.D. Ushinskogo pri Spb. Pedagogicheskom Obshchestve Vzaimopomoshchi. St. Petersburg, 1896.

BIBLIOGRAPHY

Dopolnenie ko vtoromu izdaniiu pamiatnoi knizhki okonchivshikh kurs na S-Peterburgskikh vysshikh zhenskikh kursakh. St. Petersburg, 1897.
Downs, Robert B. *Friedrich Froebel.* Boston: Twayne Publishers, 1978.
Drozdov, I. "Kak nas 'uchili' v gimnazii." *Russkaia mysl'* 7 (July 1902): 164–77.
Dudgeon, Ruth. "The Forgotten Minority: Women Students in Imperial Russia, 1872–1917." *Russian History* 9 (1982): 1–26.
Dvadtsatipiatiletie nachal'nykh uchilishch goroda S.-Peterburga, 1877–1902. St. Petersburg, 1904.
Edmondson, Linda Harriet. *Feminism in Russia, 1900–1917.* Stanford: Stanford University Presss, 1984.
Eklof, Ben. *Russian Peasant Schools: Officialdom, Village Culture, and Popular Pedagogy, 1861–1914.* Berkeley and Los Angeles: University of California Press, 1986.
―――. "Worlds in Conflict: Patriarchical Authority, Discipline, and the Russian School, 1861–1914." *Slavic Review* 50 (Winter 1991): 792–806.
El'nitskii, K. "Prepodavanie obshchei pedagogiki v zhenskoi gimnazii." *Russkaia shkola* 3 (March 1905).
Emmons, Terence. *The Formation of Political Parties and the First National Elections in Russia.* Cambridge: Harvard University Press, 1983.
―――"Russia's Banquet Campaign." *California Slavic Studies* 10 (1977): 45–86.
Engel, Barbara Alpern. *Mothers and Daughters: Women of the Intelligentsia in Nineteenth-Century Russia.* Cambridge: Cambridge University Press, 1983.
Engelstein, Laura. "Gender and the Juridical Subject: Prostitution and Rape in Nineteenth-Century Russian Criminal Codes." *Journal of Modern History* 60 (September 1988): 458–95.
―――. *Moscow, 1905.* Stanford: Stanford University Press, 1982.
Erman, L. K. *Intelligentsia v pervoi russkoi revoliutsii.* Moscow, 1966.
―――. "Sostav intelligentsii v Rossii v kontse XIX i nachale XX v." *Istoriia SSSR* 1 (1963): 161–77.
Etzioni, Amitai, ed. *The Semi-Professions and Their Organization: Teachers, Nurses and Social Workers.* New York: Free Press, 1969.
Fediaevskaia, V. "Vospominaniia uchitel'nitsy muzhskoi gimnazii." *Vestnik vospitaniia* 2 (February 1907): 145–63.
Feliksov, N. A. "Pedagogicheskie kursy i uchitel'skie s"ezdy." *Russkaia mysl'* 9 (1896): 1–28, 10 (1896): 38–56, 11 (1896) 32–56.
Filatova, A. V. *Vospominaniia uchitel'nitsy, 1874–1907.* Moscow, 1929.
Fitzpatrick, Sheila. *The Commissariat of Enlightenment: Soviet Organization of Education and the Arts under Lunacharsky, October 1917–1921.* Cambridge: Cambridge University Press, 1970.

Freeze, Gregory. *The Parish Clergy in Nineteenth-Century Russia*. Princeton: Princeton University Press, 1982.

———. *The Russian Levites: Parish Clergy in the Eighteenth Century*. Cambridge, 1977.

———. "The *Soslovie* (Estate) Paradigm and Russian Social History." *American Historical Review* 96 (1986): 11–36.

Friedan, Nancy Mandelker. *Russian Physicians in an Era of Reform and Revolution, 1865–1905*. Princeton: Princeton University Press, 1981.

Fuller, William C., Jr. *Civil-Military Conflict in Imperial Russia*. Princeton: Princeton University Press, 1985.

Galai, Shmuel. *The Liberation Movement in Russia, 1900–1905*. Cambridge: Cambridge University Press, 1973.

Geison, Gerald. *Professions and Professional Ideologies in America*. Chapel Hill, 1983.

———. *Professions and the French State, 1700–1900*. Philadelphia: University of Pennsylvania Press, 1984.

Gerdzei-Kapitsa, N. M. "N.V. Chekhov." *Russkii uchitel'* 1 (1912): 131.

Glickman, Rose L. *Russian Factory Women: Workplace and Society, 1880–1914*. Berkeley and Los Angeles: University of California Press, 1984.

Golovachev, P. "K voprosu o prepodavanii pedagogiki v zhenskikh gimnaziiakh." *Vestnik vospitaniia* 8 (August 1893): 68–76.

"Gorodskoe po Polozheniiu 1872 goda uchilishche." *Vestnik vospitaniia* 7 (1898): 163–202.

Govorov, S. *Brachnyi vopros v bytu uchashchikh nachal'noi shkoly*. Moscow, 1903.

Gremiachenskii, D. "Nachal'noe obrazovanie v Moskve." *Izvestiia Moskovskoi gorodskoi dumy*, June–July, 1908, 1–23.

Haimson, Leopold. "The Problem of Social Stability in Urban Russia, 1905–1917." *Slavic Review* 23 (December 1964): 619–42.

Harcave, Sidney. *The Russian Revolution of 1905*. London, 1964.

Hayashida, Ronald Hideo. "The Unionization of Russian Teachers, 1905–1908: An Interest Group Under the Autocracy." *Slavic and European Education Review* 2 (1981): 1–16.

Heafford, Michael. *Pestalozzi: His Thought and Its Relevance Today*. London: Methuen, 1967.

Herbart, Johann Friedrick. *The Science of Education*. Trans. Henry Felkin and Emmie Felkin. Boston: D.C. Heath, n.d.

Herbst, Jurgen. *And Sadly Teach: Teacher Education and Professionalization in American Culture*. Madison: University of Wisconsin Press, 1989.

Hinshaw, Christine Ruane. "The Soul of the School: The Professionalization of Urban Schoolteachers in St. Petersburg and Moscow, 1890–1907." Ph.D. diss., University of California, 1986.

BIBLIOGRAPHY

———. "A Source for the Social History of Late Imperial Russia." *Cahiers du monde russe et sovietique* 25 (October–December 1984): 455–62.
Hosking, Geoffrey. *The Russian Constitutional Experiment: Government and Duma, 1907–1914.* Cambridge, 1973.
I., P. "O nekotorykh slabykh storonakh uchebnogo dela v dukhovnykh seminariiakh i uchilishchakh." *Vestnik vospitaniia* 8 (August 1895): 23–40.
Iablonskii, A. "Iz gimnazicheskoi zhizni." *Mir Bozhii* 6 (1901): 28–64, 7 (1901): 145–185, 8 (1901): 28–70, 9 (1901): 172–215.
Ianzhul, I. I. *Ekonomicheskaia otsenka narodnogo obrazovaniia.* St. Petersburg, 1896.
International Labor Office. "Discrimination in Employment or Occupations on the Basis of Marital Status." *International Labor Review* 85 (March–April 1962): 262–83, 368–89.
Istoriia Moskvy. 6 vols. Moscow, 1955.
Ivanovskii, V. "O prepodavanii pedagogiki v universitetakh." *Vestnik vospitaniia* 7 (July 1906): 109–35.
"Iz uchitel'skogo byta." *Voprosy i nuzhdy uchitel'stva* 6 (1910): 90–95.
Johanson, Christine. *Women's Struggle for Higher Education in Russia, 1855–1900.* Kingston and Montreal: McGill–Queen's University Press, 1987.
Johnson, Robert. "Liberal Professionals and Professional Liberals: The Zemstvo Statisticians and Their Work." In *The Zemstvo in Russia: An Experiment in Local Self-Government,* ed. Terence Emmons and Wayne S. Vucinich, 343–64. Cambridge: Cambridge University Press, 1982.
K. "Voprosy narodnoi shkoly na II s″ezde deiatelei po tekhnicheskomu i professional'nomu obrazovaniiu." *Russkaia mysl'* 4 (April 1896): 79–94.
K., N. "Nachal'noe obrazovanie v bol'shikh russkikh gorodakh." *Vestnik vospitaniia* 6 (1899): 144–82.
K., N. V. "Vasilii Aleksevich Latyshev." *Dlia narodnogo uchitelia* 3 (March 1912): 24–26.
K., O. "O Moskovskikh gorodskikh uchilishchakh (Pis'mo iz Moskvy)." *Zhenskoe obrazovanie* 2 (February 1885): 133–38.
Kapterev, P. F. *Istoriia russkoi pedagogiki.* Moscow, 1910.
Kassow, Samuel D. *Students, Professors and the State in Tsarist Russia.* Berkeley and Los Angeles: University of California Press, 1989.
Kelleher, Frances. "Gender, State Policy and Professional Politics: Primary Schoolteachers in France, 1880–1920." Ph.D. diss., New York University, 1988.
Kh., U. "K voprosu ob obshchenii uchashchikh s uchashchimisia." *Vestnik vospitaniia* 7 (July 1907): 193–203.
Kir'iakov, V. "Vystavochnye vpechatleniia narodnogo uchitelia." *Russkii nachal'nyi uchitel'* 1 (1898): 10–12, 3 (1898): 28.

BIBLIOGRAPHY

Kleinbort, L. "Chego khotiat narodnye uchitelia?" *Obrazovanie* 3 (March 1903): 95–119.
Kluzhinskii, Ia. "Rabochii den' uchenika srednei shkoly." *Pedagogicheskoe obozrenie* 8 (August 1913): 20–31.
Kommissiia po narodnomu obrazovaniiu. *Nachal'nye narodnye uchilishcha S-Peterburga i gorodskie chetvertye klassnye uchilishcha.* 8 vols. St. Petersburg, 1900–1907.
———. *S-Peterburgskie gorodskie nachal'nye uchilishcha.* 9 vols. St. Petersburg, 1891–1899.
Konstantinov, N. A., E. N. Medynskii and M. F. Shabaeva. *Istoriia pedagogiki.* 5th ed. Moscow: Prosveshchenie, 1982.
Koreneva, F. "V vechernei shkole dlia vzroslykh." *Vestnik vospitaniia* 5 (1899): 141–52, 8 (1899): 113–22.
Kra-kaia. "Pis'mo uchitel'nitsy (Otvet na pis'ma uchitelei)." *Russkii nachal'nyi uchitel'* 8–9 (August–September 1883): 530.
Kuchepatov, N. G. "Gorodskie uchilishcha i ikh mesto v sisteme narodnogo obrazovaniia dorevoliutsionnoi Rossii." In *Uchenye zapiski Karel'skogo pedagogicheskogo instituta* 9 (1959).
Kusov, N. A. *Dvadtsatipiatiletie S-Peterburgskoi sed'moi gimnazii (Byvshei vtoroi progimnazii)* [1867–1892]. St. Petersburg, 1893.
Kuz'min, N. N. *Uchitel'skie instituty v Rossii.* Cheliabinsk, 1975.
Larson, Magali Sarfatti. *The Rise of Professionalism: A Sociological Analysis.* Berkeley and Los Angeles: University of California Press, 1977.
Leikina-Svirskaia, V. R. *Intelligentsiia v Rossii vo vtoroi polovine XIX veka.* Moscow: Mysl', 1971.
———. *Russkaia intelligentsiia v 1900–1917 godakh.* Moscow, 1981.
Letnie kolonii Moskovskikh gorodskikh nachal'nykh uchilishch. Moscow, 1894.
Likhacheva, E. O. *Materialy dlia istorii zhenskogo obrazovaniia v Rossii, 1856–1880.* St. Petersburg, 1901.
Lincoln, W. Bruce. *The Great Reforms: Autocracy, Bureaucracy, and the Politics of Change in Imperial Russia.* DeKalb: Northern Illinois University Press, 1990.
———. *In the Vanguard of Reform: Russia's Enlightened Bureaucrats, 1825–1861.* DeKalb: Northern Illinois University Press, 1982.
Lindenmeyer, Adele. "Charity and the Problem of Unemployment: Industrial Homes in Late Imperial Russia." *Russian Review* 45 (January 1986): 1–22.
———. "A Russian Experiment in Voluntarism: The Municipal Guardianships of the Poor, 1884–1914." *Jahrbücher für Geschichte Osteuropas* 30 (1982): 429–51.
Malinovskii, N. "Chto sdelano za sorok let moskovskim gorodskim upravleniem po narodnomu obrazovaniiu." *Russkaia mysl'* 4 (April 1904): 40–67, 12 (December 1904): 1–38.

Manaseina, N. "V gorodskoi shkole." *Mir Bozhii* 7 (1899): 19–40, 8 (1899): 41–66, 10 (1899): 97–113.
Manning, Roberta Thompson. *The Crisis of the Old Order in Russia: Gentry and Government*. Princeton: Princeton University Press, 1982.
Margadant, Jo Burr. *Madame le Professeur: Women Educators in the Third Republic*. Princeton: Princeton University Press, 1990.
"Material'noe polozhenie uchitelei srednei shkoly v Moskve." *Vestnik vospitaniia* 4 (April 1908): 151–66.
Matern, E. "O s˝ezde uchashchikh v nachal'nykh uchilishchakh g. Moskvy." *Dlia narodnogo uchitelia* 7 (1910): 1–4.
McClelland, James. *Autocrats and Academics: Education, Culture and Society in Tsarist Russia*. Chicago: University of Chicago Press, 1979.
Medynskii, E. *Istoriia russkoi pedagogiki*. Moscow, 1941.
Meehan-Waters, Brenda. "The Authority of Holiness: Women Ascetics and Spiritual Elders in Nineteenth-Century Russia." In *Church, Nation and State in Russia and Ukraine*, ed. Geoffrey A. Hosking. London: Macmillan, 1991.
Meyers, Peter V. "From Conflict to Cooperation: Men and Women Teachers in the Belle Epoque." *Historical Reflections* 7 (1980): 493–505.
Mezhinskaia, L. "Peterburgskoe uchitel'stvo v 1905 godu." *Narodnyi uchitel'* 11 (November 1925): 38–45.
Moskovskaia gorodskaia uprava. *Otchet o sostoianii gorodskikh nachal'nykh uchilishch uchrezhdennykh Moskovskoi gorodskoi dumoi za 1905/06 uchebnyi god*. Moscow, 1907.
"Moskovskaia gorodskaia uprava." In *Sovremennoe khoziaistvo goroda Moskvy*, ed. I. A. Verner. Moscow, 1913.
Nash, Carol S. "Educating New Mothers: Women and the Enlightenment in Russia." *History of Education Quarterly* (Fall 1981): 301–16.
———. "The Education of Women in Russia, 1762–1796." Ph.D. diss., New York University, 1978.
Nikiforova, Natalia. "Pis'mo uchitel'nitsy." *Russkii nachal'nyi uchitel'* 12 (December 1883): 688.
O., M. D. "O nauchnoi i pedagogicheskoi podgotovke v uchitel'skikh institutakh." *Vestnik vospitaniia* 7 (July 1904): 129–39.
"Obshchestvo popecheniia ob uluchshenii byta uchashchikh v nachal'nykh uchilishchakh g. Moskvy." *Vestnik vospitaniia* 3 (March 1903): 91–101.
Ocherki istorii Leningrada. Vol. 3. Moscow-Leningrad, 1956.
Odesskii, I. "Iz vesennikh vpechatlenii uchitelia." *Vestnik vospitaniia* 3 (March 1896): 96–116.
Okorokova, B. "Dva tipa pedagogicheskikh kursov." *Vestnik vospitaniia* 3 (March 1897): 170–90.
Osokov, A. V. *Nachal'noe obrazovanie v dorevoliutsionnoi Rossii, 1861–1917*. Moscow: Prosveshchenie, 1982.

"Otmena bezbrachiia uchitel'nits." *Zhenskii vestnik* 12 (December 1913): 290.
P. "Iz zhizni korporatsii Moskovskikh gorodskikh uchitelei." *Uchitel'* 5 (31 March 1907): 26–31.
Panachin, F. G. *Pedagogicheskoe obrazovanie v Rossii: istoriko-pedagogicheskie ocherki.* Moscow, 1979.
———. *Uchitel'stvo i revoliutsionnoe dvizhenie v Rossii (XIX–nachalo XX v.) Istoriko-pedagogicheskie ocherki.* Moscow: Pedagogika, 1986.
Parsons, Talcott. "Professions." In *International Encyclopedia of the Social Sciences,* 12: 536–47.
Partington, Geoffrey. *Women Teachers in the Twentieth Century.* Windsor, 1976.
Perkin, Harold. *The Rise of Professional Society: England Since 1880.* London: Routledge, 1989.
"Pervoe godovoe sobranie S.-Peterburgskogo pedagogicheskogo obshchestva vzaimnoi pomoshchi." *Russkaia shkola* 3 (March 1894): 212–14.
"Pervyi s˝ezd russkikh deiatelei po tekhnicheskomu i professional'nomu obrazovaniiu v 1889–1890 gg." *Zhurnal Ministerstva narodnogo prosveshcheniia* 278 (November–December 1891): 19–22.
Petrishchev, A. "Iz zametok shkol'nogo uchitelia." *Russkoe bogatstvo* 9 (1904): 59–85, 10 (1904): 80–115, 11 (1904): 128–61.
Petrov, V. "O chetyrekhletnem obuchenii v nachal'nykh narodnykh shkolakh." *Vestnik vospitaniia* 6 (June 1904): 165–94.
Pirumova, N. M. *Zemskaia intelligentsiia i ee rol' v obshchestvennoi bor'be.* Moscow: Nauka, 1986.
Piskunov, A. I., ed. *Ocherki shkoly i pedagogicheskoi mysli narodov SSSR: vtoraia polovina XIX v.* Moscow, 1976.
Poliakov, G. "Obshchestvo vzaimopomoshchi pri Spb. Uchitel'skom Institute." *Russkii uchitel'* 1 (January 1912): 61–74.
Pope, Barbara Corrado. "The Influence of Rousseau's Ideology of Domesticity." In *Connecting Spheres: Women in the Western World, 1500 to the Present,* ed. Marilyn J. Boxer and Jean H. Quataert, 136–45. New York: Oxford University Press, 1987.
Popova, N. "K istorii vserossiiskogo uchitel'skogo soiuza (Moskovskaia oblastnaia organizatsiia Vserossiiskogo Uchitel'skogo Soiuza)." *Vestnik vospitaniia* 4–5 (April–May 1917): 97–130.
Potekhin, P. "M. M. Stasiulevich, kak chlen i predsedatel' gorodskoi kommissii po narodnomu obrazovaniiu." *Vestnik Evropy* 3 (March 1911): 400–05.
Povaliev, F. "Otvety na pis'mo uchitel'nitsy N. Nikiforovoi pomeshchannoe v zhurnale R.N.U. za 1883g." *Russkii nachal'nyi uchitel'* 12 (December 1885): 538.
Prelinger, Catherine M. "The Nineteenth-Century Deaconessate in Germany:

The Efficacy of a Family Model." In *German Women in the Eighteenth and Nineteenth Centuries: A Social and Literary History,* ed. Ruth-Ellen B. Joeres and Mary Jo Maynes. Bloomington: Indiana University Press, 1986.

Protopopov, D. D. *Istoriia S.-Peterburgskogo komiteta gramotnosti.* St. Petersburg, 1898.

R., E. "Kartinki shkol'noi zhizni." *Russkaia shkola* 10 (October 1898): 26–38.

Razd-kii, A. "Tri goda v uchitel'skom institute." *Obrazovanie* 12 (December 1900): 91–103.

Reichman, Henry. *Railwaymen and Revolution: Russia, 1905.* Berkeley and Los Angeles: University of California Press, 1987.

Robbins, Richard G., Jr. *Famine in Russia, 1891–1892: The Imperial Government Responds to a Crisis.* New York: Columbia University Press, 1975.

Rokov, G. "Iz zapisok shkol'nogo uchitelia." *Vestnik vospitaniia* 7 (1909): 200–14, 8 (1909): 186–200.

———. "Russkii uchitel' srednei shkoly." *Russkii uchitel'* 3 (1912): 241–54.

———. "Shkol'nye volneniia 1905 goda." *Vestnik vospitaniia* 9 (September 1905): 105–49.

Rozanov, Vasilii V. *Semeinyi vopros v Rossii.* 2 vols. St. Petersburg, 1903.

Rozhdestvenskii, S. V. *Istoricheskii obzor deiatel'nosti Ministerstva narodnogo prosveshcheniia 1802–1902.* St. Petersburg, 1902.

Ruane, Christine. "The Vestal Virgins of St. Petersburg: Schoolteachers and the 1897 Marriage Ban." *Russian Review* 50 (April 1991): 163–82.

Ruckman, Jo Ann. *The Moscow Business Elite: A Social and Cultural Portrait of Two Generations, 1840–1905.* DeKalb: Northern Illinois University Press, 1984.

S., L. "Dva moskovskikh obshchestva vzaimopomoshchi dlia lits pedagogicheskoi professii." *Vestnik vospitaniia* 3 (March 1900): 92–99.

S., N. "Po voprosu o spetsial'noi podgotovke prepodavatelei v srednie shkoly." *Pedagogicheskii sbornik* 8 (August 1899): 128–36.

Sakharov, I. V. "O soiuznom dvizhenii uchashchikh tserkovno-prikhodskikh shkol." *Dlia narodnogo uchitelia* 2 (1907): 12–16.

Sakulin, P. "Moskovskoe pedagogicheskoe obshchestvo v 1905 godu." *Vestnik vospitaniia* 3 (March 1906): 45–58.

Samsonov, V. A. "Anketnye dannye o prakticheskoi i teoreticheskoi podgotovke uchitelei gorodskikh po Polozheniiu 1872 goda uchilishch." In *Trudy pervogo vserossiiskogo s"ezda uchitelei gorodskikh po polozheniiu 1872 g. uchilishch.* 2 vols. St. Petersburg, 1910.

Sanders, Jonathan. "Drugs and Revolution: Moscow Pharmacists in the First Russian Revolution." *Russian Review* 44 (1985): 351–77.

———. "The Union of Unions: Political, Economic, Civil and Human Rights Organizations in the 1905 Russian Revolution." Ph.D. diss., Columbia University, 1985.

Sankt-Peterburgskie vysshie zhenskie (Bestuzhevskie) kursy 1878–1918. Sbornik statei. Leningrad, 1973.

Satina, Sophie. *Education of Women in Pre-Revolutionary Russia.* New York, 1966.

Schneider, Joanne. "*Volksschullehrerinnen:* Bavarian Women Defining Themselves Through Their Profession." In *German Professions,* ed. Geoffrey Cocks and Konrad H. Jaraush, 85–103. New York: Oxford University Press, 1990.

Scott, Joan Wallach. "Gender: A Useful Category of Historical Analysis." *American Historical Review* 91 (December 1986): 1053–75.

"Sel'skie uchitelia o sel'skikh uchitel'nitsakh (Tri pis'ma v redaktsiiu)." *Russkii nachal'nyi uchitel'* 6–7 (1883): 413–18.

Semenov, D. D. *Gorodskoe samoupravlenie.* St. Petersburg, 1901.

———. "Nuzhdaiutsia li nashi zhenskie gimnasii v preobrazovanii i kakom imenno?" *Vestnik vospitaniia* 3 (March 1892): 19–27.

———. "Ocherki narodnogo obrazovaniia v Rossii." *Obrazovanie* 12 (December 1895): 264–67.

———. "Ocherki narodnogo obrazovaniia v Rossii: Moskovskie nachal'nye uchilishcha." *Zhenskoe obrazovanie* 4 (April 1891): 388–97.

———. "Ocherki narodnogo obrazovaniia v Rossii. S-peterburgskie nachal'nye uchilishcha." *Zhenskoe obrazovanie* 3 (March 1891): 298–307.

———. "Pervoe desiatiletie Spb. gorodskikh nachal'nykh uchilishch v vedenii stolichnogo obshchestvennogo upravleniia." *Russkaia starina,* September 1887, 669–703, October 1887, 163–95.

Sent-Iler, K. "Neskol'ko slov po povodu stat'i *Tserkovnykh vedomostei* ob uchitel'skikh seminariiakh." *Zhurnal Ministerstva Narodnogo Prosveshcheniia* 273 (January–February 1891): 39–55.

Seregny, Scott J. "Professional and Political Activism: The Russian Teachers' Movement, 1864–1908." Ph.D. diss., University of Michigan, 1982.

———. *Russian Teachers and Peasant Revolution: The Politics of Education in 1905.* Bloomington: Indiana University Press, 1989.

"S″ezd deiatelei po tekhnicheskomu i professional'nomu obrazovaniiu." *Russkaia mysl'* 2 (February 1896): 224–27.

Shchepkin, M. "Upravlenie gorodskimi uchilishchami v Moskve: Istoricheskii ocherk." *Russkaia mysl'* 26 (March 1905): 231–56.

Shorin, M. "Ob 'uchitel'skikh domakh' pri uchitel'skikh obshchestvakh vzaimopomoshchi." *Voprosy i nuzhdy uchitel'stva* 3 (1909): 30–35.

Showalter, Elaine. *The Female Malady: Women, Madness and English Culture, 1830–1980.* New York: Penguin, 1985.

Sinel, Allen. *The Classroom and the Chancellery: State Educational Reform in Russia under Count Dmitrii Tolstoi.* Cambridge: Harvard University Press, 1973.

Sitnikov, P. "Po povodu pisem sel'skikh uchitelei o sel'skikh uchitel'nitsakh." *Russkii nachal'nyi uchitel'* 8–9 (August–September 1883): 532.
Skowronek, Stephen. *Building a New American State: The Expansion of National Administrative Capacities, 1877–1920*. Cambridge, 1982.
Smith, Bonnie G. *Ladies of the Leisure Class: The Bourgeoises of Northern France in the Nineteenth Century*. Princeton: Princeton University Press, 1981.
Smith-Rosenberg, Carroll. *Disorderly Conduct: Visions of Gender in Victorian America*. New York: Knopf, 1985.
Solov'ev, I. "Pedagogika kak uchebnyi predmet v zhenskikh gimnaziiakh." *Vestnik vospitaniia* 4 (April 1913): 183–88.
S-ov, M. "Pervyi v Rossii Uchitel'skii Dom." *Dlia narodnogo uchitelia* 1 (1912): 9–14.
" 'S.-Peterburgskoe pedagogicheskoe obshchestvo vzaimnoi pomoshchi' ili 'Pedagogicheskii fond.' " *Russkaia shkola* 5–6 (May–June 1894): 283.
Stakhovich, A. "O bibliotekakh pri uchilishchakh—uchenicheskoi i uchitel'skoi i o katalogakh dlia nikh." *Russkaia mysl'* 1 (January 1902): 150–64.
Staryi uchitel'. "Nedavnee i vriad li proshloe moskovskoi gorodskoi shkoly." *Russkaia mysl'* 5 (May 1900): 201–07.
Stasiulevich, M. M. "Nuzhny li ekzameny v nachal'nykh uchilishchakh?" *Vestnik Evropy* 5 (May 1904): 423–25.
Statisticheskii ezhegodnik Moskovskoi gubernii za 1915 god. Moscow, 1916.
Stepanov, A. N. "Eksperty po uchebnoi chasti Peterburgskoi gorodskoi dumy." *Narodnoe obrazovanie* 5–6 (1946): 63–72.
———. "Shkola gorodskogo samoupravleniia v Rossii." *Sovetskaia pedagogika* 2 (February 1939): 119–26.
———. "Uchastie uchitel'stva Peterburga v pervoi russkoi revoliutsii." *Sovetskaia pedagogika* 1 (1941): 86–93.
Stepanskii, A. D. *Samoderzhavie i obshchestvennye organizatsii Rossii na rubezhe XIX–XX vv*. Moscow: Moskovskii gosudarstvennyi istoriko-arkhivnyi institut, 1980.
Stites, Richard. *The Women's Liberation Movement in Russia: Feminism, Nihilism, and Bolshevism, 1860–1930*. Princeton: Princeton University Press, 1978.
Strannoliubskii, A. "Nesostoiatel'nost' S.-Peterburgskoi Gorodskoi Dumy v dele narodnogo obrazovaniia." *Obrazovanie* 10 (October 1987): 143–70.
Surh, Gerald. *1905 in St. Petersburg: Labor, Society and Revolution*. Stanford: Stanford University Press, 1989.
T., E. "Pedagogicheskie kursy pri Moskovskom Obshchestve vospitatel'nits i uchitel'nits." *Obrazovanie* 3 (March 1893): 183–92.
Thurston, Robert W. *Liberal City, Conservative State: Moscow and Russia's Urban Crisis, 1906–1914*. New York, 1987.
Timberlake, Charles. "Higher Learning, the State and the Professions in

Russia." In *The Transformation of Higher Learning, 1860–1930*, ed. Konrad H. Jarausch. Chicago: University of Chicago Press, 1983.

Tishkin, G. A. *Zhenskii vopros v Rossii v 50–60gg. XIX v.* Leningrad, 1984.

Titov, A. "Postoiannyi i podvizhnoi pedagogicheskii muzei v Moskve." *Dlia narodnogo uchitelia* 20 (1908): 17–20.

Tsvetkov, I. L. "Pervyi s"ezd deiatelei po narodnomu obrazovaniiu v Moskovskom gorodskom obshchestvennom upravlenii." *Russkaia shkola* 9–10 (September–October 1912): 74–84.

———. "Uchitel'skoe dvizhenie 1905 goda." *Narodnyi uchitel'* 11 (November 1925): 20–24.

Tul'tseva, L. "Chernichki." *Nauka i religiia* 11 (1970): 81–82.

Tulupov, N. V. "Pervyi vserossiiskii s"ezd predstavitelei Obshchestv vspomoshchestvovaniia litsam uchitel'skogo zvaniia." *Russkaia mysl'* 3 (March 1903): 111–35.

———. "Petr Mikhailovich Shestakov." *Dlia narodnogo uchitelia* 1 (January 1915): 2–6.

———. "Uchitel'skii dom Obshchestva Vzaimnoi Pomoshchi pri Moskovskom Uchitel'skom Institute." *Dlia narodnogo uchitelia* 10 (1909): 3–7.

Tyack, David B. *The One Best System: A History of American Education.* Cambridge: Harvard University Press, 1974.

"Uchebnye programmy Peterburgskikh gorodskikh uchilishch, soderzhimykh dumoi." *Zhenskoe obrazovanie* 5 (May 1885): 407–14.

Uchenik, "Pamiati F. I. Egorova." *Dlia narodnogo uchitelia* 10 (May 1915): 1–6.

"Uchitel'skaia zabastovka v S-Peterburge v dni 14–21 oktiabria 1905 g." *Vestnik VSU* 1 (November 1905): 1–8.

Ushakov, A. V. *Revoliutsionnoe dvizhenie demokraticheskoi intelligentsii v Rossii 1895–1904.* Moscow: Mysl', 1976.

Ushinskii, K. D. *Man as the Object of Education.* Moscow, 1978.

Vakhterova, E. "O vserossiiskom uchitel'skom soiuze." *Vestnik vospitaniia* 1 (January 1906): 119–47.

V-ch. "Professional'nye nuzhdy moskovskogo uchitel'stva." *Russkii uchitel'* 3 (March 1912): 281–98, 4 (April 1912): 337–48.

Velikosel'skii, N. "Dumskie 4-kh-klassnye uchilishcha v Spb." *Russkii uchitel'* 10 (October 1913): 679–93.

Veysey, Laurence. "Who's a Professional? Who Cares?" *Reviews in American History* 4 (December 1975): 419–23.

Vipper, P. "Spetsial'naia podgotovka prepodavatelia srednei shkoly ili podniatie ego polozheniia?" *Vestnik vospitaniia* 6 (June 1898): 52–74.

Vitten, O. "Nekotorye etapy, proidennye uchitel'stvom v minuvshem godu." *Vestnik soiuza uchitelei* 1 (April 1906): 11–15.

Volkov, S. "Pervyi s"ezd narodnykh uchitelei i uchitel'nits." *Russkaia mysl'* 10 (October 1901): 208–18.

W., N. "Uchen'e i zdorov'e v zhenskikh gimnaziiakh." *Vestnik vospitaniia* 5 (May 1892): 85–107.
Whittaker, Cynthia. *The Origins of Modern Russian Education: An Intellectual Biography of Count Sergei Uvarov, 1786–1855*. DeKalb: Northern Illinois University Press, 1984.
Worobec, Christine. *Peasant Russia: Family and Community in Post-Emancipation Russia*. Princeton: Princeton University Press, 1991.
Wortman, Richard. *The Development of a Russian Legal Consciousness*. Chicago: Chicago University Press, 1976.
Zaionchkovsky, Peter A. *The Russian Autocracy in Crisis, 1878–1882*, trans. Gary Hamburg. Gulfbreeze: Academic International Press, 1979.
"Zakrytie uchitel'skogo s˝ezda." *Dlia narodnogo uchitelia* 4 (1912): 27–28.
"Zametka po povodu novoi organizatsii S.-Peterburgskikh nachal'nykh gorodskikh uchilishch." *Russkaia shkola* 9–10 (September–October 1897): 170–87.
"Zapiski prepodavatelei moskovskikh srednikh uchebnykh zavedenii." *Pravo* 6 (13 February 1905): 424–25.
Zelnik, Reginald E., ed. and trans. *A Radical Worker in Tsarist Russia: The Autobiography of Semen Ivanovich Kanatchikov*. Stanford: Stanford University Press, 1986.
——. "The Sunday School Movement in Russia, 1859–1862." *Journal of Modern History* 27 (June 1965): 151–70.
Zenchenko, S. "O podgotovke prepodavatelei srednikh uchebnykh zavedenii k pedagogicheskoi deiatel'nosti." *Vestnik vospitaniia* 4 (April 1896): 60–96.
Zhulev, P. "Uchitel'skie obshchestva vzaimopomoshchi." *Russkaia shkola* 1 (January 1912): 1–20.
——. "Vtoroi Vserossiiskii s˝ezd predstavitelei uchitel'skikh obshchestv vzaimopomoshchi." *Russkii uchitel'* 3 (1912): 253–66, 5 (1912): 455–60.
Zolotarev, S. "Vtoroi s˝ezd prestavitelei uchitel'skikh obshchestv." In *Professional'nye uchitel'skie organizatsii na Zapade i v Rossii: sbornik statei*, 282–93. Petrograd, 1915.
Zp., N. "K voprosu o material'nom polozhenii uchitelei gorodskikh uchilishch." *Obrazovanie* 5–6 (May–June 1901): 69–75.
Zviagintsev, E. "Iz zhizni moskovskikh prosvetitel'nykh obshchestv." *Vestnik vospitaniia* 3 (March 1911): 20–51.

Index

Abused students, 14–15, 42
Administration: and meetings with teachers, 94, 172–75; of primary schools, 15, 16, 45–47, 171; reforms demanded of, 138, 160; and relations with teachers, 34–35, 42–43, 45, 49, 93, 159, 188; representation of teachers in, 19, 87–88, 111, 135–36, 174, 181
Admission, open, to schools, 132, 138, 160–61
Adult education, 167
Advanced primary schools, 35–36, 37–40, 111–12
Age: of Petersburg women teachers, 78–79; of graduates of teachers' institutes, 37, 39
Alexander I, 24, 25
Alexander II, 3, 24, 30, 185
All-Russian Industrial Exhibition (1896), 92, 105–06
All-Russian Pedagogical Society, 182
All-Russian Teachers' House, 181
All-Russian Teachers' Union, 115, 130, 133. *See also* VSU
All-Russian Union of Secondary Schoolteachers, 160–62, 163
All-Russian Union of Teachers and Education Activists. *See* VSU
All-Russian Women's Congress, 168–69
Alumni organizations, after teacher training programs, 35, 41
Amnesty, for insurgent teachers, 139–40
Antigovernment sentiment, 44; in teachers' movement, 67, 91, 122–23, 189; in teacher training programs, 23, 35, 41
Arbitrary treatment (*proizvol*), 44–49, 60–61. *See also* Legal rights, lack of
Arkhangel'skii, N. A., 120
Army, 10, 154, 155–56, 164
Arrests, 162, 165; of activists, 115, 147–48, 154
Artisans, 12–13
Arts, and women's education, 29
Authority. *See* Power and authority

Autocracy: and civil society, 91, 109–10, 185, 187, 188–89; and individuals, 10, 44, 50, 60–61, 89, 159, 170; strength of, 156–57, 163, 164
Autonomy: of the child, 22; in definition of the professional, 6, 8, 9, 11, 61; and marriage ban, 76, 119, 120; and pedagogy, 23, 44, 50; and professional identity, 43, 91, 108, 122, 133–34, 141; of secondary schools, 152; of universities, 147

Bairak, A. S., 178
Baltalon, I. P., 148
Banquet campaign (1904), 113, 124
Bestuzhev (St. Petersburg Higher Women's) courses, 32–33, 35, 215n36
Black Hundreds, 131–32, 148, 153
Bloody Sunday, 128, 130–31, 139
"Bloody Sunday of the schools," 131–32
Bolsheviks, 16–17, 144–45
Books, 95, 109, 123. *See also* Texts
Bourgeoisie, 17, 56
Boycotts, 150, 153
Boys' schools, 57
Bulygin, Minister of Interior, 133
Bureaucracy, 5, 6–7; educational, 16, 44–47, 131; government, 10, 12–13, 53, 59–60, 89, 98; teachers as bureaucrats, 18, 21, 133, 134
Business, 53; by merchants, 8, 12–13, 56, 186

Capitalism, 6, 186
Centralization: of schools, 80–81, 167; in union, 160–61
Chaikovskii, S. K., 72
Charnoluskii, V. I., 144
Chebysheva-Dmitrieva, E. A., 169
Chekhov, "man in the footlocker" image of, 18, 42
Chekhov, Mariia, 223n29
Chekhov, N. V., 75, 121, 122, 180, 223n29
Chekhova, Maria, 168

249

INDEX

Child-centered pedagogy, 22, 24–25, 28–29, 40, 55, 95
Children, 12–13, 69–70, 130, 181; and marriage ban for women teachers, 71, 118, 157–58. *See also* Students
Cholera epidemic (1891–1892), 97–98
Citizenship, 3–5, 87. *See also* Civil society
City teachers, 16–17, 212n30; organizations of, 14, 94–97, 133–37, 152, 192–95; and pedagogy, 34–35, 94: politics of, 114, 142–47, 165; problems of, 14–15, 42, 108–09, 188; profile of, 13–15, 16, 187–88, 195–97; reaction to citywide teachers' meeting, 173–75; reforms proposed by, 47, 80–81, 110–11, 135, 137–38, 165, 170–71, 174, 181; and religious education, 51–52; salaries of, 56–60
Civil rights: demand for, 4–5, 124, 138; for women, 29–30. *See also* Legal rights; Marriage ban
Civil service. *See* Bureaucracy
Civil society, 98; and conflict with autocracy, 50, 55, 85–86, 91, 187; creation of, 3–5, 55–56, 61, 195–97
Classical training, in boys' secondary education, 53
Clergy, 10, 21, 51–52. *See also* Religion; Religious education
Cohn, Samuel, 81
Commission for Investigating Lives . . . of Primary Schoolteachers, 101
Commission on Education, 130; and teachers, 51–52, 77, 94, 151, 159. *See also* Marriage ban; Petersburg
Community, sense of: in schools, 46, 80; in teacher training programs, 40–41
Competition: between men and women, 68–71, 83–85; in the professions, 7; in Russian society, 13, 21
Congresses: of advanced primary schoolteachers, 111–12, 177–78; importance of, 92, 103–04, 107, 172–75, 179; of mutual-aid societies, 121–22, 166–67, 179–83; technical, 92, 104–06, 121–23; of VSU, 142–47, 161–62, 162; women's, 168–69; zemstvo congress, 123–24
Congress for Advanced Primary Schoolteachers, 177–78
Congress of 1912, 172–75
Congress on Women's Education, 168–69
Conservatives, 30, 53, 138

Counterreforms, 185
Court of honor, 110, 135, 174
Crimean War, 29, 185
Cultural centers (teachers' houses), 177–79
Cultural missionaries, teachers as, 13, 22, 65–66, 70
Cultural organizations for teachers, 95, 101
Curators, of teacher training institutions, 26–27, 107, 110
Curriculum: in Russian schools, 12–13; problems with, 14–15, 42, 50; reforms of, 29–30, 112, 171–72; in teacher training programs, 22–23, 31–32, 37–40

December Uprising, 154, 157
Demkov, M., 38
Democraticization of school system, 13, 95, 160–61
Department of the Institution of the Empress Maria, 30–31, 57–58
D'iakonova, E., 32
Directors, of schools, 57, 58
Discipline, 34, 54, 55
Discrimination: against Jews, 179; against women, 63, 65, 73, 84, 170. *See also* Marriage ban
Disease, 97–98, 118; among students, 42, 188
Dismissals. *See* Firings
Dolgorukov, P. D., 121, 123, 124
Dushechkin, Ia. V., 137

Education: adult, 167; control of, 45, 142; in definition of teaching profession, 7, 8, 9; need for, 12, 56, 80, 98, 105; philosophy of, 25, 50–51; rewards of, 43, 57, 60; and social classes, 12–13, 19, 53; of teachers' children, 59, 115, 181; technical, 104–06, 121–23; for women, 29–35, 62–63. *See also* Reform; Religious education; Vocational education; types of schools
Educational Exhibition, at the All-Russian Industrial Exhibition (1896), 105–06
Educational policy: discussion of, 93, 99; power over, 46–47, 159; proposed reforms of, 135, 136, 160–61, 167
Eklof, Ben, 65
Eksperty (pedagogical advisors), 46–47, 77–78, 171
Elite: education of, 12–13, 21; as source of professionals, 13–14, 68–71; rewards for,

250

4, 10, 55–56; secondary school teachers as, 60, 141
Employer/employee relations, 60–61
Employment, 4–5; women's right to, 29–30, 169
Engel, Barbara Alpern, 74
Engelstein, Laura, 135–36
Entrance exams, 12
Equality: among teachers, 192, 193; in society, 129–30, 166, 182–94. *See also* Social justice
Era of the Great Reforms. *See* Great Reforms
Estate system. *See* Social classes
Ethics: standards for, 8, 9, 136. *See also* Court of honor; Values
Ethos, of professional teachers, 89, 165, 174; creation of, 15, 18, 28, 41, 61, 83–84
Europe. *See* Western Europe
Eval'd, F. F., 77
Exclusion: strategy of closure, 7, 17; of women, 62–63, 71, 73, 83
Executive Commission on Education (Petersburg), 46; hiring women teachers, 77–80, 81
Experience, for teachers, 81–82; in classroom, 19, 33, 37–38
Expertise, technical: and educational policy, 69–71, 93; and teachers' professional identity, 43, 49, 61, 108; value of, 8, 57, 172
Experts: professionals as, 5, 10, 21–22; teachers' self-image as, 18, 26, 40–41, 45, 83, 87–88. *See also* eksperty

Facilities: educational, 15; and housing for women teachers, 69, 72, 80, 119; in Moscow Teachers' House, 178
Factory workers, 13, 128. *See also* Workers
Fal'bork, G. A., 158
Families: of teachers, 47–49, 59, 60, 78–79; women's education for, 29–30, 31–32. *See also* Marriage ban; Parents
Famine of 1891, 90, 97–98
Famintsyn, A. S., 121
Feminist organizations, 17, 168–70, 223n29, 230n8
Firings: causes for, 44, 47, 49; and denial of right of appeal, 47, 188; and marriage ban, 70, 76–77, 117, 118; for political activity, 73, 97, 148–49, 165; proposals about, 135, 174, 181

First All-Russian Congress of Representatives of Teachers' Mutual-Aid Societies, 107–11
First Congress of Russian Participants in Technical and Vocational Education, 104
First Congress of the All-Russian Teachers' Union, 142–47
First Technical Congress, 104
Foreign languages, and women's education, 29, 53
Fourth Congress of the VSU, 162
France, 7
Freedoms: as civil liberties, 138–39, 140, 151–52, 153; educational, 16, 94–95, 122, 136, 142, 160–61; professional, 10
Frieden, Nancy Mandelker, 11–12, 59
Froebel, Friedrich Wilhelm, 95

Gender: role of in professions, 7–8, 62–63; role of in teaching profession, 17, 30, 69–71
Gender roles: and political passivity of women, 137; of women and teachers, 64, 67, 69–70, 73–74, 81, 83, 118, 119, 190
General Questions Section at Second Technical Congress, 105
Gerd, A. Ia., 77–78
Gerd, V. A., 144
Girls. *See* Women
Girls' schools, 57
Government: and education reform, 13, 87–88; and professionals, 6–7, 9–12; relief, 97–98; responses to unrest by, 122–23, 147–48, 155; and teachers, 42, 44–49, 59–60, 92; and women, 73, 74, 100. *See also* Autocracy; Government-sponsored professionalization; Local government; Ministry of Education; Moscow; Petersburg; Reform
Government institutions, 3, 5, 11–12
Government schools, 133
Government-sponsored professionalization, 21–24, 41, 48–49, 85–86, 87, 187, 189
Govorov, Sergei, 115–16, 117
Great Britain, 7–9
Great Reforms, 3–5, 21–24, 44, 87, 185
Guerrier (Moscow Higher Women's) courses, 32–33, 215n36
Gymnasiums, 53, 131–32; for women, 30, 31–32, 78–79

251

INDEX

Head teachers, 16, 46, 135
Hierarchies: in government, 18; of status and power, 129–30, 145–46; 166; in teaching profession, 146, 182–84; women in, 62–63, 81–82, 83
Higher women's courses, 32–33, 35, 215n36
Hiring issues, 76–78, 135, 174, 181
Holy women image, 64, 74–76
Hunger, among students, 14–15, 42, 188

Identity: formation of teachers, 27–28, 35, 39–41, 92, 96, 104; professionals, 10, 11; of secondary school teachers, 26, 141; social, 4; student, 27–28; Teachers' House as symbol of, 178–79; teachers' professional, 14, 18, 23, 61, 64–65, 133–34, 145–46, 195–97
Il'in, A., 149–50
Illness: 97–98, 118; among students, 42, 188
Image: of public servants, 183–84; of teachers, 18; and teachers' self-image, 23, 73–74, 78, 82, 195–97; of women, 100; of women teachers, 63–65, 69, 71–72, 76, 78, 80, 83, 191
Imperial Russian Technical Society, 95
Individualism: and government authority, 61, 159; and professionals, 6, 11; among teachers, 43, 44, 49, 55, 61, 76, 165
Industrialization, 56, 81
Initiative, of teachers, 18–19, 87–89, 91, 105
Inspectors, of schools, 57, 58, 148, 153
Intelligentsia: professional, 5, 9–10, 11, 184; radical, 11, 43, 108, 133–34, 185–86; service ideal of, 49, 56, 114–15, 143, 195–97; and teachers, 13, 66–67, 68
Interactive pedagogy, 25
Isolation, 109–10; of city teachers, 94, 95; and lack of power, 88, 92; of rural teachers, 14, 108–09; of secondary school teachers, 160, 161
Ivanovskii, P., 26

Japan, and Russo-Japanese War, 123, 128
Jews, 179

Kaluga Mutual-Aid Society, 107
Khar'kov Society to Aid Working Women, 120
Korporatsiia, in Moscow City Teachers' Association name, 124–25
Kraevskii, A. A., 77
Kursk, 132

Labor unions. *See* Unions
Ladder system of education, 12–13; call for, 112, 137–38, 142, 152, 160–61
Languages: foreign, 29, 53; local vs. Russian, 122, 131, 138, 142
Larson, Magali Sarfatti, 6
Latyshev, V. A., 94
Law, rule of. *See* Legal rights
Leaders: of organizations, 103, 121, 144, 153; of teachers' movement, 47–48, 97, 98, 109, 121–22, 137; of Union of Teachers, 114, 115
Lectures, for teachers, 102, 105–06, 139
Legal rights, 3, 110; and proposed reforms, 122, 135, 139; teachers' lack of, 44–49, 47
Legislative body: formation of, 132, 133; rights for women in, 139. *See also* State Duma
Lesson plans, 34, 37
Liberal arts, 12, 13, 29–30
Liberation movement, 19, 120, 152. *See also* Union of Liberation
Libraries, of teachers' resource materials, 34, 99, 101, 102, 178
Literacy, in Russian society, 12, 13, 21; societies for, 98. *See also* Education
Literacy Committee of the Free Economic Society, 95
Literacy Committee of the Moscow Agricultural Society, 95
Local government: and Great Reforms, 185; and schools, 19, 21, 45, 167–68; and teachers, 88. *See also* Moscow; Petersburg
Lower classes, 10, 12–13, 33–34. *See also* Peasants

Manifesto of the Petersburg Union of Secondary Schoolteachers, 140–41
"Man in a footlocker" (Chekhov story), 18, 42
Mariinskaia Gymnasium, 78–79
Marriage: and women teacherrs, 72, 117–18. *See also* Marriage ban
Marriage ban: and acceptance of women teachers, 191, 192; in St. Petersburg, 78–80, 113, 115–20, 156–59, 166, 168–70, 181–82, 193–94; purpose of, 81–82; and sexuality of teachers, 116, 118
Meehan-Waters, Brenda, 74
Meetings, 26, 51, 122; of city teachers, 14, 34, 172–75; places for, 178; restrictions on, 90, 94, 105–06, 112. *See also* Congresses; Mutual-aid societies; Pedagogical societies

252

Membership: of mutual-aid societies, 97, 98, 101, 175; of pedagogical societies, 93, 102; of teachers' organizations, 113, 124, 133–34; of VSU, 144, 162
Methodology, pedagogical, 34, 112; modern, 24–25, 44, 52, 187–88; in secondary schools, 15, 25–27, 53–54; in teacher training programs, 32, 37. *See also* Child-centered pedagogy
Middle class, 63, 184; development of, 210–11nn20; and professionals, 5–6, 8–9; in Russia, 8–9, 195–97
Ministry of Education, 13, 53, 159; and local control, 15, 94, 167; and reform, 21–24, 30–31, 55, 89; restrictions on organizations imposed by, 96, 98, 99, 101–02, 103–04, 106, 107–08, 179; and shutdown of organizations, 93, 110–11, 139, 182; and teachers, 26–27, 57–60, 66, 67–68, 88, 108; teacher training programs of, 23, 24–28, 35–41
Ministry of Finance, 57–58, 104–06, 216n1
Ministry of Internal Affairs, 101, 148–49, 179–80, 182
Monitor (nastavnik), 54
Moral education, 54; and women as teachers, 70–71, 73–74, 75. *See also* Religious education
Morozova, V. A., 140
Moscow: city government of, 134, 148–50, 170–71; primary schools of, 15–16, 45–47; strikes in, 150, 155–56; teachers in, 14–15, 96, 172–75. *See also* City teachers
Moscow Advanced Primary Schools Congress, 111–12
Moscow City Teachers' Association, 124–25
Moscow District Teachers' Congress, 92, 106
Moscow Higher Women's (Guerrier) Courses, 32–33, 215n36
Moscow Mutual-Aid Society, 175
Moscow Pedagogical Society, 102–03, 130–31, 132, 137
Moscow Society for the Improvement of Living Conditions, 96, 101–02, 110, 113, 179–80; projects of, 107, 123, 124, 177
Moscow Soviet, 155
Moscow Teachers' Association, 133–36, 148, 150, 155, 164; divisions within, 152, 153–54
Moscow Teachers' House, 177–79
Moscow Teachers' Institute, 38–39, 111–12

Moscow Teachers' Institute Mutual-Aid Society, 177
Moscow Union of Secondary Schoolteachers, 152
Mothers: image of women teachers as, 64, 80–81, 83; and marriage ban, 119, 158; training to aid women as, 28–29, 30, 31–32
Municipal Employees' Union, 148
Museums, pedagogical, 101, 102, 109
Mutual-Aid Congress, 113, 115–16
Mutual-Aid Fund for Teachers in the Moscow City Public and Private Schools, 96
Mutual-aid societies, 96–103; congresses of, 107–08, 121–22, 166–67, 179–83; importance of, 106–07, 125–26, 177; membership of, 124, 175; purposes of, 91, 176; spiritual assistance provided by, 176–78; union of, 109–10
Mutual-Aid Societies' Congress, 92
Mutual-Aid Society at the Moscow Teachers' Institute, 96
Mutual-Aid Society for Former Students of the St. Petersburg Teachers' Institute, 96
Mutual-Aid Society for Male and Female Primary Schoolteachers in the St. Petersburg Province, 96
Mutual-Aid Society for Members of the Teaching Profession in the City of Moscow, 96

Nabokov, V. D., 158
Nastavnik (monitor), 54
Networks: during and after teacher training programs, 27–28, 35, 40–41; of teachers, 88, 92
Nicholas II: and October Manifesto, 151, 154; reforms of, 132–33, 147, 163
Nikiforova, Natalia, 72, 73, 74
1905 Revolution. *See* Revolution of 1905
1908 school bill, 167
1912 Congress, 172–75
1912 resolution, 174
Ninth Pirogov Congress, 122, 123
Nizhnii Novgorod Exhibition (1896), 107
Nobility, 10, 12–13, 56, 154
"Notes of the Moscow Secondary Schoolteachers," 132

Observers, government, 107, 110
October General Strike, 150–51, 152

253

INDEX

October Manifesto, 151–52, 154
One-room schoolhouses, 16, 80–82, 220–21n46
Open admission to schools, 132, 138, 160–61
Oppression: of students, 36, 37, 54; of teachers, 112, 164, 189; of women, 49. *See also* Marriage ban
Organizations: alumni, 35, 41; feminist, 17, 168–70, 223n29, 230n8; increasing number of, 124, 151–52; of professionals, 9, 91, 96; of teachers, 88–92, 92, 137–41, 175, 182; and women in teachers' groups, 17, 73, 100. *See also* Leaders; Mutual-aid societies; Pedagogical societies; Unions
Orthodox Church, 49, 51–52, 100
Outsiders: women excluded as, 190–91; women teachers described as, 17, 65–71, 73, 84
Overcrowding, of classrooms, 14–15, 42

Parents, of schoolchildren, 19, 150; and relation to teachers, 49, 132, 159, 160
Parents' committees, 159
Parsons, Talcott, 5–6
Peasants: and education, 12, 97–98; and Great Reforms, 3–4; revolts of, 154, 164; as teachers, 14, 36–37, 67, 68; and women teachers, 65–71, 75
Peasant's Union, 153
Pedagogical councils, 94, 112, 132, 160–61
Pedagogical societies, 91, 93–94, 95, 102–03, 124. *See also* Congresses; Meetings
Pedagogical Society of the University of Moscow, 58–59
Pedagogical training, 19, 95; ongoing, 106, 181; in teacher training programs, 25–27, 37–41; for women, 28–29, 31–32, 33, 78–79, 215n35
Pedagogy. *See* Child-centered pedagogy; Methodology
Peer review board. *See* Court of honor
Pensions, 57, 58, 79–80, 82, 136
People's university, 167
Perkin, Harold, 7, 17
Pestalozzi, Johann, 22, 24–25
Petersburg: and marriage ban, 78–80, 81–83, 119, 120, 156–59, 168–70; organizations in, 96–101, 136, 140–41, 179–80; primary schools in, 15–16, 45–47, 77; strikes in, 151; teachers in, 14–15, 51–52. *See also* City teachers

Petersburg Commission on Education. *See* Commission on Education
Petersburg Froebel Society, 95
Petersburg Literacy Society, 98
Petersburg Mutual-Aid Society, 96–101, 113, 120, 136–38, 175–76; and Second Congress of Mutual-Aid Societies, 121–22, 179–80
Petersburg Pedagogical Society, 93–94. *See also* Ushinskii Commission
Petersburg Soviet, 154
Petersburg Teachers' Association, 156–59
Petersburg Teachers' Institute, 36–37
Petitions: direct to throne, 132–33; by students, 131; by teachers, 130–31, 136, 150; by workers, 128
Petrunkevich, M. I., 158
Pirogov, N. I., 29
Pirogov Society, 102, 109, 122, 123
Pleve, Minister of Internal Affairs, 123
Pokrovskii, M. N., 137
Police, 47, 115, 131–32, 142
Political activity, by teachers, 82–93, 93, 113, 176; government definition of, 89, 90–91
Political affiliations: of teachers, 137, 194; in teachers' organizations, 126–27, 148–49, 165–66
Political impact: of rural teachers, 66–67, 68, 71–72; of women teachers, 73, 84
Political parties, 113–14, 140, 144, 166. *See also* Social Democratic Party; Social Revolutionary Party
Political passivity, 66, 68, 137, 142–43, 156–59
Political reliability, of teachers, 14, 22–23, 35–41, 47–48, 53–54, 72, 148–49
Political self-interest, 8–9, 11; of teachers, 114–15, 194, 196–97
Pomoshchniki (assistants), 171, 172
Potehkin, P. A., 157, 169
Poverty, effects of on education, 14–15, 42, 98
Power and authority, 185; in the classroom, 42, 55, 83, 173–74; denial of to women, 62–63, 81–82, 100; in educational bureaucracy, 44–47, 94; government's reluctance to share, 4, 85–86, 88; in society, 129–30, 138, 145–46, 166, 185–86; in teachers' organizations, 145, 160–61, 193
Primary schools: administered by government, 15; control of, 45, 167–68; problems of, 42, 50–52, 99–100; trustees in, 45–47.

See also Advanced primary schools; Moscow; Petersburg

Primary schoolteachers, 22, 28–29, 133–34, 151; salaries of, 56–57, 60; in teachers' organizations, 101, 122, 141, 192–195

Private life: of holy women, 75; of students, 54; of teachers, 52, 136. *See also* Marriage ban; Surveillance

Professional consciousness, 47; affronts to, 48–49, 50, 82; creating, 27–28, 41, 43, 83–84, 96; results of, 178–79, 182–84

Professional organizations. *See* Mutual-aid societies; Pedagogical societies; Organizations; Teachers' movement; Unions

Professional-political platform, 176–77; in teachers' movement, 140, 142–47, 161–62, 191–93, 194–95

Professions: at banquet campaigns, 124; development of, 5–11; and gender, 17–18, 62–63; and government, 5, 19, 91, 98; identity of, 4, 195–97; institutions governing, 6, 8; organizations of, 90, 102, 122, 124–25, 125; and politics, 144–45, 164, 169–70; rewards for, 10, 59, 186

Pro-gymnasiums, 30

Proizvol (arbitrary treatment), 44–49, 60–61. *See also* Legal rights

Public Education Section, of Petersburg Mutual-Aid Society, 99–100, 120, 136

Public service, 22–23, 88; and Russian professionals, 9, 10–11, 195–97; values of, 57, 61, 183–97; values of, 57, 61, 183–84, 186

Public sphere, concept of, 11, 14, 195–97

Puzyrevskii, G. A., 149, 173, 175

Quality of education, 21–22, 26, 39–40, 87

"Questions of Life" (Pirogov), 29

Radicals, 53; image of women teachers as, 69, 71–72; and revolution, 92, 128; and service image of women, 64, 74; in teacher's movement, 114–15, 124–25, 126, 133–34, 149

Redkin, P. G., 93, 95

Reform, 19, 29, 60–61; and connection of issues, 19, 89–90; of education by government, 26–27, 29–30, 52–53, 55, 80–81, 85–86, 161; and proposals for education, 110–11, 122–23, 131, 132, 135, 137–38, 165, 174, 181; social, proposals for, 124, 129–30, 137–38, 165; of teachers and education, 13, 47, 87–92, 99, 105, 159, 170–71; urged, 92, 95. *See also* Great Reforms

Relief efforts, after famine of 1891–1892, 90, 98

Religion: Orthodox Church, 49, 51–52, 100; and women teachers, 64, 74

Religious education, 51–52; elimination of, 132, 138, 142

Reports: at congresses, 105, 107, 108–09, 115–16, 121–22, 169; at meetings, 102–03, 172–75

Rescript, issued by Nicholas II, 132–33

Resolutions, 122–23, 130–31, 137–38, 169, 174

Restrictions: on mutual-aid societies, 99, 101–02, 107, 179; on teachers' congresses, 106, 111–12; on teachers' organizations, 89–90, 98

Revolutionary movement, 18, 64, 92, 113–15, 128, 133

Revolution of 1905: beginning of, 91, 128; ending, 152, 163; groups in, 92, 130, 168; results of, 159–60, 164–65, 167, 170, 194–95

Rewards: desired by teachers, 10, 43, 55–56, 141, 145–46, 165; in ideal society, 129–30, 182–84, 186; traditional, 4

Reztsov, N. A., 178

Rights. *See* Civil rights; Legal rights

Role models, 51–52, 74–75; teachers as, 47, 49, 61

Rote memorization, 22, 24, 27

Rousseau, Jean-Jacques, 83

Rozanov, Vasilii, 119

Rozhkov, N. A., 137, 144

Rule of law. *See* Legal rights

Rumiantseva, Nadezhda P., 115–16, 180, 181

Rural teachers, 14, 21, 36–37; organizations of, 176–77, 192–95; politics of, 114, 143, 144, 164; problems of, 16, 108–09, 153, 162; women as, 63, 65–71. *See also* Primary schoolteachers

Russia: modernization of, 3, 13, 21, 87, 89, 185; transformation of, 129–30, 185–87. *See also* Government

Russian language, 21, 50; versus local dialects and languages, 122, 131, 138, 142

Russian Women's Mutual Philanthropic Society, 168–69

Russo-Japanese War, 123, 128; and Social Democratic Party platform, 140, 142, 143

255

INDEX

Sacrifice: radical intelligentsia's, 43, 49, 56; of sexuality, 75, 84. *See also* Service
Salaries: effects of low, 27, 44; relation to status, 10, 55–57, 59–60; of teachers, 14–15, 21–22, 112, 115–16, 136, 181; and women teachers, 70, 77–78, 78, 80, 81–82
Sanatoriums, 107, 109
Scholarships, for teachers' institutes, 36
School bill of 1908, 167
Schools: increasing numbers of, 21, 87; subsidies for, 167; supplies for, 42, 95; transformation of, 18–19, 138. *See also* Primary schools; Reform; Secondary schools; Vocational education
"Schools of democracy," 96–97
Secondary schools, 45; problems of, 42, 52–55, 140–41; reforms proposed for, 132, 160–61; students in, 12, 131–32, 159–60
Secondary schoolteachers, 21, 55; organizations of, 152, 159, 192–95; politics of, 132, 138–39, 145–46, 151; salaries of, 57–60; training of, 24–28, 32–33
Secondary Teachers' Union, 151
Second Congress of Mutual-Aid Societies, 121–22, 179–83
Second Mutual-Aid Society Congress, 182–84
Second Technical Congress, 104–05
Self-reliance, 6, 11, 61
Seregny, Scott J., 66, 197
Serfs. *See* Peasants
Service, 10–11, 43, 135, 166; groups devoted to, 13–14; to the people, 10, 56, 114–15, 133–34, 143, 183–84, 188–89, 195–97; to tsar, 10, 89, 188–89; and women, 30, 64, 84, 117
Sexuality, 75, 84. *See also* Marriage ban
Shestakov, P. M., 47–48, 121
Shvarz, Aleksandr, 152
Social classes: cooperation of, 135–36; and government, 3–5, 12–13; professionals' place in, 5–6, 8–9; in rural schools, 63, 65–71, 72; teachers' identification with, 57, 194; in teachers' movement, 84–85, 129, 134, 145–46, 182–84
Social Democratic Party, 114, 126–27, 137; and VSU, 140, 142, 144
Social Democratic Teachers' Union, 151
Socialism, 113–15, 143, 186–87
Social justice, 13, 145–46, 146. *See also* Equality; Hierarchies

Social mobility, 5–6, 8
Social Revolutionary Party, 126–27, 144, 224–25n69
Society for the Dissemination of Technical Knowledge, 95
Society for the Welfare of Women Educators and Teachers in Russia, 96
Soldiers, 10, 154, 155–56, 164
Soviets, 16–17
Specialization, of teachers, 22, 26, 31, 32, 187–88
St. Petersburg Higher Women's (Bestuzhev) Courses, 32–33, 35, 215n36
St. Petersburg Mutual-Aid Society, 96. *See also* Petersburg Mutual-Aid Society
Staff meetings, for teachers, 94
Stasiulevich, M. M., 77, 157–58
State Duma, 151, 161, 163
Status, social: criteria for, 165, 186; and hierarchy, 166, 182–84; raising one's, 67, 68, 83; relation to salaries, 55–57, 59–60; as reward for service, 13–14, 145–46; of teachers, 13–14, 23; of teaching, 21–22, 30, 40; and women, 7–8, 17–18, 62–63, 100
Stolypin State Duma, 163
Strike committees, 150, 151, 155
Strikes, 131, 147, 153, 168; general, 150–51, 152, 154–55
Students, 93; and government, 24, 36–37, 91, 131–32, 159–60, 189; identity as, 27–28, 229n67; problems of, 14–15, 42, 188; and relations with teachers, 15, 39, 42, 54, 118, 161, 188
Suffrage, 139, 140, 151–52
Supervision, 27, 171; and gender, 62–63, 78, 83
Surveillance: of students, 15, 54, 131, 132, 189; of teachers, 46, 47–49; at teachers' institutes, 36, 37
Sviatopolk-Mirskii, Petr, 123
Synthetic turnover, marriage bans as, 81–82
Sytin, I. D., 178

Teachers: commitment of, 40, 181; and the governmment, 12, 13, 19, 130–41, 168; quality of, 21–22, 32, 38, 59, 76, 77–78, 81, 99; supply of, 26, 31, 36, 67–68, 74, 78–79, 81–82, 169; working conditions of, 14–15, 16, 42, 99–100, 108–09, 115–16, 135–36, 181, 188. *See also* City teachers; Primary schoolteachers; Secondary school-

256

teachers; Reform; Rural teachers; Teacher training programs; Women
Teachers' clubs, 27, 137–41
Teachers' houses, 166, 177–79, 181
Teachers' institutes, 22, 35–41
Teachers' movement: development of, 85–86, 87–92, 96–97, 104, 106–07, 128–29; leaders of, 15, 97, 98, 121–22, 137; politics in, 146–47, 165–67, 191–93, 194–95; women in, 100
Teachers' seminaries, 22, 36, 39
Teacher training programs, 24–28, 35–41, 51, 189; reform of, 21–22, 187; women's, 28–35, 78–79, 215n35
Technical congresses. *See* Congresses, technical
Technical education, 167. *See also* Congresses, technical; Vocational education
Tenure, 25–26, 59, 100; for women teachers, 28, 66, 76, 78, 79, 81–82
Texts, choice of, 46, 54, 171–72
Third Congress of the VSU, 161–62
Third Element, 108, 133
Third Technical Congress, 121–23
Tolstoi, Dmitrii, 12, 25, 89, 93
Tolstoi system of education, 12–13, 54–55
Transfers, of teachers, 66, 135, 136, 174, 181
Transformation: of schools, 18–19, 160–61; of society, 9, 138, 145–46, 185–87. *See also* Reform
Trustees, of schools: elimination of, 171, 174; and teachers, 45–47, 173, 216n2
Tsvetkov, I. L., 148–50, 180
Tuition, for students, 12, 36; for teachers' children, 59, 181
Tulupov, N. V., 109, 177–78
Tutors, 21, 33, 59

Ukaz, of Nicholas II, 132–33, 134
Unification: and deemphasis on differences, 92, 113, 166–67, 182–83, 189–93; obstacles to, 11, 84–85, 114, 130, 140–47, 145–47, 161–62; power of, 88, 103, 106, 126–27, 178–79
Union of Liberation, 114–15, 122, 124, 138–39
Union of Municipal Employees, 134, 136; strikes of, 150, 155
Union of Petersburg Secondary Schoolteachers, 146
Union of Railroad Workers, 154–55
Union of Teachers, 113–15, 123, 224–25n69

Union of Unions, 147–48
Union of Women's Equality, 168
Unions, 153; and government, 134, 154, 168, 193; illegal, 113–15, 128; locals, 139, 146–47, 159; professional, 124, 133, 144–45; teachers, 107, 109–10, 124–25, 133–34, 137–41, 152, 160–62, 224–25n69
United States, 5–9
Universal education, 132, 138, 142, 167
Universities, 13, 27–28, 147, 229n67; people's, 167; and teacher training, 24–28, 32–33
Upper class, 63, 68–71, 145–46. *See also* Elite
Universities, 13, 27–28, 147, 229n67; people's, 167; and teacher training, 24–28, 32–33
Ushinskii, Konstantin D., 25, 30, 180
Ushinskii Commission, 99, 122, 139
Uvarov, Sergei, 25

Vakhterov, V. P., 100, 105
Values: and impact of teachers, 104, 165, 172; of the intelligentsia, 11, 114–15, 133–34; of civil society, 85–86; of professionals, 43–44, 61, 89, 108, 181, 183–84; of teachers, affronts to, 76, 82. *See also* specific values, e.g. Autonomy; Service
Virginity, of prospective teachers, 49
Visions: of ideal schools, 160–61; of ideal society, 129–30, 138, 141, 145–46, 166, 185–87
Vocational education, 12, 13, 95. *See also* Congresses, technical
VSU (All-Russian Union of Teachers and Education Activists), 151, 153; congresses of, 142–47, 161–62, 162; formation of, 137, 140; politics in, 140–41, 165–66, 176

Western Europe, 53, 90, 112; professionalization of, 5, 7–9
What Is to Be Done? (Chernyshevskii), 30
Witte, Sergei, 56
"Woman question," 28–29, 63, 67
Women, 17, 59; education of, 15, 45, 53; image of, 63–71, 73–76; liberation of, 63; in organizations, 97, 105–06, 146, 173, 181–82; and politics, 66, 137; in professions, 7–8, 62–63; status of, 100, 139; as teachers, 17–18, 49, 63, 67–74, 77–78, 99–100, 138, 190–92; in teacher training programs, 28–29, 31–32, 33, 215n35. *See also* Marriage ban; Primary schoolteachers; Rural teachers

257

INDEX

Women's liberation, 63
Workday, eight-hour, 140, 142, 143
Workers: education of, 12–13, 13, 95; living conditions of, 56, 60, 138, 143; organizations of, 91, 128; teachers' solidarity with, 135–36, 139, 150, 151; uprisings of, 128, 155–56
Work force, modern industrial, 3, 13, 21–22, 50
Working conditions, of teachers, 14–15, 16, 42, 100, 188; discussions of, 99, 108–09; reforms proposed, 115–16, 135, 136, 181

"Yearbook of Teachers' Societies," 182

Zemstvos, 5; activists, 114; congress, 123–24; schools, 169; Third Element, 108, 133
Zenchenko, S., 27
Zhulev, P., 176–77
Zolotarev, S., 180, 182

Pitt Series in Russian and East European Studies
Jonathan Harris, Editor

At the Price of the Republic: Hlinka's Slovak Peoples' Party 1929–1938
James Ramon Felak

The Bolshevik Party in Conflict: The Left Communist Opposition of 1918
Ronald I. Kowalski

Building Socialism in Bolshevik Russia: Ideology and Industrial Organization, 1917–1921
Thomas F. Remington

The Disabled in the Soviet Union: Past and Present, Theory and Practice
William O. McCagg and Lewis Siegelbaum, Editors

The Distorted World of Soviet-Type Economies
Jan Winiecki

Gender, Class, and the Professionalization of Russian City Teachers, 1860–1914
Christine Ruane

Jan Wacław Machajski: A Radical Critic of the Russian Intelligentsia and Socialism
Marshall S. Shatz

Midpassage: Alexander Herzen and European Revolution, 1847–1852
Judith E. Zimmerman

The Moscovia of Antonio Possevino, S.J.
Hugh F. Graham, Trans.

Parables from the Past: The Prose Fiction of Chingiz Aitmatov
Joseph P. Mozur, Jr.

Perceptions and Behavior in Soviet Foreign Policy
Richard K. Herrmann

Plekhanov in Russian History and Soviet Historiography
Samuel H. Baron

The Russian Empire and Grand Duchy of Moscovy: A Seventeenth-Century French Account
Jacques Margeret (Chester S. L. Dunning, Trans.)

The Soviet Socialist Republic of Iran, 1920–1921: Birth of the Trauma
Cosroe Chaqueri

The Soviet Union and the Threat from the East, 1933–41: Moscow, Tokyo and the Prelude to the Pacific War
Jonathan Haslam

That Alluring Land: Slovak Stories by Timrava
Norma L. Rudinsky, Trans.

Troubled Waters: The Origins of the 1881 Anti-Jewish Pogroms in Russia
I. Michael Aronson

The Truth of Authority: Ideology and Communication in the Soviet Union
Thomas F. Remington

Varieties of Marxist Humanism: Philosophical Revision in Postwar Europe
James H. Satterwhite